Echoing Silence: Essays on Artic Narrative

Echoing Silence:
Essays on
Artic Narrative

Edited with a Preface by
JOHN MOSS

University of Ottawa Press

REAPPRAISALS
Canadian Writers

GERALD LYNCH
General Editor

Canadian Cataloguing in Publication Data

Main entry under title:
Echoing Silence: Essays on Arctic Narrative

(Reappraisals, Canadian Writers; 20)
Papers originally presented at the Symposium on Arctic Narrative,
    University of Ottawa, spring 1995.
Includes bibliographical references.
ISBN 0-7766-0441-4

1. Canada, Northern, in literature. 2. Canadian literature—History and criticism
3. Canadian literature—Inuit authors—History and criticism. 4. Canadian
literature—Women authors—History and criticism. I. Moss, John, 1940-
II. Symposium on Arctic Narrative (1995: University of Ottawa). III. Series.

PS8101.A73E34 1997   C810.9'32719   C97-900552-3
PR9185.5.A7E34 1997

This book has been published with the help of a grant from the University of Ottawa
Faculty of Arts Research Fund.

University of Ottawa Press gratefully acknowledges the support extended to its publishing programme by the Canada Council, the Department of Canadian Heritage,
and the University of Ottawa.

 UNIVERSITY OF OTTAWA
UNIVERSITÉ D'OTTAWA

Cover Design: Robert Dolbec
Cover Illustration: Judith Currelly, *Phantom Herd*, 1993, Oil on panel, 48 × 72 in.,
Diane Farris Gallery.

ISBN 0-7766-0441-4

Printed and bound in Canada

Contents

Echoing Silence: Preface

JOHN MOSS

The Honourable Nellie Cournoyea said, "call me Nellie." Graham Rowley, thirty-some years my senior, although I'm a grandfather, was equally casual. Rudy Wiebe, whom I've known since before he won the first of two Governor General's Awards, was character-istically informal. Nellie spoke not as the premier of the Northwest Terri-tories but as an Inuk on the values in collecting the elders' stories; she was followed by Graham, after whom a district of Baffin is named, who related to us his experience as an Arctic explorer between the Wars, when it still seemed there was an unexplored Arctic; and Rudy completed the panoply with a wonderous conflation of historical document and the literary imag-ination. This was the opening session of the Symposium on Arctic Narra-tive held at the University of Ottawa in the spring of 1995. Variant authority and casual eloquence anticipated the program to follow, in which from the apparent silences of the Arctic we could hear echoing among us the words of its innumerable stories.

It is important to acknowledge that this book began as a social event. The essays gathered here were shared first in oral presentation, many of them having been conceived for oral delivery. Their arrangement now, as it was then, is orchestrated to generate and convey maximum res-onance. Through the course of a highly charged weekend, proscriptive limitations inherent in the contemporary academic version of oral tradi-tion were again and again challenged by the power of spoken language, from such a broad variety of perspectives, to gather listeners into a spon-taneous community. Disparities of opinion or ideology, race or sex, resolve to the ear in a way they cannot when read—not in harmony but, through tolerance, in symphonic diversity. The reader must listen to this text, if it is to be appreciated as more than a document of passing common interests.

Consider the closing stories by Mary Carpenter. The first is expository, words of her own experience as an Inuk woman in the modern world, a song in praise of memory, when the elders dance like shadows in front of you; the second and third she relays, her voice a medium, from deep within her cultural heritage. She tells of Skeleton Woman, a disarmingly grotesque love story, and of Nuriviq, a variation of Sedna, the woman of the sea whose long hair must be combed by shamans to have her bounty released for the survival of the people. In Mary's words, recorded and transcribed, you can hear the cadence, the sounds of a landscape inseparable from the stories of its inhabitants.

As Sean Kane tells us in *Wisdom of the Mythtellers*, the very nature of story transforms with our changing relationship to the environment. What once was a means of relating to the natural world became an account of separating from it, subduing it to our purpose as visitors who are passing through. From making connection, story came to establish difference. This shift, in what Shelagh Grant decribes below as a movement from narrative informed by spirituality to narrative informed by imagination, coincides with the transition from orature to literature. The oral tradition and the literary tradition articulate fundamentally different conceptions of reality; that is, reality itself is a different experience in what Kane identifies as hunter-gatherer and agrarian/post-agrarian cultures.

In the Arctic as a context of landscape and historical event, these two realities address each other in sometimes delightful, sometimes dismaying, ways. As content, the Arctic has been story in the Western world since Pythias wrote of it for the ancient Greeks, and in the memory of indigenous peoples since the times before time began. And time began with history, with the arrival of text into what outsiders perceived as frozen waste and what was, for the people living there, their home. What we know of the Arctic now, even of the oral tradition, is largely filtered through a screen of literacy, so that the Arctic of scholars, adventurers, and to some extent of the Inuit themselves, is a literary construct. Yet as we experience it through story, barriers crumble, boundaries blur; we can, if we listen, hear ourselves breathe.

Story is narrative—which is a good word to designate something that has already happened—a recounting, the conveyance of a sequence of events, real or imagined. But story is more. Story refuses to lie still as a noun. It is action, an activity, ongoing and elusive, allusive, generative, volatile, and, for all that, curiously self-reliant. We study narrative, gather in conferences to discuss narrative, but we come alive within stories. Narrative is artifact; what is there. Story is experience; how we perceive what is happening. This is a book about narrative, yes, but it is a book of stories. The worlds spoken here, written here, are overlaid, one upon another, in words and in ways that refuse to lie still.

Alootook Ipellie, a contemporary Inuk, speaks in a context where H. G. Jones explores Inuit stereotypes as perceived by Martin Frobisher's voyagers, encountered precisely where Alootook grew up along the shores of Frobisher Bay; Alootook speaks of difficulties in capturing his fragmented heritage in words and images, in a context where David Woodman's valorization of Inuit accounts leads to at least a partial resolution of the Franklin mystery, and where Shelagh Grant relates literary and oral traditions in ways that make Alootook's radical new forms of narrative seem almost inevitable.

Jones and Woodman, along with Edward Parkinson who extrapolates an intriguing narrative of the Third Franklin Expedition from the most meagre of fragments, speak in a context that entertains Graham Rowley's remembered expeditions and Wayne Grady's delightfully offbeat account of icebreaking adventures in pursuit of an elusive North Pole in 1994. Joan Strong places Harold Horwood's *White Eskimo* under critical scrutiny, while Horwood, himself, listens and then shares a panel with Farley Mowat on the Arctic *as* narrative; papers on Wiebe, van Herk, myself, are given by Kenneth Hoeppner, Marlene Goldman, Lorrie Graham, Tim Wilson, and Aron Senkpiel, while Rudy, Aritha, and I attend from the audience; Aritha van Herk engages in a splendid dialogue between her scholarly and creative selves, oddly echoing Constance Martin's commentary on the divided response to the Arctic of artist-scientist Dewey Soper.

There is much going on in this text: different generations of writers representing diverse aesthetics, different visions, sharing the rhetorical stage; a mixing of academic and non-academic voices; scholarly discourse in a context of enthusiasm and actual experience; intellectual rigour reinforcing and sometimes contradicting expressions of personal conviction; matters of difference addressed, matters of race, of cultural perspective, and especially of gender. In an Arctic context, the sex of the writer shapes narrative profoundly. So few women travelled from outside to the Arctic until recently, our present perceptions of the oral tradition so little differentiate between male and female orators, narrative literary conventions have been so shaped by masculine imperatives, that matters of gender, as Sherrill Grace argues, in how Arctic becomes content are of signal importance. Her commodious dialectic is anticipated by Marlene Goldman's consideration of gender in the writings of Aritha van Herk, and reinforced by Renée Hulan's commentary on gender stereotypes in nineteenth-century stories of the Arctic for boys, written by men. Each of these writer/speakers in effect comments on the other, as surely as Michael Kennedy, in his scholarly treatise on the Sedna myth, in context between Shelagh Grant's commentary on spirituality and imagination and Mary Carpenter's electrifying stories, goes well beyond the academic to participate in procedures of cultural change.

If the notions of an evolving continuum between oral and literary traditions, of cultural development as cultural improvement, are subverted in these pages, perhaps in the rich narrative voices of Alootook Ipellie or Aritha van Herk or Wayne Grady, perhaps in the scholarly tones of researchers, conspiratorial tremulations in the voices of Arctic enthusiasts, then the reader will have truly listened and will be well served. Conversation between differing traditions, irreconcilably opposing ontologies, disparate genres, and the conventions of various disciplines, sometimes within a single presentation, conveys more in its cadences, echoes, and silences than any editorial commentary could anticipate. Add to that, personalities—Farley Mowat and Harold Horwood were a marvelous complement to each other, a splendid foil to almost everyone else—and the shared conviction that the Arctic is both a real and an imagined place of great consequence, and you have a book I hope worth listening to.

In the summer of 1995, several months after the symposium, near a lake which in my journal, with my granddaughter Clare in mind, I called Isungituq, for the clearwater blues that spill into Kimiatuktujuk, called Cormack Bay on the maps, at the western end of Clyde Inlet, named for the River Clyde by Scottish whalers, on the northeast shore of Baffin Island, named after William Baffin who sailed by under the flag of the Virgin Queen, while backpacking with my brother Steve, we discovered a Dorset hunting site, pre-Dorset, perhaps, the people extinct, named with a time-shifting prefix for a shire in England, the site untouched in a thousand years, the solitude inviolate except for a single rusting tin can half buried in lichen; and there were fifteen small fortresses of stone funnelling to a wall above a cliff so that fifteen hunters waiting and waiting for caribou to pass, waiting motionless for hours and days, could each year, on the leap of a signal, secure a season's meat and sinew and clothing and stories to take back to the village on the shore of Kimiatuktujuk, for these were the days when there were communities all year round, before the dispersal, the death of the people whose name we don't know, whose names we don't know; and as I lay curled in one of their small stone fortresses, peering down the caribou path, knowing we had nearly walked by under the burden of our packs and seen nothing, I thought of the conference, the symposium on Arctic narrative, as a model for the manifold nature of the Canadian community and I envisioned writing this, which I'm writing now, about us, about Canada: these hunters are kin—if you have to go back before God to make the genetic connection, the bones of my people, of your people and of these our unnamed ancestors merge within the echoing silence of this weathered and weathering land.

The Arctic is a landscape of lichens and mountains, snowflakes and icebergs, saxifrage, creeping willow, pebbles ground to gemstone perfection, and vast formations of ice, contours of rock, sweeping geomorphic crenellations draped with greys and smokey greens, draped with the shadows of wind and the colours of snow. This is the home of the Inuit. This is their homeland. But just as a township is part of a county, a country a part of the world, this is the home of the Qallunaat as well, Canadians from the south who know the Arctic as an idea, a dimension of our experience of ourselves, although many may never have been there. We are a northern nation and, more significantly, we are a northern people. The white of our flag is the winter. The Arctic is a condition of our imagination. As we become increasingly a part of the global community, as our history, written by geography, is rewritten by ethnic diversity, we cannot survive as a people without coming to terms with how we imagine ourselves. The white of our flag is the winter, but the Arctic has seasons. Those who live there know that. For the rest of us, who visit or who read, we must explore beyond winter, find what is there and what we think is there, find what we missed. Then we may know ourselves.

I would like to express a profound debt of gratitude to the contributors who, when anticipated funding collapsed, rallied to bring it all together. Among my colleagues who helped us through the financial maelstrom, no-one deserves more credit than Camille LaBossiere. I would like to thank Gerald Lynch for his help as General Editor of the series in which this book appears. I would also like to thank Ian MacLaren for his contribution to the proceedings, Sherrill Grace for the generosity of her enthusiasm, and Angela Robbeson for her organizational and editorial work, without which neither the symposium nor the book might ever have happened. And this is a book that, if it works, happens.

Documenting the Oral History of the Inuvialuit

NELLIE COURNOYEA

$\mathbf{F}$irst, I want to thank Professor Moss for the invitation to speak at this symposium and for including the Committee for Original Peoples Entitlement Project in the deliberations on Arctic narrative. Although the COPE Collection also includes historical and traditional information gathered in interviews with the Gwich'in and North Slavey, its focus is on documenting the oral history of the Inuvialuit. The Inuvialuit oral histories are a significant and valuable part of the Arctic narrative. In an academic sense, they are a primary text of the Arctic. They represent an integral body of cultural knowledge, history, and traditions gathered over a period of thirty years or more in a project involving more than 150 individuals. The information was recorded on tape and obtained orally in the Inuvialuktun language from elders whose lifestyles may have changed, but who had or have a living memory of a truly traditional past.

Before I describe the documentation project, it would be helpful to sketch some background historical information for those who may not be aware of who the Inuvialuit are and where they live. The western areas of the Canadian Arctic have long been the home of the Inuvialuit. Spread between the Alaska-Yukon border and Cape Bathurst, the Inuvialuit were the largest group of people in the Canadian Arctic when Europeans first arrived. The earliest written records from this area, as well as oral histories, describe the Inuvialuit as a people who lived throughout the winter in large villages of driftwood and sod houses, surviving on stored supplies of beluga whale, caribou, and fish which were extremely plentiful in the summer months. The large population, relatively stable villages, and abundant resources contributed to a rich social and cultural life.

Trade and other interactions with Europeans became common after about 1850, initially in the south, as fur traders moved down the

Mackenzie River and, later, along the Beaufort coast, as Yankee whalers began to move into that area. As was too often the case in North America, this meeting of races introduced diseases and social disorders that brought about alarming reductions in the number of Inuvialuit. The pre-contact Inuvialuit population can be conservatively estimated at about 2500; in a little more than a generation of sustained contact the population was reduced by over ninety percent.

Two main groups currently make up the Inuvialuit. The people of the Tuktoyaktuk area who speak the Siglit dialect of Inuvialuktun are the more established Inuvialuit. Around the 1850s, the Alaskan Inupiat, who constitute the second group, began migrating to the Mackenzie Delta area, partly because of the abundance of wildlife and partly because of a growing relationship between the Inupiat and the traders and whalers. This migration continued into the 1920s, when Alaskan Inuit migrated to the Delta during the great reindeer re-location project. Today, Inuvialuit occupy their land claim area stretching from the Yukon border to Victoria Island.

By 1963 many individuals were involved in documenting the oral histories of Inuvialuit elders, and it became apparent that an expanded and in-depth program of documenting the elders was necessary to record and preserve the Inuvialuit culture. The documentation project began in 1963, and although the oral histories were collated into one complete inventory in 1990, the project continues today. It requires additional development, especially in documenting elders who have yet to be recorded, and who can provide oral clarification to the many questions that still need to be answered. Just such a person who could have done this task was Raymond Mangelana of Tuktoyaktuk, who passed away last week. His knowledge and experience of Inuvialuit culture was vast, and his connection to an older, more traditional past is a deep loss to the Inuvialuit.

The Inuvialuit only recently established a written language. The oral transmission of knowledge has always been the key means for passing on knowledge. Inuvialuit culture was passed from generation to generation orally by the elders. There are now only about six hundred speakers of Inuvialuktun, mostly elders. With their numbers declining, it is urgent that the process of documenting elders continue. Although the COPE and Oblate tapes are considered the important collections that relate to the Inuvialuit, they are said to have only scratched the surface of the historical and traditional knowledge of the Inuvialuit.

The COPE Collection is the largest compilation of work involving the Inuvialuit. In 1962 a great deal of concern was raised that the history and traditions of the Inuvialuit had not been documented. A number of individuals including Father LaMeur, an Oblate missionary in Tuktoyak-tuk, began to accelerate the recording of the elders' stories. Funding was minimal, though small grants were received from the Secretary of State and the Council for Young Canadians. Most of the work was done on a volunteer basis. The recording and documenting phase was an ongoing activity carried out over a twenty-year period. One of my own primary responsibilities was to ensure the material collected was safe and accessible. Initially the tapes were stored at CBC because if CBC broadcast them, which it did fairly regularly, then we could pay fifteen or twenty dollars to the elders for their contribution. This continued until I left CBC, where I was regional director, in the 1970s. The CBC Inuvik station served a very culturally diverse area; we were not confined to the Inuvialuit, but also served the Gwich'in and Slavey who were part of the COPE oral history project. The CBC's need for space threatened the survival of the original material and quick action had to be taken to find another home for it.

Since then, this invaluable collection has had a number of homes, one of which was the filing cabinets at the offices of the Committee for Original Peoples Entitlement. Consequently the name became the "COPE Collection." In the 1980s efforts continued. Working in conjunction with the Inuvialuit Regional Corporation on a grant, first from the Canadian Council of Archives, and then the Donner and Walter and Duncan Gordon Foundations, all the tapes were duplicated and the available transcripts and translations were computerized. In 1990 a complete set of the original recordings, transcripts and translations was presented to the NWT Archives, and relevant copies provided to the Inuvialuit, Gwich'in and Slavey communities.

Another notable collection of oral history on the Inuvialuit resulted from the work of two Oblate missionaries: Father LeMure and Father Meteyer. Both men came to the Beaufort and Central Arctic under the auspices of the Catholic Church in the 1950s and they remained there until their passing. Both men became fluent in Inuvialuktun and Innuinaqtun. Records of their work with elders date back to 1954. Throughout the 1960s, 1970s, and into the 1980s they were involved in a number of other projects to document the history of the Inuvialuit. These included gathering genealogical information, traditional place names, and producing Inuvialuit dictionaries. Their archives were sent south to the Oblate Archives in St. Albert, Alberta. Both men, in their wills, expressed the desire that their work should be made freely available to the Inuvialuit. Because of the Oblates desire to carry out the wishes of the two men, the NWT Archives was able to borrow and duplicate the collection.

Both collections are quite extensive. The COPE Collection is made up of 1013 stories which represent six hundred full hours of recording. The Oblate material is made up of almost three hundred full hours of recordings. In addition the Archives has other oral history recordings on the Inuvialuit from a variety of different sources such as the Yukon North Slope Project and the Banks Island National Park Project. These recordings represent an invaluable and irreplaceable source of information on the Inuvialuit, as the majority of the elders interviewed are no longer alive.

One thing that should be pointed out about the sporadic nature of the recording of oral history and oral traditions is that it is an expensive business and to ensure that it is done properly requires team effort. It has been estimated that the actual interview is only ten percent to fifteen percent of the work involved; and to preserve it properly and make it accessible requires a number of different specialties. The interviews should be conducted by individuals who are very familiar with the culture and who cannot only conduct an effective interview but also know what questions should be asked. Linguists who are familiar with the language and can faithfully translate and transcribe the interviews are essential to the process. Then information contained on the tapes has to be arranged, described and catalogued by archivists.

The last step is conservation. The need for permanent preservation, which requires a significant and ongoing commitment, is often overlooked. Material recorded on an analogue cassette tape has an expected life of roughly ten years. In order to be sure that no information is lost tapes have to be periodically rerecorded. The NWT Archives has had to build a sophisticated sound lab devoted to conserving the four thousand hours that it has in its holdings. The Archives recently started to duplicate all their recordings on to a digital format. Digital tapes have a longer useful life than the ordinary analog cassette tape—up to thirty years. More importantly, however, is that with digital technology there is no loss of information when the tapes are rerecorded on to new cassettes.

The NWT Archives is making significant efforts to make the material it has in its holdings accessible. An electronic oral history data base has been developed and a catalogue of all the Archives' sound recordings is being entered on to it. This data base will be placed on the "North of 60," an electronic bulletin board service that reaches every school in the NWT. The Archives also tries to make the actual recordings available at the community level. Recently the entire Oblate collection—all three hundred hours—was duplicated for the Beaufort Divisional School Board, which is using it to confirm field research required for locally produced curriculum for use in the schools. The Archives is also exploring the opportunities presented by CD ROM technology to make oral history even more accessible. One possibility is to produce searchable CD ROM disks which will contain selections of oral history recordings on various subjects.

The oral histories represent much of Inuvialuit culture. For scholarly purposes one can consider oral histories as being composed of two categories: first, the oral histories are a series of personal accounts or narratives which constitute the history of Inuvialuit culture; and, second, they are a rich literature which details an Inuvialuit view of the world.

The personal narratives of the elders speak about the *Ingilraani,* which means "the long past"; *taimani,* which means "the recent past"; and *qangma,* which means "the present time." The histories paint a picture of what life was like for the Inuvialuit. They describe the seasonal lifestyle of the people and their intimate relationship to the land. The histories detail the technology the Inuvialuit employed, and the strategies the people used to survive from the land's resources. The histories of the elders speak of the nature and behaviour of the land, animals, and people. They describe in detail the places the people journeyed to and inhabited. They identify and outline the significance and importance of family relationships, what is really the "Inuvialuit Family Tree." The importance and role of kinship in Inuvialuit culture is one of the most important functions of the oral histories. The historical aspect of oral tradition, documentation, and recordings speaks to and describes the depth of Inuvialuit culture through an extensive series of personal narratives.

The oral histories are the literature of the people. The stories and legends represent a cosmology of Inuvialuit culture. They describe how the earth was made and how the people of the earth came about. The legends paint a picture of the mythical "other worlds" of the Inuvialuit, the worlds under the ocean and in the sky. Mythical creatures and locations are detailed, as well as the journeys and the special powers needed by the *angakok* to travel to these places. Many of the stories and legends contain morals which were used as social standards or behaviour re-inforcement for children.

The personal narratives, and the stories and legends, are tied together by one central, common and dominating fact and theme: the control the environment had over the people forced the intimate relationship the Inuvialuit have had and still have with the land. By living under the dominance of the environment, aboriginal cultures still possess a worldview influenced by the whole scope of nature itself. Historically, the Inuvialuit did not use an orthography, and, as a result, the oral passing of knowledge was the only medium and instrument that connected and brought meaning to the past (the *ingilraani*), the near past (the *taimani*), and the now (the *qangma*).

A lot of people have put in many long hours of volunteer work on this project because they believe in the value and worth of their culture. Addi Tobac worked on the Sahtu-Dene recordings. Alestine Andre and Jim Koe both worked hard on the Gwich'in documentation. From the Inuvialuit side Charlie Smith, one of the most skilful storytellers anywhere, devoted much time and effort to documenting the elders. Bertram Pokiak and all the youth volunteers were steady workers on the project. Other persons who dedicated their time were Larry Osgood (now in New York), the priests of the Roman Catholic Church, and even Nick Cooper, descendent of the American author James Fennimore Cooper, who roamed the communities of the western Arctic giving a helping hand. Organizations which assisted include the Inuvialuit Regional Corporation, the Donner and the Walter and Duncan Gordon Foundations, the Prince of Wales Museum in Yellowknife, and the CBC. Many other persons and groups assisted, and it would take another presentation to show how they all fit in. The most recent gatherer of Inuit history is Richard Condon, an American anthropologist with the University of Arkansas, who has spent seven seasons with the Inuit of Holman on Victoria Island.

In closing, here is an historical segment told by an Inuvialuit lady, Agnes Nigiyok:

> When I started to wake up, my adoptive parents would tell me stories about the past. I was born during the spring down in Prince Albert Sound. I was adopted because my (biological) parents (Pitu-itok and Kupeuna) wanted to throw me away. They had put me into a caribou sling with a looped drawstring. And for my mouth, they had a mouthpiece ready for me. Then Nilgaks entered the tent (Nilgak and Annie Otoayok). When they were told that my parents were going to throw me out—these were relations to Otoayok (Otoayok was Kupeuna's sister)—when they said all that, Nilgak picked me up without hesitation right away from the skin that was for me. Otoayok could not bear any more children. That's when Nilgak had married her. Nilgak had married Otoayak even though she wasn't able to bear anymore children. They had had only one child— Akkowakiut—when they first got together.
>
> When I was older (approximately nine or ten), I was taken away by Hikoaluks for a daughter-in-law. I was taken from my adoptive mother even though she didn't want them to take me. She told them that I was still too young and hadn't learned enough to be a wife. Hikoaluks told my adoptive mother that they would teach me all those things. Hikoaluks took me down around the Coppermine area. That summer we travelled west of Coppermine hunting caribou and trapping. When winter came we were near Pierce Point on the coast. That's when I was left behind, on a big bay near Pierce Point. I don't know why I was left behind. I tried really hard. Maybe it was because I didn't know how to sew very well or do anything because I was too young. Sewing is hard when you first leave your family. It's very hard. I hadn't even sewn my first pair of mitts. I was just a young girl then. When they left me, I came near freezing. It was during the winter and I was left out on the ice. My body was partly frozen, but just on the surface—the skin on some parts of my body. My feet weren't so bad. I kept on walking. I walked all the way on the ice to the land following their trail. I tried not to lose their trail. The daylight was short. The day was over so soon. It must have

been around December. I would cry every so often, then start on the trail again. I would find a snowhouse and enter, but there would be nothing inside. Not even a piece of meat. They wouldn't even leave a piece of food for me, and they knew that I was following their trail. There were two policemen and two Inuit who found me. The Inuit were Simon Bennett and Alex Lester. I don't remember the names of the policemen. That was the first time I saw white people. They took me to a place near Paulatuk where Inglanasaks and Ningasiks were camped. Before the day was out, I found out that Hikoaluks were at that camp, too. Ningasiks took care of me and gave me clothes. They had to cut the clothes off my body because they were frozen so stiff. I stayed with them for about a year. Then Nikoaluks took me back, but left me again. After that, I was adopted by Lennie Inglangasak and his wife Sarah. They had a ship. Lennie was a trapper and we would spend year to year at different places.

An Arctic Affair

GRAHAM ROWLEY

When you saw on the program that I was to speak on "An Arctic Affair" you may have wondered what "an Arctic affair" was. I did too, although the phrase was taken from the subtitle of my book, then in preparation, *Cold Comfort: My Love Affair with the Arctic;* so I asked our convenor, and he said I was to talk about the Arctic before the war—why I went there, how I got there, and what I did there. I shall do my best to compress three or four years into half an hour, but I'll have to leave much unsaid.

The north has changed so much since the war. Before the war one year was very like the year before, with living and travel conditions almost the same as they had been throughout the previous century. Since the war, air travel, radio, television, telephones, schools, health services, and so on have been introduced; houses have replaced igloos, in winter skidoos have replaced dog teams, and in summer four-wheel Hondas have replaced feet. It is a different world from the north I first knew. (There is another north, as well—a north that a writer may describe but which never existed except in imagination.) The real north has changed so much and so fast that even the young Inuit today have little concept of how their parents and grandparents used to live. As you can imagine, this makes oral history particularly important, provided it is collected from the rapidly diminishing group of elders without reinterpretation by those who have little first-hand experience of living in the old north. Oral history is quickly lost in the wide gaps between generations.

My story begins in Cambridge in 1935. I had graduated in natural sciences and then read archaeology, and I had no idea how to earn a living. One morning early in June a man called Tom Manning came to see me. I did not know him, but he gave me a letter from the curator of the

Archaeological Museum there. The letter was short: "My dear Rowley, This is to introduce Mr. Manning with whom, I hope, you will go to the Arctic. He will explain things to you. Yours sincerely, Louis Clarke."

Tom told me he was planning to lead a small expedition to the Eastern Canadian Arctic, leaving in the spring of 1936, and asked me to join it as the archaeologist. As nobody else had said they wanted an archaeologist, I agreed, though I knew little of what I was letting myself in for. Still less did I realize that in seeking to evade the issue of what to do I had in fact determined how I would spend most of the rest of my entire life.

There were five in our party. Tom Manning; Reynold Bray, who was an ornithologist; Pat Baird, a geologist; and Dick Keeling, who had just qualified as a doctor and said he would spend the first summer with us until he could be replaced by Peter Bennett, an army surveyor.

In 1935 parts of the Arctic were described as unexplored and shown on maps with dotted lines. The largest such area in Canada, and indeed in the whole circumpolar north, was part of the west coast of Baffin Island. No white man had yet been there, and it was rarely visited by Inuit because the hunting was unpredictable and several parties had starved to death there. This was where Tom proposed we would go, by thirty-foot whaleboat in summer and dog team in winter. Support was hard to find in those days, so we would have to do everything as cheaply as we could, and pay most of the cost ourselves.

There were then a few Hudson's Bay Company (HBC) posts in the Eastern Arctic. About half of them had also a two-man RCMP detachment and possibly an RC or Anglican mission. Few of the five thousand or so Inuit in the Eastern Arctic lived at these posts; they hunted and trapped from small camps scattered along the coasts. The economy was based on white fox, which the Inuit trapped and traded, mainly for tea and tobacco, guns and ammunition, and blanket cloth. Virtually the only link between north and south was a ship that called at each post once a year to bring in supplies and take out the fur.

We sailed for Canada in March 1936, going first to Ottawa. Here I saw Dr. Diamond Jenness, the renowned anthropologist, and asked him what an archaeologist could most usefully do in the Arctic. He suggested that I try to find out more about the Dorset Culture, an extinct Eskimo culture that he thought had existed. If I could find a pure Dorset Culture site—a place where only the Dorset people had lived—it would be convincing evidence that there had been such a culture.

We went by train to Churchill where we helped to finish the thirty-foot whaleboat a Norwegian trapper was building for us. She was low in the water when we loaded our gasoline, supplies, equipment, and then our dogs. All Churchill was at the dock to see us off and to hear an old trapper's farewell sally, "If one of them dogs pisses she'll sink." We sailed north along the floe-edge. It was early in June—this was much earlier than the port opened and than small boats usually sailed. It was then believed that Hudson Bay remained open throughout the year. Not until the war, when aircraft first flew over the bay, was it found to freeze over in the winter. We thought we were sailing on the open sea when we were really following a wide lead that an east wind would quickly close.

After calling at Chesterfield we headed for the Bay of God's Mercy on Southampton Island and left Reynold to spend the summer at the snow goose breeding ground there. There was also an archaeological site which I dug but found no Dorset. Our next stop was Walrus Island in South Bay, where we were caught on a lee shore and nearly wrecked. We watched anxiously as the waves lifted our boat time after time and dashed her on the rocky beach, but she was strongly built and we could repair most of the damage. An excavation here yielded some Dorset artifacts but they were mixed with later material. We reached the post at Coral Harbour before the annual supply ship, the *Nascopie*, which would bring Peter to replace Dick. We were able to tell the post manager that Italy had invaded Abyssinia, that there was Civil War in Spain, and that King George V had died and been succeeded by Edward VIII, all of which was news to him.

The *Nascopie* left after less than a day and Tom and Peter sailed in our boat to pick up Reynold. Pat and I went with some Inuit to Coats Island and then sledged across Southampton Island with an Inuk to meet the others. The first day or two were difficult, as there was little or no snow and we were often sledging over bare limestone.

After rejoining the others, we sailed across Frozen Strait and laid up the boat for the winter, before walking to the HBC post at Repulse Bay. Unfortunately, we had no tents, which had been lost when a canoe we had been towing broke away in the darkness. We had no winter clothing, and little food for a journey we thought would take three days, but in fact took nine. It is cold in October and it was a miserable walk.

We spent the fall learning how to drive dogs, build snow houses, look after our fur clothing, among other necessary skills. Our main problem was lack of dog food, and it was decided that Reynold and I would take one team to Igloolik, three hundred miles away, where there was certain to be plenty of walrus. This was a journey which could be described as learning on the job. We started on December 21. We expected to find that it was cold, dark, and windy. It was, but what delayed us most was mist sometimes so thick we could not see our way ahead. Each day we plodded by the sledge as we slowly made our way north. As it grew dark we would look for suitable snow for the igloo that I would build, while Reynold fed the dogs. Once inside the igloo with our candle flame reflected by the snow crystals in the wall, and a polar bear skin and our fur sleeping bags spread on the snow bed, Reynold said it was like living in a fairy tale. After a meal the pleasure of not feeling hungry was added to the pleasure of not feeling cold, and we slept.

Towards the end of January we had completed the worst part of the journey and were getting short of food. One morning we were having breakfast in our igloo and wondering how long our dogs could haul, as we had just finished the dog food, when we heard an unusual sound outside. Reynold quickly cut a door in the wall and a boy crawled in. From that point our lives changed.

Aipilik, for that was his name, shared our breakfast and then led us to a solitary igloo where he lived with two couples and a baby, and where we soon felt ourselves part of the family. They fed us and our dogs for a week of bitter weather and then one of the men went with us to the next camp. It was larger, but everyone was as kind as those in the camp we had left. In this way we were relayed along the coast to Igloolik—the objects of much interest because other white men never travelled alone and rarely travelled in mid-winter. We also had tea and tobacco and they had run out of both.

At Igloolik a solitary RC priest, Father Bazin, lived in an igloo, dependent on what supplies the Inuit could carry for him by dog team from the nearest post, about three hundred miles away. He could have had little difficulty in observing his Oblate vow of poverty. He helped us in every way he could and he gave me an archaeological collection the Inuit had brought him from a neighbouring island. Almost everything in it appeared to me to be Dorset material.

Reynold and I had learned a lot on our journey. We had learned that we could travel on our own by dog team at the worst time of the year. We had also learned that it was much quicker, much more interesting, and far more comfortable to travel with Inuit. We wrote to Tom and said we would now be on our own and Tom, to his great credit, did not resent our leaving his expedition.

When we asked the Inuit about the coast of Baffin Island to the east—the part marked unexplored on maps—two hunters said they would take us there if we wanted, so this became our next journey. Sometimes our wish to map and our companions' enthusiasm for hunting caribou conflicted, but we always reached a compromise. To our surprise we were able to complete the map of Baffin Island without much difficulty. The coast proved to be farther west than the dotted lines on the map, so we added some two thousand square miles to the area of Canada, as well as a large island we could clearly see to the south.

On our return trip to Igloolik we met Jack Turner, an Anglican missionary returning from his annual circuit of his enormous parish, and I joined him for his journey across Baffin Island to Pond Inlet. I then went with two young Inuit to Arctic Bay, where I rejoined Reynold. We were now able to plan for the summer. Reynold decided that the Igloolik area would be best for birds, and I was told about some archaeological sites near Arctic Bay where I could resume my search for the Dorset Culture. Archaeologically, my summer was disappointing. I was able to excavate at three places, but I found no indication that the Dorset people had ever lived there. At the end of the summer I went south in the *Nascopie,* which first had to establish the HBC post at Fort Ross, at the entrance to Bellot Strait. In Ottawa, I showed the collection Father Bazin had given me to Dr. Jenness, who confirmed that it was Dorset with no significant amount of later material.

Back in Cambridge I worked on all I had excavated and realized I had made a big mistake in not returning to Igloolik to excavate the site where the Dorset collection had been found. One Wednesday afternoon in the summer I suddenly made up my mind. I had to excavate that site. On Thursday I went to my bank in Manchester and then bought a ticket to Canada. I took the train to London on Friday and on Saturday I sailed from Southampton. This was not the careful planning an expedition is said to need.

At Winnipeg I had a few days to buy supplies and visit a dentist before the weekly train left for Churchill, where the HBC schooner was ready to sail to Repulse Bay. The HBC had planned to open a post at Igloolik that summer, but the ship had been turned back by ice, so I would have to take everything I needed by sledge from Repulse. My greatest needs would be tea, tobacco, and a shovel. I would find plenty to eat there, although not always what I would choose, and I could arrange for any Inuit who helped me to be paid through the HBC at Repulse.

In October Kutjek, one of two Inuit who had been with Reynold Bray and me, unexpectedly walked into the post. He had been unable to return to Igloolik in the spring and was at a nearby camp. He said he would take me to Igloolik starting in December, the earliest time that travel by sledge would be practicable. Christmas and New Year were spent at Kutjek's camp; we then started the long journey to Igloolik. We followed much the same route that Reynold and I had taken two years earlier and again reached Igloolik early in February.

Digging the Dorset site would keep me busy once the ground started to thaw in June. I had four months to spend, and it was the best time of year for travel by dog team. We had completed the coastline of Baffin Island, but most of the interior of the island was unknown, particularly between Pangnirtung and Pond Inlet, where the coast was mountainous, often with vertical cliffs two thousand or more feet high. A map made by an anthropologist last century had indicated a route right across the mountains to Foxe Basin. The Inuit must have told him about it, but nobody now alive had crossed the island here. I decided to try to find if this route existed and what the interior was like. When I mentioned my plan to Kutjek, he said he would come with me. Mino, the other Inuk who

had been with Reynold and me, decided to join us. I believed his real reason was to look for a suitable wife at the camps we would visit, as he had
recently become a widower. There were four of us as Kutjek brought his
ten-year-old son.

Inuit who sometimes went inland to hunt caribou advised us to follow a river that ran into Foxe Basin from the northeast. For two days it
gave us good, though not very direct going, but then we came to a narrow,
steep, and rocky ravine that would defeat any dog team. We had to go
some way back to find a way around it, through difficult country which
always seemed to lead us in the wrong direction. At the end of our fourth
day on the land we were only about ten miles from the coast. Nearly three
weeks had passed since we had left Igloolik and we had little dog-food
remaining to feed our two dog teams and, by now, ourselves as well. Next
day we reached the river again at an altitude several hundred feet higher
that where we had left it; the only surprises it had for us now were pleasant
ones. It connected a chain of narrow lakes all running in the way we
wanted through an upland plateau where we were able to kill enough caribou for our needs.

Eventually the river turned away from the direction we wanted. We
knew we must be approaching the watershed and each of us set out on
foot to try to find a way to the sea. Kutjek returned saying he believed he
had found a possible way. I frequently doubted this as we struggled all the
next day down a steep rocky valley with hardly any snow, wondering
whether it would end in a precipice. The following day we came to where
we could see far below us a frozen river in a wide valley that must lead to
Baffin Bay. Our only problem was how to descend to it. At the most difficult part we had to throw our load over a precipice, turn our sledges over,
and take them upside down to the bottom of a steep snow bank in a series
of short traverses, with the sledges often overriding the dogs, which
became a brake. We recovered our possessions, mostly caribou meat, and
in another day reached the sea to drive along a spectacular fiord with ice-
capped cliffs on both sides. It was an easy journey to Pond Inlet, stopping
at camps en route, to the surprise of the Inuit there.

I knew some of the white population at Pond Inlet from my previous visit. They had a radio and told me what had been happening in
Europe during the past few days. Czechoslovakia had dissolved, Moldavia
and Bohemia had been occupied by the Nazis, and Madrid had been
taken by Franco. To me it seemed far away, and to belong to a different
world. There was nothing I could do about it, and I was sure the situation
would change greatly before I could become directly involved.

After a week we left for Arctic Bay and then for Igloolik, which we
reached with Mino still single, though we had visited every camp on our way.

The snow remained deep on the land and it was clear I would not
be able to excavate for at least three weeks. I decided to go with Kutjek to

the river we had followed across Baffin Island to see if there was a waterfall at the head of the narrow ravine which had stopped us. I was no more successful at this second attempt. I walked or climbed some distance along the ravine, but many of the stones in my way appeared to be recent arrivals from the cliffs above, and I could hear rocks falling ahead of me. I did not want to be even a random target and, since it seemed a lonely place to be brave, I turned back. Kutjek and I decided to go instead to Kagiuyak, a fairly large island that had been seen but not visited by a Danish expedition fourteen years earlier. There was a hill on this island; from the top I could see the north coast of a much larger island to the south, several hundred square miles in area, which was another addition to the map of Canada. We could not visit it because there was open water between it and us.

By now the land was nearly bare of snow and I could start to excavate the site on Abverjar Island where the Dorset Culture collection had been found. In spite of the weather, which was unusually wet and cold, it was a perfect summer. Aipilik, the boy who had found Reynold and me in our igloo two years earlier, came to help me, as did the young son of Kutjek. Apart from a few fragmentary pavements of flat stones there were scant signs of dwellings, but we found about fifteen hundred artifacts, all Dorset, unmixed with other cultures. Our finds included many small superbly carved, ivory pendants—walrus and bear heads and other animals and birds. One piece of antler had twenty-eight faces carved on it. There could now be no doubt that the Dorset Culture had existed and that it was a much richer culture than had been thought.

Our camp became a favourite stopping place for Inuit, and once the ice went out we had visitors almost every day. They would stop for tea on their way to and from hunting, but I think their real reason was to make sure that nothing had happened to us. I was delighted to hear from one of these visitors that Mino had at last succeeded in finding a wife.

A ship had been expected at the end of August, so I moved back to Igloolik Island to test an archaeological site there. By mid-September we were sure the ship had been stopped by ice. It had turned back in August the previous year. I was looking forward to another year in the north when I saw the ship approaching. She carried an HBC store for Igloolik. She also brought news that Germany had invaded France two weeks earlier and that we were at war. As I packed I realized that the last year had been more successful than I could have hoped in both geographical exploration and in archaeology. I realized also how much I owed to the Inuit, because they had made my work possible. As I said goodbye to them one old man who could speak a little English, said to me "War again?" "Yes." "Germans again?" "Yes." "You go fight war?" "Probably." "Damn fool. You stay here."

We reached Montreal in mid-October. I reported my geographical discoveries to the mapping authorities in Ottawa, and with the great help of Dr. Jenness wrote a short article for *American Anthropologist* on the Dorset Culture and what I had found. I then joined the Canadian Army, and sailed for England with the First Canadian Division in January. I would not return to the Arctic until the war in Europe was over.

Coursing a Naked Country

RUDY WIEBE

Canadians are so generally uninformed about their Arctic existence—one might as well say, not only *uninformed* but resolutely *blind*—that I think we need the guidance of a poet for our northern considerations in Ottawa this weekend. I thank Nellie Cournoyea for invoking an Inuvialuit elder's story, and I would call upon Leonard Cohen, his inimitable voice and words:

> There is a crack in everything;
> that's how the light gets in,
> that's how the light gets in.

The tiny crack in our northern ignorance that I want to explore is a moment in the afternoon of Friday, December 14, 1821, in Fort Providence, which at that time was a spruce-palisade Hudson's Bay Company post on the shore of what is now called Yellowknife Bay on Great Slave Lake. Three days before, Captain John Franklin, Dr. John Richardson, sailor John Hepburn, and Metis translator Jean Baptiste Adam have been carried into it by the Yellowknife Dene, who have just barely saved this remnant of the English exploration party from death by starvation on the tundra. Now, in the momentary December daylight, the Yellowknife leader, Akaitcho, and his band come into the fort to bid the two English officers farewell; this is how Richardson in his journal describes what happened:

> [Akaitcho] smoked his customary pipe with Mr Weekes [the trader at the post] and learnt from him that our expected supplies had not come in [that summer for us to pay them for their services].

He spoke of this circumstance as a severe disappointment [to him and his people], but without attaching any blame to us.

"The world goes badly," he said, "all are poor. You are poor, the traders appear to be poor, and I and my party are poor likewise, and since the goods have not come in, we cannot have them. But I do not regret having supplied you with provisions, for a Red Knife can never permit a White man to suffer from want on his lands without flying to his aid.... At all events," he added in a tone of good humour, "it is the first time that the White people have been indebted to the Red Knife Indians."

He then cheerfully received the small present we made to himself, and although we could give a few things to those only who had been most active in our service, the others who perhaps thought themselves equally deserving, did not murmur on being left out in the distribution.... [But] we felt a deep sense of humiliation at being compelled to quit men capable of such liberal sentiments and humane feelings in the beggarly manner in which we did. (178–179)

George Back does not record this incident in his journal—he had already proceeded to the next fort—and Robert Hood was of course dead; Franklin in his enormously popular *Narrative,* published two years later, prints Richardson's account, word for word. The only part he omits is "the deep sense of humiliation we felt" on leaving; rather, Franklin writes that Akaitcho "bade us farewell with a warmth of manner rare among the Indians."

In a letter to his wife, written from Great Slave Lake in April, 1822, Richardson is even more explicit about the kind nature of the Dene. He writes to his wife:

I shall not attempt to describe the miseries we endured in this journey ... the bare detail would be too harrowing to your feelings ... half our party perished through cold, famine, and fatigue. [He does not mention that 2 of the 11 men who died were shot, one of them by himself.] The survivors were found by the Indians on Nov. 7, and these savages (as they have been termed) wept on beholding the deplorable conditions to which we were reduced. They nursed and fed us with the same tenderness they would have bestowed on their own infants, and, finally, on December 11, conveyed us to Fort Providence, the nearest post. (*Life,* 112)

Thomas Hobbes on human nature can help us explore what is going on here. In *Leviathan* (1651), Hobbes speculates that when "men live without other security than what their own strength and their own invention shall furnish them"—which is what the English generally assumed was the way of life of the aboriginal people they met—such people, Hobbes writes, live with "no arts; no letters; no society; and which is worst of all, continual fear, and danger of violent death; and the life of man [is] solitary, poor, nasty, brutish, and short."

In my reading of them, the officers of the First Franklin Expedition might disagree with Hobbes on his "no society" and "solitary" definitions regarding Dene life, but I am convinced they would agree with him on every other: for them, the Yellowknives had "no arts; no letters;" they lived in "continual fear, and danger of violent death;" life for them was certainly "poor, nasty, brutish, and short." As a result, their journals again and again express surprise, even outright astonishment when, as Richardson notes on Nov. 16, 1821, the Indians "evinc[e] a degree of humanity that would have done honour to the most civilized of nations"—by which of course he means Great Britain. How can Indians, even occasionally, behave in so "most civilized" a manner when Franklin has already warned possible "future travellers" of the Indians' "avaricious nature, and . . . that little reliance can be placed upon them when their interests jar with their promises" (276)?

Contemporary Canadian scholars may be too informed to paste a "noble savage" label on aboriginal peoples, but from my experience we tend still to see the pre-white-contact world as homogenous and, basically, unchanging: it was the the arrival of Europeans that brought change, fundamentally *civilizing* change, to the peoples of the Americas. When, however, one reads the best of contemporary studies, like Kerry Abel's *Drum Songs: Glimpses of Dene History* (1993), one begins to see a much larger picture; if you add to that books like *Life Lived Like a Story,* the life accounts of Angela Sidney, Kitty Smith, and Annie Ned as edited by Julie Cruikshank (1990), or George Blondin's *When the World Was New: Stories of the Sahtu Dene* (1990), one may start finding ways to begin to understand that encounter on the shore of Tucho between the Yellowknives, whose complete home and country it is, and the Englishmen who have been in that land for a year and a half, and who have been devastated, almost totally destroyed, by it.

Why were the Yellowknives so kind to the English? If we turn the story around, can we, for example, imagine the English being kind and considerate to strangers landing on their shore and demanding that the English leave their own pursuits and livelihood to labour for them, the strangers, to achieve their particular and indecipherable purposes of exploring, even exploiting, the resources of the country? English hostility towards invaders is only too well known: for over a thousand years their proudest boast—and challenge—to the entire world has been "This island is ours; you stay out. Or invade at your peril." Well, was there something so obviously impressive about English men, was their superiority so inherent and instantly overwhelming, and were these local denizens so "child-like" and "ignorant" that they were just naturally, immediately over-awed into treating the English like kings and gods?

I would suggest that we not continue the stupidities of our ancestors. It is perfectly obvious from the record that, on first encounter with the land of the Dene, the English, despite their extraordinary resolution and courage (or perhaps because of it), the English were as helpless as infants in arms. In fact, one might even argue from their three hundred years of futile attempts to sail through the Arctic ice (as far as I know, no English vessel of any kind has ever traversed the so-called Northwest Passage to this day—they haven't tried to for over a century), one could argue that not only were the English in the Arctic inferior to most nations, they were also at a certain bull-headed point fundamentally unteachable.

The Third Franklin Expedition illustrates this point perfectly. It seems to me that by 1845 our Arctic world had finally had enough; at that point the Arctic finally declared, "All right, you have been poking around at me for 270 years—ever since Martin Frobisher so confidently decided China was just a whistle and turn beyond my most eastern island. So, send me now the most scientifically outfitted ships you can equip, staff them with your brightest, strongest men, and I will show you once and for all what I am really like. I will destroy them, both ships and men, destroy them so utterly you will find barely a trace of them for ten years; destroy them so completely that a hundred-and-fifty years later people will still be searching with every bit of science they know, and still finding nothing."

Clearly, if the Dene had been living in the difficult Arctic world for some thousands of years—as they had, for hundreds of generations—then they were no incredulous children to be simply over-awed by the mere arrival of white-skinned people carrying a lot of strange stuff. Contemporary research has shown that it was the complex pre-contact trade between aboriginal groups that made possible the rapid economic development of the European companies trading their industrial goods of hatchets, knives, needles, kettles, cloth, guns, shot, and powder. These basic goods were more efficient than the Dene had been able to develop without a knowledge of iron, and their quick adoption showed their ability to change, to adapt. The long-range effect on Dene society, of changing them from a relatively independent nomadic moose-and-caribou hunting culture to the more restricted life of trapping and being indebted—that is, bound—to a trader at a fixed white post, that change was in no way lost on the Dene; but they changed consciously, for the reasons that all cultures adapt, alter themselves, when other patterns of less labourious living become possible.

I am not an anthropologist, and have no desire to explicate those reasons here; rather, I wish to indicate one aspect of Dene thinking which has, I believe, been too little researched, though for the Dene it may be at least as significant as the economics of cultural change. In his book *When the World Was New,* Great Bear Lake elder George Blondin makes it clear that until as late as the 1920s, the Dene world was dominated by what he calls "medicine," powerful medicine that was used by the persons who had it for both very good and very bad purposes. He does not define what "medicine" is; one difficulty is that, to quote Blondin, "most medicine people don't talk about their medicine; it is sacred and secret" (102). And indeed, the English language may not actually have a vocabulary that can reveal much of what that concept would or can mean to a Dogrib or a Sahtu Dene. English can only talk around it: special persons, either male or female, receive particular powers to do certain things; often these powers are associated with a certain animal, like the raven, beaver, bear, squirrel, etc., and it would seem they can be used for good, that is, for the good of others, or for bad, that is, for personal, individual aggrandizement. The use of this power either way is determined, at least to some extent, by the personal decision of the individual who has it since, as some stories reveal, someone who has always used the power for good, under extreme provocation can also apply it for evil effect upon the community. As far as the Dene were concerned, this power was not in any way restricted to the psychological effects it had on gullible believers, which is the way whites who encounter it often describe it. Blondin's stories tell of Europeans and their goods being affected by it as well—a bullet fired by a medicine person travels 320 kilometres in thirty minutes; a prophet foretells the white discovery of uranium on the shore of Great Bear Lake.

The early explorers say literally nothing about this power; indeed, the supernatural powers of the Dene are to them veiled in secrecy: it would seem the Dene refused to tell them anything. Franklin writes in 1823: "Of their notions of a Deity, or future state, we never could obtain any satisfactory account; they were unwilling, perhaps, to expose their opinions to the chance of ridicule" (256).

When I first read this, I was puzzled: what an odd statement. The English officers were the only listeners there—so the Dene could only be apprehensive about being ridiculed by them—but why would the officers be so foolish as to ridicule them? Perhaps Franklin assumed that the Christianity to which he was devoted was so obviously superior to anything the Dene could espouse that they must immediately recognise its quality and be ashamed for their spiritual poverty. In any case, he does not explain, but George Back's journal on the same subject provides an amazing connection. He writes, with typical Back superiority, that these "savage tribes [are] extremely superstitious, relating many *ridiculous* stories of bears and squirrels being the origin of creation" (122).

Franklin's book is more circumspect, noting only that: "Akaitcho generally evaded our questions on these points, but . . . [he], and many others of his tribe, possess a laudable curiosity . . ." (256). But "ridiculous"—

"ridicule"—are words not easily dismissed in this context. To understand we need to remember the incident recorded by Richardson at Fort Enterprise on January 5, 1821:

> This evening whilst we were at dinner old [Keskarrah] came in for medicine for his wife. He received it and wrapped it up with such extraordinary carefulness that we could not help smiling at his gestures. [Franklin states it more strongly; he admits that Keskarrah's actions "excited the involuntary laughter of Mr. Hood and myself".] This aroused the old fellow's suspicion, and his wife afterwards fancying that it had not produced its wanted good effects, they came to the conclusion that I had intentionally given them some bad drugs. The whole night was spent in singing and groaning—next morning, the whole family were crying in concert and it was not until evening of the second day that we succeeded in pacifying them. The old woman began to feel better and her faith in the efficacy of the medicine was renewed. (25)

Clearly, as far as the Dene were concerned, when powerful people laugh at you, you are in trouble. Even when, as Franklin notes about their relationship with Keskarrah, they are accustomed to joke with you in easy camaraderie. The laughter of powerful people is ridicule, and that is always dangerous.

This Dene sensitivity, their reticence and curiosity in the matter of "medicine" are corroborated by Richardson in the second volume of his *Arctic Searching Expedition: A Journal of a Boat-Voyage through Rupert's Land and the Arctic Sea, in search of the Discovery Ships under Command of Sir John Franklin*, (1851). Speaking of the northern Tinne, as he called them:

> Of the peculiarities of their religious belief I could gain no certain information. The interpreters . . . disliked the task, and invariably replied, "As for these savages, they know nothing; they are ignorant people." [With translators like that, how could he learn anything at all?] The majority of the nation recognise a "Great Spirit", at least by name, but some doubt his existence, assigning, as a reason for their atheism, their miserable condition; or they say, "If there be such a being, he dwells on the lands of the white people, where so many useful and valuable articles are produced." (20–21)

A strange fact, this: in the mid nineteenth century many Dene question the very existence of a Great Spirit. It seems that not even in fundamental religious beliefs were the Dene as lock-step as we generally assume them to have been.

This strange fact was already elaborated thirty years earlier by the Dene elder just mentioned, Keskarrah. Only Franklin mentions this incident in his *Narrative*:

> Old Kerskarrah alone used boldly to express his disbelief of a Supreme Deity, and state that he could not credit the existence of a Being, whose power was said to extend everywhere, but whom he had not yet seen, although he was an old man. The aged sceptic is not a little conceited, as the following exordium to one of his speeches evinces: "It is very strange that I never meet with any one who is equal in sense to myself." (256)

Keskarrah then goes on to tell a long continuing creation story which involves a contest between a bear and a squirrel; it may be that this is the story Back found "ridiculous," although he does not mention Keskarrah in his journal.

In his turn, Franklin finds the acuity of mind that will doubt the existence of a supreme being as "conceited." However, it is clear from Keskarrah's long life and his skilful behaviour both as a hunter, a guide, and an elder that, whatever his ideas about a "god" might have been, he knew a good deal about the supra-human powers that make things happen in the Dene world. Since he went to Richardson for drugs for his wife's ulcer, he obviously recognized that doctor had some powerful "medicine" against the evils of sickness, an area where he himself seems to have had little power, though he made prayers and offerings to the Water Spirit at the Winter River rapid below Fort Enterprise "whose wrath," as Richardson records, "he apprehends to be the cause of her malady" (22). But it would seem that Keskerrah had power ... medicine from and with animals: his skill at finding caribou during the long winter and bringing them in to feed the hungry officers and voyageurs is highlighted several times, and in his book, *The Zoology of the Northern Parts of British America, First Part: The Mammals* (1829), Richardson tells an enlightening story about Keskarrah's "strong medicine":

> Keskarrah ... was seated at the door of his tent, pitched by a small stream not far from Fort Enterprise, when a large [barren-ground] Bear came to the opposite bank, and remained for some time apparently surveying him. Keskarrah considered himself to be in great danger, and having no one to assist him but his aged wife, made a speech to the following effect: "Oh Bear! I never did you any harm; I have always had the highest respect for you and your relations, and never killed any of them except through necessity. Go away, good Bear, and let me alone, and I promise not to molest you." The Bear walked off, and the old man, fancying that he owed

his safety to his eloquence, favoured us, on his arrival at the fort,
with his speech at length. (251)

It seems to me that, in telling Richardson this story, Keskarrah is
not at all parading his "eloquence"; rather, he is powerful enough in his
own medicine to freely explicate it to someone who has good medicine in
another area. This particular strength is also evident in what Franklin
records: the familiar, joking relationship the old man has with all the officers. Despite what the English may literally record in their journals, it is
obvious that the Dene have no sense of inferiority in their relations with
them; rather, in this long winter of first encounter for both races, of
enduring life together in the growing harrowing cold and darkness at the
edge of the tree-line from August, 1820, to June, 1821, the Dene were
completely confident within themselves. And why should they not be?
They have accepted these whites into their country; these visitors are
learning from them how to live in it. And how little they actually do learn
is quickly, horribly evident from the disaster they experience when they
leave the Yellowknife territory.

Which brings us back to that afternoon of December 14, 1821, the
"crack" which might allow in a bit of light to illumine our ignorance of
our northern past. Akaitcho is still speaking with that thoughtful ease, that
gentilesse which flavours and shapes the speech of perceptive, thoughtful
human beings; he is joking with the traumatized, physically ravaged officers whom the Yellowknives have just carried here, rescued from the brink
of death by starvation which has destroyed more than half of their companions. And, of all things, Akaitcho is joking! A complex joke involving
the traders, the explorers who of course have been indebted to the Dene
for everything, all winter, and his people.

Joking. As people often do when they have been forced to experience how nothing of themselves there is except—perhaps—the bare bodies of their existence; when no one has any words to explain the mysteries
of the life we all, somehow, live—until we all die anyway, somehow.

"The world goes badly," Akaitcho says. "We are all poor." Who in
that room was quite aware of how poor they truly were? Within a year the
white devastation of smallpox would reach the Yellowknives from the
neighbouring Chipewyan, and within three years the Dogribs would come
into full-scale war with them. The problems between the two tribes were
fundamentally exacerbated by the fur trade: though there were enormous
caribou herds from the tree-line to the Arctic Ocean, the numbers and
territories of fur-bearing animals was much more limited, and so the more
numerous Dogribs, driven beyond endurance by the territorial arrogance
of the Yellowknives, would have begun the ultimate destruction of that
tribe. As for the English—they are probably overwhelmed by their most
evident present poverty: they can only remember the miserable death of

their young fellow officer, Robert Hood, and the deaths of the ten voyageurs who literally carried them into the country and whose bones are now scattered by the hunting animals of the tundra. Poor indeed.

"Nevertheless," Akaitcho adds, "we do not regret bringing you into the country, and supplying you with provisions. Tetsot'ine can never permit a white person to suffer on their land without coming to his aid." He is telling them, again, if they will listen: This is our land. You came here without us inviting you, but we fed and clothed you so that you could live here. After you left us and we heard you were dying, we went to your aid immediately. We saved your lives because it is the nature of Dene people to help everyone.

Apparently Keskarrah, the elder with animal medicine, the old sceptic, is not there. At least he is not mentioned as being there; nor that he speaks. But in the Dene book of etiquette neither action would be necessary for him. His understanding, his humane wisdom, is there in the words and manner of the younger man, Akaitcho, who has from the moment when these whites first arrived in their land eighteen months before, spoken for all the Testsot'ine.

But John Richardson is certainly there, listening, alertly aware, the Scots doctor who will become the outstanding Arctic scientist of the first half of the nineteenth century. The man who has already "deprived a fellow-creature of life", as he describes it, by shooting the only Indian voyageur "through the head with a pistol" for having killed Ensign Robert Hood. Hood, whom Richardson and Hepburn had refused to leave, whom they had so tenderly nursed for two weeks as they all slowly died of starvation on the tundra.

John Richardson first saw the tundra on September 9, 1820. He wrote in his journal:

> By noon we reached a remarkable hill with precipitous sides called by the Copper Indians Agnaatheh or the Dog-rib rock. . . . From the time we quitted the banks of the Winter River [at Fort Enterprise] we saw only a few detached clumps of trees, but after passing Dog-rib rock even these disappeared, and we travelled through a naked country. (8)

Oddly enough, Keskarrah was with Richardson on that short trip to the Coppermine River, acting as both guide and hunter. No doubt the Dene elder told the naturalist the name of that immense rock, which remains truly remarkable to this day. He might also have told the long, continuing story of that rock; if Keskarrah had felt free to do so, I believe that Richardson would have understood, among other things, that the immense country lying all around before him was not quite so naked as it appeared to be to his logical, scientific, European, eye.

In any case, it is now a hundred and seventy-five years later. Surely we no longer need to make the mistake he made. Surely by now we are ready to understand that the nakedness of our country lies most purely in the uninformed eye of the beholder.

WORKS CITED

Abel, Kerry. *Drum Songs. Glimpses of Dene History.* Kingston: McGill-Queen's University Press, 1993.

Blondin, George. *When the World Was New.* Yellowknife: Outcrop, 1990.

Back, George. *Arctic Artist: The Journal and Paintings of George Back, Midshipman with Franklin, 1819–1822,* ed. C. S. Houston. Kingston: McGill-Queen's University Press, 1995.

Cruikshank, Julie. *Life Lived Like a Story; Life Stories of Three Yukon Elders.* Vancouver: University of British Columbia Press, 1990.

Franklin, John. *Narrative of a Journey to the Shores of the Polar Sea in the Years 1819–'20–'21–'22.* London: Everyman, n.d., Introduction by Captain R. F. Scott, c. 1910.

McIlraith, John. *Life of Sir John Richardson.* London: Longmans, Green, 1868.

Richardson, John. *Arctic Ordeal: The Journal of John Richardson, 1820–1822.* ed. C. S. Houston. Kingston: McGill-Queen's University Press, 1984.

———. *Arctic Searching Expedition: A Journal of a Boat Voyage through Rupert's Land and the Arctic Sea, in Search of the Discovery Ships under Command of Sir John Franklin.* 2 vols. London: Longman, Brown, Green and Longmans, 1851.

———. *Fauna Boreali-Americana, or The Zoology of the Northern Parts of British America. First Part, the Mammals.* London: John Murray, 1829.

An Early Meeting of Cultures: Inuit and English, 1576–1578

H. G. JONES

The setting of this paper is Frobisher Bay, southern Baffin Island, approximately 1300 air miles (2080 km) north of Ottawa. For background, a seventy–second review: although there had been earlier contact between the Norse and the Greenlandic (and possibly Canadian) Eskimos, and although a drawing published in Augsburg in 1567 suggests that at least one Arctic captive may have been taken to Europe earlier, the first well-documented contact between Europeans and the American Eskimos, hereafter referred to as Inuit in the plural and Inuk in the singular, occurred in 1576 when Martin Frobisher led the first of his three expeditions in search of a northwest passage. The Englishman assumed that he had found an isthmus between the American continent on the south and an arm of Asia on the north, and he gave the waterway the name Frobisher Strait, much as Magellan had given his own name to the strait at the opposite end of the Americas.

Frobisher never knew where he had been, although he was able to find his way back twice, and for two centuries mapmakers shifted "Frobisher Strait" to southern Greenland. It was nearly three hundred years before Charles Francis Hall utilized Inuit oral history in 1862 to locate the ruins of the sixteenth-century mining operations and restore Frobisher's name to the waterway, which is in fact a dead–end bay rather than a strait.

Chief legacies of the three Frobisher voyages are the archaeological remains now being explored by a joint Canadian–American team, of which the University of Ottawa geologist Donald Hogarth is a key member, and the descriptions left behind of the icy waters, the treeless land, and, especially, the inhabitants of this harsh but already occupied world. Remarkably, we have eyewitness accounts from four participants of the voyages, two of whom may have sailed on all three. The remainder of my paper is limited to these first–hand accounts of contacts between the English and the Inuit—from, of course, the English point of view.

Let George Best describe the very first meeting of two cultures:

> . . . being ashore upon the top of a hill, he [Frobisher] perceived a number of small things fleeting in the sea afarre off, which he supposed to be porposes or seales, or some kinde of strange fish; but comming neerer, he discovered them to be men in small boats made of leather. And before he could descend downe from the hill, certaine of those people had almost cut off his boat from him, having stollen secretly behinde the rocks for that purpose, where he speedily hasted to his boat, and bent himselfe to his halberd, and narrowly escaped the danger, and saved his boat. (Best, 59)

Whether or not the intentions of the Inuit were as hostile as the invaders interpreted, seeds of distrust were thus sown during the very first encounter, and future dealings would be burdened by distrust. Warily, however, Christopher Hall, captain of the *Gabriel* (the only one of the three original vessels to reach Baffin) and several of his men rowed ashore again and, through sign language, conversed with a native group, to each of whom he gave a "threadden point." Hall persuaded an Inuk to come aboard the *Gabriel,* leaving a crew member ashore as hostage. The visitor "made great wondering at all things," and when he was offered a taste of the ship's meat and drink, "he made no countenance of liking any." He did, however, joyously return to shore with a tinkling bell and "other tryfles." This auspicious visit led to another by a delegation of nineteen Inuit, who brought aboard with them raw meat and fish, which, to the disgust of the English, they "greedily devoured . . . before our men's faces." Hall reported, ". . . they spake, but we understoode them not," but both sides were well pleased with the exchange of "coats of seales, and beares skinnes, and such like" for bells, buttons, looking glasses, and cheap toys (Hall, 31; Best, 59).

This amicable relationship did not last. Another Inuk was enticed aboard the *Gabriel* and given a bell and a knife, and, through sign language, was apparently persuaded to row in his kayak in front of the English ship in its negotiation of the shallow and treacherous "strait." Frobisher had five of his men row the Inuk ashore to get his kayak, but the crewmen ignored the general's orders to drop the visitor off at a rock in clear view. Instead, intent upon exchanging more gifts with a group of "countrie people" known to be waiting out of sight, they disappeared behind an island, never to be seen again. Sounds of trumpet, falconet, and human cries brought no response from the shore (Best, 59; Hall, 31).

Frobisher, having lost his only rowboat and thus being incapable of sending a party ashore to retrieve his men, was now down to a crew of only thirteen, several of them ill. He now regretted that he had not taken hostages earlier, so when a number of native kayaks appeared on the water the next day,

> to deceive the deceivers he wrought a prety policy; for knowing wel how they greatly delighted in our toyes, and specially in belles, he rang a prety lowbell, making signes that he would give him the same that would come and fetch it. And because they would not come within his danger for feare, he flung one bell unto them, which of purpose he threw short, that it might fall into the sea and be lost. And, to make them more greedy of the matter he rang a louder bell, so that in the end one of them came nere the ship side to receive the bel; which when he thought to take at the captaines hand, he was thereby taken himselfe: for the captaine being readily provided let the bell fall and caught the man fast, and plucked him with maine force boat and all. . . . Whereupon when he found himselfe in captivity, for very choler and disdaine he bit his tongue in twaine within his mouth: notwithstanding, he died not thereof . . . (Best, 59)

Knowing nothing but suspecting the worst fate of his missing men, Frobisher could not afford to linger in the icy waters as inhospitable as the natives and, after a few days of repeatedly sounding its trumpet and firing its falconet with no response from the shore, the crippled *Gabriel* turned its bow toward England. Six harrowing weeks later the ship astounded the nation—because its cowardly sister ship had deserted and reported the *Gabriel* lost on the voyage over—by sailing into Harwich with its souvenirs, including the "strange infidell, whose like was never seene, read, nor heard of before, and whose language was neither knowen nor understood of any" (Best, 59). A London observer described the captive as a "strange man and his bote, which was such a wonder onto the whole city and to the rest of the realm that heard of yt as seemed never to have happened the like great matter to any man's knowledge." The poor man became a national curiosity and was sketched by Lucas de Heere and Adriaen Coenen before succumbing to white man's disease (Sturtevant and Quinn, 72–76).

It was another souvenir, a heavy black rock containing shiny flecks, that made Frobisher a national hero and assured his return to Meta Incognita, as Queen Elizabeth named the newfound land. Both the 1577 and 1578 expeditions, with the queen's *Ayde* as flagship, were specifically for the mining of what was believed to be gold ore, and there was little time for confirming the northwest passage. But Frobisher did have another important objective: to recover the five men captured by the Inuit during the first voyage. Contact started off hopefully in 1577:

> . . . we espied certaine of the countrey people on the top of Mount Warwick with a flag wafting us backe againe and making a

great noise, with cries like the mowing of Buls seeming greatly
desirous of conference with us: whereupon the Generall being
therewith better acquainted, answered them againe with the like
cries, whereat and with the noise of our trumpets they seemed
greatly to rejoyce, skipping, laughing and dancing for joy. And
hereupon we made signes unto them, holding up two fingers, commanding two of our men to go apart from our companies, whereby
they might do the like. So that forthwith two of our men & two of
theirs met togither a good space from company, neither partie having their weapons about them. Our men gave them pins and points
and such trifles as they had. And they likewise bestowed on our
men two bow cases and such things as they had. They earnestly
desired our men to goe up into their countrey, and our men
offered them like kindnesse aboord our ships, but neither part (as
it seemed) admitted or trusted the others curtesie. (Best, 63)

As the Englishmen turned toward their boats, the Inuit "with great
tokens of affection . . . called us backe againe . . . whereupon our Generall
taking his Master with him, who was best acquainted with their maners,
went apart unto two of them, meaning, if they could lay sure hold upon
them, forcibly to bring them aboord, with intent to bestow certaine toyes
and apparell upon the one, and so to dismisse him with all arguments of
curtesie, and retaine the other for an Interpreter." The unsuspecting Inuit
exchanged such things as they had left, and one of them, "for lacke of better marchandise, cut off the tayle of his coat (which is a chiefe ornament
among them) and gave it unto our Generall for a present." The ungrate-
ful Englishmen then grabbed both Inuit, but in the slippery snow the
natives broke away, recovered their hidden bows and arrows, and "with
such fury assaulted and pursued our Generall and his Master, being altogether unarmed . . . and hurt the Generall in the buttocke with an arrow . . ." (Best, 64). Ignominiously, Martin Frobisher was probably the first
casualty in European–Inuit contact.

Nevertheless, a Cornishman chased down one of the natives, who
was captured and carried aboard. The captive appears to have become
somewhat co-operative, for later he accompanied the English on searches
for the five men lost the previous year. At a camp hastily abandoned by the
Inuit, the hostage explained the use of various sleds, bridles, kettles, and
knives. Best wrote, ". . . taking in his hand one of those countrey bridles, he
caught one of our dogges and hampred him handsomely therein, as we
doe our horses, and with a whip in his hand, he taught the dogges to draw
in a sled as we doe horses in a coach" (Best, 66). The Inuk disbelieved his
eyes when the men showed him a drawing of his countryman captured
and taken to England the year before, "thinking that we could make men
live or die at our pleasure" (Best, 67).

The most violent encounter between the invaders and the natives occurred when the English caught up with a group of sixteen or eighteen Inuit, who, being forced ashore, broke their oars and

> desperatly returning upon our men, resisted them manfully in their landing, so long as their arrowes and dartes lasted, and after gathering up those arrowes which our men shot at them, yea, and plucking our arrowes out of their bodies incountred afresh againe, and maintained their cause untill both weapons and life fayled them. And when they found they were mortally wounded, being ignorant what mercy meaneth, with deadly fury they cast themselves headlong from off the rockes into the sea, least perhaps their enemies should receive glory or prey of their dead carcaises, for they supposed us belike to be Canibals, or eaters of mans flesh. (Best, 68)

In the battle at Bloody Point, immortalized by John White's watercolour, one Englishman was hurt in the belly by an arrow, and five or six of the Inuit were slain. The remainder fled, except for two women. An older one—so ugly that the Englishmen took her to be a witch—was left, but the younger one, who was "cumbred with a sucking childe" in her amautiq, was taken. In the melee, the child's arm had been pierced by gunshot. When the English medic applied ointment to the wound, the mother "plucked those salves away, and by continuall licking with her owne tongue, not much unlike our dogs, healed up the childes arme." George Best gloomily reported, "And now considering their [the other Inuit] sudden flying from our men, and their desperate maner of fighting, we began to suspect that we had heard the last newes of our men which the last yere were betrayed of these people. And considering also their ravenous and bloody disposition in eating any kind of raw flesh or carrion howsoever stinking, it is to bee thought that they had slaine and devoured our men . . ." (Best, 68).

The English later encountered and conversed with another group of natives in sign language, seating the woman and child on a rock as hostages. Frobisher was led to believe that he was being told that three of the five missing men were still alive and that they asked for pen, ink, and paper. Consequently, he prepared a letter in which he stated, "I have aboord, of theirs, a man, a woman, and a child, which I am contented to deliver for you. . . . Moreover you may declare unto them, that if they deliver you not, I will not leave a man alive in their country" (Best, 70). He also left writing materials to be taken to the men.

As the days passed there was no response from the lost Englishmen, but the Inuit continued to wave and call for negotiations. But for each of the few Inuit who actually came within speaking distance, several more were spied hiding behind rocks. They mistook the gullibility of the English when one Inuk, pretending to be terribly lame, hobbled down to the beach pleading for treatment. To test his lameness, a shot was fired near the man. His duplicity was proven, in the words of Dionyse Settle, when "The counterfeit villeine deliverly fled, without any impediment at all . . ." (Settle, 36).

This second expedition returned to England with three new captives. Their likenesses by John White are especially significant because they predate White's more numerous watercolours of the Algonquin Indians in North Carolina by less than a decade. None of the three Inuit lived more than a few months.

In terms of contact with the Inuit, the third expedition in 1578, consisting of fifteen vessels and nearly four hundred men (making it the largest Arctic expedition down to the present time), was anticlimactic. The wary Inuit kept their distances, and Frobisher was under strict orders to concentrate on digging and loading ore. More than 1100 tons were taken back to England and proved worthless except as paving and building materials.

Thus, as I indicated earlier, the Frobisher voyages are significant today because of their archaeological opportunities and their accounts of Europe's first documented encounter with the Eskimos of North America. On the first voyage, Christopher Hall made notes, carefully observing the strange people of Meta Incognita: "They be like to Tarters," he wrote, "with long blacke haire, broad faces, and flatte noses, and tawnie in colour, wearing Seale skinnes . . . the women are marked in the face with blewe strekes down the cheekes, and round about the eyes. Their boates are made all of Seales skinnes . . ." (Hall, 31). Hall also took a brief language lesson by pointing to seventeen parts of the body and pieces of clothing and having them identified by the Inuit. I am no linguist, but more than four hundred years later I can recognize several of his badly misspelled words: *Attegay* (*atigi,* meaning parka or coat); *Callagay* (*karlik,* meaning breeches); *Chewat* (*suit,* meaning ear); *Coblone* (*kublu,* meaning thumb), *Teckkere* (*tikerk,* meaning forefinger), and *Yacketrone* (*ikritkrok,* meaning little finger) (Hall, 32).

Dionyse Settle's account of the second voyage gives us a much fuller picture of the natives. His description of their skin—"their colour is not much unlike the Sunne burnt Countrey man, who laboureth daily in the Sunne for his living"—may help explain the English reference to them as "countrie people." A few other observations by Settle:

> They eate their meat all raw, both flesh, fish, and foule, or something per boyled with blood and a little water which they drinke. . . . They neither use table, stoole, or table cloth for comlines. . . .

They apparell themselves in the skins of such beasts as they kill, sewed together with sinewes of them. All the foule which they kill, they skin, and make thereof one kind of garment or other to defend them from the cold. They make their apparel with hoods and tailes, which tailes they give when they thinke to gratifie any friendship shewed unto them: a great signe of friendship with them. . . .

Upon their legges they weare hose of leather, with the furre side inward two or three paire on at once, and especially the women. In those hose they put their knives, needles, and other things needful to beare about. . . .

They dresse their skinnes very soft and souple with the haire on. In cold weather or Winter they weare the furre side inward: and in Summer outward. Other apparell they have none but the said skinnes. . . .

Their houses are tents made of Seale skins, pitched up with 4 Firre quarters foure square meeting at the top, and the skins sewed together with sinewes, and laid thereupon: they are so pitched up, that the entrance into them is always South or against the Sunne. They have other sorts of houses . . . which are raised with stones and Whale bones, and a skinne layd over them, to withstand the raine, or other weather: the entrance of them being not much unlike an Ovens mouth. . . .

As the Countrey is barren and unfertile, so are they rude and of no capacitie to culture the same to any perfection: but are contented by their hunting, fishing, and fouling, with raw flesh and warme blood to satisfie their greedy panches, which is their only glory. (Settle, 32–39)

Not surprisingly, Dionyse Settle exhibited the disdain of an Englishman toward a culture other than his own, but after more than four centuries, a final comment demonstrates the perceptiveness of his observations of a society without a written language and previously unknown to Europeans: "Those beasts, fishes, and foules, which they kill, are their meat, drinke, apparell, houses, bedding, hose, shooes, threed, and sailes for their boats, with many other necessaries whereof they stand in need, and almost all of their riches" (Settle, 37). For, indeed, that was a fair evaluation of the ways of the Inuit until the invasion of trade goods deprived them of their subsistence living and made them, too, dependent upon a consumer economy.

Eight years after Englishmen initially came into contact with Baffinlanders, Richard Hakluyt, in his manuscript popularly known as "A Discourse on Western Planting," made the first known use of the term "Esquimawes" (Quinn and Quinn, 66). Now, more than four hundred years later, the descendants of the "Esquimawes," the Inuit of Baffin Island, are joining with their kin throughout the Northwest Territories in establishing a new government, Nunavut—"Our Land." The English did, indeed, as Hakluyt proposed, "plant" the North American continent; fortunately, however, they did not entirely *supplant* their predecessors who, after four centuries of marginalization, will soon regain their dominant role in the Arctic narrative.

WORKS CITED

Best, George. *A true Discourse of the three Voyages of Discoverie, for the finding of a passage to Cathaya, by the Northwest, under the conduct of Martin Frobisher General. . . .* In Richard Hakluyt, *The Principal Navigations, Voyages, Traffiques and Discoveries of the English Nation . . .* 3 vol. in 2. London: George Bishop, Ralph Newbie, and Robert Barker, 1598–1600, vol. 3: 47–96.

Collinson, Richard, ed. *The Three Voyages of Martin Frobisher, in Search of a Passage to Cathaia and India by the North–West, A.D. 1576–8.* London: The Hakluyt Society, 1867.

Ellis, Thomas. *The third and last voyage unto Meta Incognita, made by M. Martin Frobisher, in the yeere 1578.* In Richard Hakluyt, *The Principal Navigations, Voyages, Traffiques and Discoveries of the English Nation . . .* 3 vol. in 2. London: George Bishop, Ralph Newbie, and Robert Barker, 1598–1600, vol. 3: 39–44.

Fitzhugh, William W. and Jacqueline S. Olin, eds. *Archaeology of the Frobisher Voyages.* Washington: Smithsonian Institution Press, 1993.

Hall, Charles Francis. *Life with the Esquimaux.* 2 vol. London: Sampson Low, Son, and Marston, 1864.

Hall, Christopher. *The first Voyage of M. Martine Frobisher, to the Northwest, for the search of the straight or passage to China, written by Christopher Hall, Master in the Gabriel, and made in the yeere of our Lord 1576.* In Richard Hakluyt, *The Principal Navigations, Voyages, Traffiques and Discoveries of the English Nation . . .* 3 vol. in 2. London: George Bishop, Ralph Newbie, and Robert Barker, 1598–1600, vol. 3: 29–32.

Hogarth, Donald D., P. W. Boreham, and J. G. Mitchell. *Martin Frobisher's Northwest Venture, 1576–1581: Mines, Minerals & Metallurgy.* Ottawa: Canadian Museum of Civilization, 1994.

Hulton, Paul and David Beers Quinn. *The American Drawings of John White, 1577–1590.* 2 vol. London: The British Museum, and Chapel Hill: University of North Carolina Press, 1964.

Kenyon, W. A. *Tokens of Possession: The Northern Voyages of Martin Frobisher.* Toronto: Royal Ontario Museum, 1975.

McFee, William. *The Life of Sir Martin Frobisher.* New York: Harper, 1928.

Oswalt, Wendell H. *Eskimos and Explorers.* Novato, CA: Chandler & Sharp, 1979.

———. "The Eskimo People: The Earliest Accounts." In *The Beaver* 308 (Autumn 1977): 21–27.

Quinn, David Beers and Alison M. Quinn, eds. *A particuler discourse concerning the greate necessitie and manifolde commodyties that are like to grow to this Realm of Englande by the western discoveries lately attempted, written in the yere 1584 by Richarde Hackluyt of Oxforde* [better known by the title of *Discourse of Western Planting*]. London: The Hakluyt Society, 1993.

Rowley, Susan. "Frobisher Miksanut: Inuit Accounts of the Frobisher Voyages." In Fitzhugh, William W. and Quinn, Jacqueline S., eds. *Archaeology of the Frobisher Voyages*. Washington: Smithsonian Institution Press, 1993.

Settle, Dionise. *The second voyage of Master Martin Frobisher, made to the West and Northwest Regions, in the yeere 1577, with a description of the Countrey, and people, written by Master Dionise Settle*. In Hakluyt, Richard. *The Principal Navigations, Voyages, Traffiques and Discoveries of the English Nation* . . . 3 vol. in 2. London: George Bishop, Ralph Newbie, and Robert Barker, 1598–1600, vol. 3: 32–39.

Stefansson, Vilhjalmur and E. McCaskill, eds. *The Three Voyages of Martin Frobisher in search of a passage to Cathay and India by the North–West, A.D. 1576–8*. 2 vol. London: The Argonaut Press, 1938.

Sturtevant, William C. "The First Inuit Depiction by Europeans." In *Etudes/Inuit/Studies* 4 (1980): 47–49.

Sturtevant, William C. and David Beers Quinn. "This New Prey: Eskimos in Europe in 1567, 1576, and 1577." In Feest, Christian F. ed. *Indians and Europe: An Interdisciplinary Collection of Essays*. Aachen: Radar–Verlag [Forum 11], 1987: 61–140.

Wallis, Helen. "England's Search for the Northern Passages in the Sixteenth and Early Seventeenth Centuries." In *Arctic* 37 (December 1984): 453–472.

"All Well": Narrating the Third Franklin Expedition

EDWARD PARKINSON

Historians, literary critics, and archaeologists have all agreed that there exists no published "narrative of a third Franklin expedition" since everyone on that tragic journey perished in the Arctic some time between the fall of 1845 and the spring and summer of 1848; David Woodman, in his book *Unravelling the Franklin Mystery,* argues that some members may have lived until 1851. In any case, no detailed journals exist, but the expedition did produce several *texts* including an official record discovered in a cairn, and some personal papers of Harry Peglar found in the clothes of a skeleton. The cairn record and Peglar's papers produce what I will call the "journal of the third expedition," a narrative more fragmented than any traditionally edited and published exploration journal, but one which reveals much about the discourse of exploration. While the cairn record is obviously meant to be a public document, scientifically detailing the time and space through which the expedition has travelled, the "papers" are largely private and personal. This combination of public and private parallels many explorers' journals wherein meteorological, cartographic, and ethnographic observations are balanced with personal reflections on the landscape and on the social interactions which occur in any expedition.

I will begin by discussing the cairn record (Figure 1), which was uncovered by Lieutenant W. R. Hobson on May 5, 1859 on King William Island, and has been interpreted extensively and its few words examined exhaustively for historical accuracy.[1] Much has been theorized about the events and characters mentioned in it, though this work has come mainly from historians and not literary critics. To begin with, the record is a *bona fide* official document, written on a naval record form supplied to Franklin by the Admiralty. It contains two entries, indicating it was deposited once,

H. M. S.hips *Erebus* and *Terror* } Wintered in the Ice in

28 of May 184 7 } Lat. 70° 5' N. Long. 98°.23' W.

Having wintered in 1846—7 at Beechey Island in Lat 74° 43'.28" N. Long 91°.39'.15" W. After having ascended Wellington Channel to Lat 77°. and returned by the West side of Cornwallis Island.

Sir John Franklin commanding the Expedition. All well

Commander.

WHOEVER finds this paper is requested to forward it to the Secretary of the Admiralty, London, *with a note of the time and place at which it was found*: or, if more convenient, to deliver it for that purpose to the British Consul at the nearest Port.

QUINCONQUE trouvera ce papier est prié d'y marquer le tems et lieu ou il l'aura trouvé, et de le faire parvenir au plutot au Secrétaire de l'Amirauté Britannique à Londres.

CUALQUIERA que hallare este Papel, se le suplica de enviarlo al Secretarie del Almirantazgo, en Londrés, con una nota del tiempo y del lugar en donde so halló,

EEN ieder die dit Papier mogt vinden, wordt hiermede verzogt, om het zelve, ten spoedigste, te willen zenden aan den Heer Minister van de Marine der Nederlanden in 's Gravenhage, of wel aan den Secretaris den Britsche Admiraliteit, te London, en daar by te voegen eene Nota, inhoudende de tyd en de plaats alwaar dit Papier is gevonden geworden.

FINDEREN af dette Papiir ombedes, naar Leilighed gives, at sende samme til Admiralitets Secretairen i London, eller nærmeste Embedsmand i Danmark, Norge, eller Sverrig. Tiden og Stædit hvor dette er fundet ønskes venskabeligt paategnet.

WER diesen Zettel findet, wird hier-durch ersucht denselben an den Secretair des Admiralitets in London einzusenden, mit gefälliger angabe an welchen ort und zu welcher zeit er gefunden worden ist.

Party consisting of 2 Officers and 6 Men left the Ships on Monday 24th May 84/5

Wm Gore Lieut
Chas F. Des Voeux Mate

Figure 1

then retrieved, re-inscribed, and deposited in the cairn a second time. Both entries are in the handwriting of Commander James Fitzjames, third in command of the expedition, though the first record was signed, dated, and deposited by Lieutenant Gore. The first message gives the routes the *Erebus* and *Terror* travelled in the first two seasons and ends "all well." The second message describes the deaths of fifteen men and nine officers (including Sir John Franklin) and ends with a brief reference to the abandonment of the ships, still beset in the ice, and the desperate and doomed attempt by the "105 souls" who remained alive to reach Back's Fish River, over two hundred kilometres away. The second entry also contains the signature of Captain Crozier. The composition of the cairn record therefore follows the pattern of John Franklin's first two published narratives, which were collective productions and included the texts and scientific observations of several officers in the expeditions. And like Franklin's *Journey to the Polar Sea* and *Narrative of a Second Expedition,* the cairn record functions as an official report, though it is obviously lacking many specific details.

One of the most famous interpretations of the record was by the Arctic veteran, Captain Francis Leopold McClintock, who commanded the expedition of which Hobson was a member. In his book, *The Voyage of the "Fox",* McClintock describes the change in tone between the first and second entries: "In the short space of twelve months how mournful had become the history of Franklin's expedition; how changed from the cheerful 'All well' of Graham Gore!" (259). And McClintock's most famous description of the record is his statement that "A sad tale was never told in fewer words" (260). Indeed, the record is brief reading, consisting largely of statements of time and place (a remarkable number of which are incorrect), along with descriptions of the men's movements and deaths. Its entirely "official" and factual documentation satisfied the public's desire for facts and dates, yet left most of the expedition's events to the imagination. McClintock's interpretation draws attention to the document's brevity, yet argues that its literary *effect* is still substantial, in spite of its compression. He implies that it does "tell a tale" and therefore its value for him is primarily narrative.

Although the record is incomplete, fragmented, and contains geographic and chronological errors, it is important to recognize its immense authority as *official text* of the third expedition. In the years following Franklin's disappearance much speculation occurred as to the length of time he and his men might have survived, the outcome of their possible contact with the Inuit in the area, and the amount of territory they might have explored. The discovery of this records, and, subsequently, a lifeboat with skeletons of Franklin's men officially ended the mystery of the expedition's fate. I am arguing that the cairn record *is* part of the "journal" of the third expedition, a document which declares its validity and importance through its singularity. While conjecture and theorization continue to this day, the record has become central to any interpretation because it stands as the only official statement from the expedition itself. Despite its immense historical importance and the considerable number of times its words have been cited, virtually no attention has been paid to its literary significance. It is as if McClintock's statements were deemed sufficient, and no further words were spent exploring its plot and technique.

The cairn record is immediately striking because of its severely formal nature. It is a standard naval form, with prompts and blank areas for the ship's name, the date, and latitude and longitude to be filled in. In fact, there is practically no space set aside to write out anything other than these barest of details. The form's formal austerity discourages any author from weaving a narrative other than what can be filled in, in the blanks, and the first entry tries vainly to stay within these officially prescribed boundaries. But the second entry overwhelms the official record's formalism and its text is literally written in the margins—the interstices between what the navy has decided is essential knowledge. Just as the journey itself has been a struggle against obstacles, ending in the unyielding bottleneck of northern pack ice, the narrative of the journey struggles with official naval decorum, threading its own way through the bureaucratic form and its maze of blanks.

The majority of the form is taken up by these instructions in six languages:

> WHOEVER finds this paper is requested to forward it to the Secretary of the Admiralty, London, *with a note of the time and place at which it was found:* or, if more convenient, to deliver it for that purpose to the British Consul at the nearest Port.[2]

As Jacques Derrida has written, "The entire history of postal *tekhné* tends to rivet the destination to identity. To arrive, to happen would be to subject, to happen to 'me'" ("Envois," 192). In other words, the postal system is part of a structure of identity, where "arriving" is a confirmation of the system itself. We can see the postal system as an *envoy* of government, and this naval message illustrates Derrida's point by expanding the location of the post office and directing *anyone who finds it and can read it* to become an imperialist messenger, thus including the whole of the "Western" and "civilized" world within the service of the British Admiralty. The message's obvious appeal to universality provokes the question: who cannot read it? And one answer would be the Inuit, who have either not found the record, or left it there deciding it was worthless. The record lay in its cairn for several years, waiting for the postman to come. The universality of the Royal Naval form, translated into all major European languages, is stopped by an untranslatable cultural barrier. Even in the nineteenth century, when the fur trade had opened routes the length and breadth of the country, there remained uncharted areas, and peoples who would not know how to find a "British Consul." Perhaps the record remained secure in the cairn precisely because of its own untranslatability, its otherness which defied interpretation.

Some Inuit oral reports claimed the Inuit had seen the *Erebus* and *Terror* after the expedition had perished, and had boarded the vessels, tearing out valuable wood and iron before the ships eventually sank. Whether or not these reports are true, the ships *did* contain resources the natives could recognize, and it is logical that they would have been stripped. In a sense, these actions would be echoing an earlier scene depicted in Franklin's *Narrative of a Second Expedition* by the engraving titled "Esquimaux Pillaging the Boats." That scene, where the "Esquimaux" are shown brandishing knives, overrunning the boats, and stealing supplies, was instigated by Franklin's attempt to initiate mercantile trading practices with a culture unaccustomed to the laws of private property and capitalist exchange. In the case of the third expedition, the Inuit ultimately "pillaged" the boats used in the last desperate attempt to reach the Back River. These examples demonstrate antagonistic relationships between the Europeans (and their private property) and the indigenes which one might expect would extend to the cairn record, yet it remained untouched and unread. Perhaps the cairn was never discovered by the Inuit, but perhaps it *was* discovered and did not appear valuable or meaningful in any sense the Inuit could recognize; it remained outside their economy and realm of exchanges.

The record exhibits a remarkable circularity: it travels outwards toward the site of discovery, and then announces its intention to return home, to rivet its identity firmly on British soil. Furthermore, it extends this circularity throughout the world by making any port a site of British identity; and by reproducing the message into other languages it reinforces a myth that this identity survives translation. Ports are architectural junctures bridging the alterity between land and sea: "a place by the shore where ships may run in for shelter from storms, or to load and unload; a harbour, a haven" (*OED*). A port must combine a good geographic location with a solid organizational infrastructure, and is also "a place where customs officers are stationed to supervise the entry of goods." Thus ports are strategic places of governmental control with each location "standing in," synecdochically, for Britain, therefore ensuring that the image of imperialism travels around the world and, through the loading and unloading of goods and the circulation of trade, that it is always tied to capitalist production.

As I began to describe above, the austere formalism of the naval record is undermined by the excessive marginalia through which the narrative of the expedition unfolds. The blanks are replete with latitude and longitude figures, but these figures overflow the designated areas and spill out into the margins. The word "Commander" is crossed out, or perhaps put *under erasure,* since there were two ships and several officers in positions of authority and this one record must represent all of them. The first note is signed by Lieutenant Gore, although Franklin is "commanding" the expedition, and the second is written by Fitzjames, although it may have been "dictated" by Crozier (now in command after Franklin's death). There is simply too much information to be conveyed, and the form is completely filled with writing. In addition to compressing the events of the voyage, the record also compresses the time: in contrast to traditional exploration journals, where each day is used to mark the progress through time and geography, here we have only two moments represented and they emphasize the expedition's march into tragedy.

Although the text greatly exceeds the space designed for it, neither Gore nor Fitzjames manage to transcend the fairly strict limits of official naval discourse. It is as if, although exceeding the blanks, each statement were designed to still fill the blanks, even in the margins. The text of the first note reads:

> 28 of May 1847. HM Ships Erebus and Terror wintered in the ice in Lat. 70°05' N. Long. 98°23' W. Having wintered in 1846–7 at Beechey Island, in lat. 74°43'28" N, long. 90°39'15" W. after having ascended Wellington Channel to Lat. 77°, and returned by the west side of Cornwallis Island. Sir John Franklin commanding the expedition. All well. Party consisting of 2 officers and 6 men left the ships on Monday 24th May 1847. Gm. Gore, Lieut. Chas. F. Des Voeux, mate. (Neatby, 262)

The date of wintering is incorrect and should read 1845–1846. This text is comprised almost solely of statements of dates, locations, and proper names. The one deviation is the two-word sentence, "All well," which Graham Gore added when he deposited the record. As McClintock states, this phrase becomes tragically inaccurate when read in the context of their ultimate deaths. These figures indicating time and place form a compressed narrative of the third expedition which historians have read and reread, in order to reconstruct events and theorize motivations and routes travelled.[3]

The second entry describes how the ships "were deserted" on the 22nd of April "[hav]ing been beset since 12th Sept. 1846" and how "The Officers & Crews consisting of 105 souls under the command [of Cap]tain F. R. M. Crozier landed here in Lat. 69° 37' 42" Long. 98° 41'." There follows one of the strangest parts of the record:

> [This] paper was found by Lieutenant Irving under the cairn supposed to have been built by Sir James Ross in 1831 where it had

been deposited (4 miles to the northward) by the late Commander Gore in May June 1847. Sir James Ross' pillar has not been found and the paper has been transferred to this position which is that in which Sir J Ross pillar was erected—Sir John Franklin died on the 11th June 1847 and the total loss by deaths in the Expedition has been to this date 9 officers & 15 men.

What is fascinating is the elaborate and lengthy discussion of the record's position, and the discussion of Ross's cairn. The events of the expedition are scarcely mentioned while much precious space is devoted to explaining how Ross's cairn could not be found. There is an obvious obsession with place, and with the self-reflexive discussion of the movement of this one text which they hope might one day be discovered. It appears almost as an afterthought that after Crozier signed his name "Captain & Senior Offr" he added "and start on tomorrow, 26th, for Backs Fish River." This is one of the most striking images of the Third Franklin Expedition, the final doomed march of the "105 souls" over frozen ground to a destination over two hundred kilometres away, and it is found here in a postscript to a supplement.

There are two extraordinary aspects of this record discovered by Hobson in 1859 (a narrative which was almost not written, and then almost not found). First, it is remarkable that such a fragile sheaf should weather several winters and provide such a large amount of information concerning the third expedition. Though it was rolled inside a metal cylinder to protect it from the elements, such care is still relatively insignificant against the severity of the Arctic climate and the vastness of the landscape. Leopold McClintock gives us several details concerning both the fragility of the records, and the difficulties involved in their production. He writes,

> [the records] were soldered up in thin tin cylinders, having been filled up on board prior to the departure of the travellers; consequently the day upon which they were *deposited* was not filled in; but already the papers were much damaged by rust, a very few more years would have rendered them wholly illegible. (273)

McClintock goes on to remark that "our gratitude [for the records] ought to be all the greater when we remember that the ink had to be thawed, and that writing in a tent during an April day in the Arctic regions is by no means an easy task" (274). The conditions of production and storage are extremely hostile to writing, yet this text survives and part of the reason for its *survival* is that it was able to remain absolutely *apart* from the environment; it did not disintegrate or rot, and was stored in a cairn to draw attention to its textual and cultural *différence* from the surrounding landscape. The cairn record also demonstrates that the technology of writing stores information efficiently, and that it subsequently provides a rich resource for interpretation. The cairn record survives because writing is flexible, durable, and has an extensive capacity for carrying knowledge.

The second extraordinary aspect of this record is that its instructions are actually followed! It *is* "forwarded to London" and the time and place of its being found have become almost legendary. The circularity of the system is completed and, to paraphrase Derrida, the letter reaching its destination "rivets" the identity of the third expedition. However, the third expedition's identity is now split: Franklin and his crew are both imperial subjects whose home is England, yet they are also historically and materially part of the Arctic territory where the record was located. Their mid-nineteenth-century disappearance has become part of Canada's history, and their narrative is being interpreted by our own historians and forensic anthropologists. When Gore and Fitzjames write their notes they are not simply recording events; they are writing their histories back to the Empire in the hope that somehow their message will be forwarded or delivered to whomever it might concern.

At almost the same time that Hobson found the cairn record, McClintock was investigating the south coast of the island where he found a skeleton which he believed to be of Harry Peglar, a Petty Officer on the *Terror.* Just as the cairn conveyed writing, so did this skeleton, though Peglar's texts have received much less attention. They are detailed in an article by R. J. Cyriax and A. G. E. Jones with the self-explanatory title, "The Papers in the Possession of Harry Peglar, Captain of the Foretop, H.M.S. *Terror,* 1845."

Cyriax and Jones list a total of thirteen items found "in the possession of Harry Peglar," of which the following are most important: "1) *The parchment certificate of a seaman serving in the Royal Navy;* 2) *A narrative of Harry Peglar's services at sea;* 3) *The words of a sea-song* beginning 'The C the C the open C it grew so fresh the Ever free,' and several other papers, some with addresses, others with assorted forms of writing. Item number nine is *A sheet of paper bearing some lines which begin:* 'O death whare is thy sting, the grave at Comfort Cove for who has any douat how ...' (192). "Most of the words are spelt backwards and so many are illegible that the subject-matter cannot be fully elucidated. The first line, 'O Death, whare is thy sting,' was obviously taken from the Burial Service or the New Testament" (192).

Among these papers we have a microcosm of the nineteenth-century British seaman's world. The papers include Peglar's Royal Navy seaman's certificate and a history of his life aboard various ships, and these two items establish his imperial identity.[4] Cyriax and Jones have attempted to trace the addresses in Peglar's possession and were successful in approximately half the examples. These addresses are additional indicators of Peglar's national identity since they link him with the British postal system and I have already described the importance of that system to the dissemination of imperialism. Cyriax and Jones were able to trace the addresses through city registry books, proving the efficacy of the archival in maintaining historical and national coherence. Peglar can be traced back to England because his texts are part of an English technology of writing, an imperial system of inscription that links a wide variety of sources and references.

Peglar's "sea-song" is a consciously literary text, and Cyriax and Jones report that "McClintock concluded that since Peglar had amused himself by writing this song on 21 April 1847, the officers and men of the Franklin expedition were at that time still cheerful and confident of success. Indeed, he regarded the song as a confirmation of the words 'All well' written on two records deposited . . . on King William Island" (190–191). McClintock links the sea-song intertextually to the cairn record I have already discussed, although his interpretation ignores the texts' formal characteristics and uses them as touchstones to speculate on the character and mood of the historical figures he reconstructs. But this "sea-song" can also be grouped with Peglar's seaman's certificate and his narrative of service because it is another text of the profession. Regardless of his mood, Peglar would have been familiar with rhymes and poems relating to the sea; they were texts he would have recited, to pass the time, or to relieve the tedium of shipboard tasks.[5] The burial service from the New Testament ("O Death, whare is thy sting") is another text which seamen might be expected to know since regular services were held on board, and it would be recited when any of their members passed away. The papers Peglar carries define his professional and personal identity; they are artifacts which he used to fix his own place within the discourse of exploration.

The combination of the cairn record and Peglar's papers offers a public and private "narrative" of the final Franklin expedition. The public record details the ships' spatial progress through the Arctic, and fixes important temporal moments of the expedition such as Franklin's death and the abandonment of the ships. That the public record is an official form only reinforces the imperialist system of regulation. Harry Peglar's "papers" show us the textual construction of a professional seaman's social domain. The addresses, seaman's certificate, and personal history link him to Britain's imperial project of exploration and communication. Peglar's diverse travels, including both to "Jamaker" and the Arctic, helped reinforce the Empire's control over its vast territories. Peglar's literary texts represent the culture of the seafaring world, oscillating between optimistic rhymes of the freedom of the sea, and sobering lines from the New Testament. Therefore, although no published journal exists, these fragmented texts provocatively narrate many events of the third Franklin expedition.

NOTES

1. There are actually two records found by Hobson on King William Island: both had nearly identical entries made in 1847, and one had an extraordinary "supplement" added in 1848. It is the latter record I will be discussing because it is by far the more interesting although, as Cyriax points out, the record with the single entry "is by no means devoid of interest or value" ("Franklin Records," 180).

2. It is intriguing that the directions in English are the most comprehensive and the translations are not all complete. For example, the French text omits informing the prospective messenger that he may deliver the paper to the "British Consul at the nearest Port" that is "more convenient."

3. Perhaps the ultimate irony is that the men who abandoned the ships a year after this portion of the record was written *did* discover the Northwest Passage when they walked south and found that "King William Land" was, in fact, "King William's Island." Leslie Neatby describes this achievement as a form of redemption when he writes that the "unburied skeletons . . . found along King William Island shore and on islets in Simpson Strait . . . prove that in those last days of misery and despair they did achieve the discovery of the Northwest Passage which they had so joyously undertaken" (*Search*, 264).

4. The narrative begins: "H Peglar has Served On board of His MS Clio 1825 Joined H M Ship Magnificent at Spit head For Jamaker Under the Command Lev( )tenent Mundel . . ."

5. I thank David Woodman for pointing out that this sea song, which expresses a desire for freedom and the ocean, also has a ribald connotation where the "C" stands for female genitalia. The double-entendre symbolizes a desire many sailors would have for both the open sea and unrestricted sexuality, particularly when contrasted with their difficult, dangerous, and restricted lives on board a typical nineteenth-century vessel.

WORKS CITED

Beattie, Owen. "Forensic Sciences Applied to Historical Problems: The Franklin Expedition." *Cultures in Contact: McMaster Anthropology Society Annual Symposium.* McMaster University, Hamilton, Ontario, 1992.

Beattie, Owen, and John Geiger. *Frozen in Time: Unlocking the Secrets of the Franklin Expedition.* Saskatoon: Western Producer Prairie Books, 1987.

Cyriax, Richard J. "The Two Franklin Expedition Records Found on King William Island." *Mariner's Mirror* 44 (1958): 179–189.

Cyriax, Richard J., and A. G. E. Jones. "The Papers in Possession of Harry Peglar, Captain of the Foretop, H.M.S. *Terror*, 1845." *Mariner's Mirror* 40 (1954): 186–195.

Derrida, Jacques. *The Post Card: From Socrates to Freud and Beyond.* Trans. Alan Bass. Chicago: University of Chicago Press, 1987.

Franklin, John. *Narrative of a Journey to the Shores of the Polar Sea, in the Years 1819, 20, 21, and 22.* London: John Murray, 1823. New York: Greenwood, 1969.

———. *Narrative of a Second Expedition to the Shores of the Polar Sea in the Years 1825, 1826, and 1827.* London: John Murray, 1828. Edmonton: M. G. Hurtig, 1971.

McClintock, Francis Leopold. *The Voyage of the "Fox" in the Arctic Seas. A Narrative of the Discovery of the Fate of Sir John Franklin and His Companions.* Boston: Ticknor and Fields, 1863. Edmonton: Hurtig Publishers, 1972.

Woodman, David C. *Unravelling the Franklin Mystery: Inuit Testimony*, gen. ed. Bruce G. Trigger. McGill-Queen's Native and Northern Series. Kingston: McGill-Queen's University Press, 1991.

Inuit Accounts and the Franklin Mystery

DAVID C. WOODMAN

Confucius said that "pale ink is better than the most retentive memory," and this prejudice against oral tradition has long held sway. Yet in the last century a great deal of research into the mechanics of saga and its transmission through folk tales has led to a re-evaluation of narrative as a valid historical source. Although historians, like the police, are reluctant to place undue emphasis on the uncorroborated statements of witnesses, they are becoming more aware that even imperfect memories are often a valuable supplement in cases where physical evidence is lacking or contradictory.

The Canadian experience shows the stress between oral and written history very well. The tales of the First Nations, passed down through generations for hundreds of years, are treated with some distrust by those who have recently arrived with a long written tradition. The tension between these two methods of dealing with the past is starkly illustrated by the way in which the story of the Franklin expedition has been treated by the two cultures involved.

Exactly 147 years ago this morning (April 22, 1995), a party of doomed men left their ice-bound ships near the northwest coast of King William Island in the central Canadian Arctic. They had endured their third winter in the ice, and twenty-four of their companions, including their commander, Sir John Franklin, had died. The survivors, now under the command of Captain Crozier, loaded their sledges with food for forty days and started a forlorn attempt to reach help or safety. Reaching shore in a shallow bay the men made camp on the gravel beach. Crozier prepared a short record of the events of the recent past, and of his intentions and placed it in a tin canister that was eventually recovered from a nearby cairn. He wrote that the next morning the entire party would commence the long journey to the south toward the Back River. None of the Crozier party survived.

The short record left at Victory Point on that cold April day is only 138 words long (the original document is kept at the Greenwich Maritime Museum, Arctic Collection document 2/121). Millions of words have been written about the fate of those lost explorers, library shelves around the world groan under the weight of much informed, and even more ill-informed, opinion. When the record was recovered eleven years after its deposition, its discoverer noted that "no log-book could be more provokingly laconic" (McClintock, 274). A trail of bleached skeletons and some personal relics were also found, but these could not help very much in resolving the details of that fateful retreat.

In the century and a half since the discovery of the fate of Franklin's men, their story has passed from the realm of objective history into mythology. It seems to have an irresistible hold on the public imagination. The story, as it has unfolded, has all of the elements of high drama—lost heroes battling the hostile elements, shipwreck, murder, and cannibalism. Since the details of the tragedy are still unknown, speculation has often replaced investigation. Until recently the lore of the doomed Franklin expedition has been told almost exclusively from the point of view of the European culture that sent it forth. Yet the stories have always held a great fascination for the Inuit of the central Arctic as well. The tales of the dead explorers and their ships were told and retold during the long winter nights. It is often forgotten that an expensive decade-long search for Franklin's crew was abandoned in the same year that a native casually told the explorers where to look.

The passage of a large group of strangers through their land could hardly go unremarked by the Inuit, but there was a great reluctance to trust their stories. This disdain for Inuit testimony emerged even before the location of the disaster was known. The year after Crozier wrote his short note, a native used sign language and a rough sketch to tell some whalers that he had visited two ships full of white men a few months earlier near King William Island (Wright, 231–232). The next year, when Franklin's first winter camp was found far to the north, the native was "proven" to have been mistaken. Even now, when we know that *HMS Erebus* and *Terror* had indeed been near King William Island at the appropriate time, the story is considered unreliable. As Crozier's record said that the ships had been abandoned in 1848, historians remark that no native could have visited the crews aboard them the following year.

The next year a native told a party of searchers a tale he had learned from the Baffin Island Inuit (Cyriax, 1962). His confused and confusing tale of men dying near abandoned ships at a place called Omanek was of no use to the searchers at the time, but there are enough points of similarity between his third-hand tale and the known details of the Franklin disaster to cast doubt on his characterisation by the searchers as a "drunken liar." Inuit stories about strange white men and their incomprehensible activities continued to emerge from the Arctic, usually told to whaling captains (Rae, 39; Gilder, 3). These were almost universally disbelieved, an attitude that has remained largely unchanged.

There were several reasons for this denigration of Inuit testimony. One was that British commentators did not wish to believe what they were being told. Given the fact that there were no survivors, it was best to picture their countrymen as having fallen in a disciplined and orderly and "civilized" manner. A primary factor in the inability of those at home to accept the Inuit testimony was undoubtedly that not all of it was flattering to their friends and loved ones. Gruesome tales of cannibalism, of skulls with apparent bullet holes in them, and of boots filled with cooked human flesh were not calculated to gain widespread acceptance. For many years the initial reaction to tales with these elements was that they must be fabrications, invented by the Inuit to cover up their own involvement. It was felt that the natives had at least abandoned, and probably murdered, the lost heroes (Dickens, 1854).

There was also a reluctance to accept that their lost comrades, who had been elevated to the status of cult heroes over the decades, had been unable to overcome difficulties in an environment in which the "savage" Inuit thrived. This is still often heard as a criticism of the conduct of the expedition. What is missing from such an equation is a consideration of scale—King William Island probably never supported more than fifty Inuit hunters, and famine was not unknown to them. The logistical demands of feeding people increase exponentially, and one cannot assume that Crozier's 105 companions would have been able to support themselves, even using Inuit techniques and skills that took a lifetime to master.

One difficulty in assessing the relevance of the Inuit traditions to the historian is that the Europeans and natives had completely different world views. The Inuit had no interest in the things the white men were most concerned with—exact numbers and dates. Their interest was in people—they remembered for seventy years the names of all of the Inuit participants in any event, the names of the relatives of those people, the state of the weather, and the hunting conditions at the time.

Long inured to the harshness of their environment, the Inuit were neither surprised nor overly dismayed by the great tragedy that had befallen Franklin's men. Although respected for their material wealth, according to most natives the sailors were like children, preoccupied with frivolous pursuits and unskilled in the ways of survival. That these men had died when they were forced to leave their artificial shipboard environment was hardly surprising. To the natives the greatest source of wonder was to be found in the nature of the expedition's abandoned technology. Inuit would often gleefully retell stories of the discovery of lifeboats containing untold wealth of wood and iron. They were fascinated by each strange thing found at a Franklin camp, although they often failed to understand its use. When they came across percussion caps, they thought they were tiny thimbles and envisioned a subspecies of midget seamen who busily used them for mending sails. Although occasionally amusing, the description of things that the Inuit found incomprehensible often lends credibility to their accounts. The discovery of a soft substance that "later became all same stone" may suggest that they encountered mortar or cement (Burwash, 115). When the Inuit speak of a boat which had holes in the side to "hold wind", they are accurately describing an inflatable dingy, a new invention that few Europeans had ever seen (Hall, 58914, 218). White men and their strange things could also be dangerous—on at least one occasion an explosion occurred when a young boy investigated a gunpowder store (Hall, Book 31).

Inuit descriptions of the campsites of the doomed men give us our best information about conditions after the ships were abandoned. The natives were sure that Franklin's men died from a sickness rather than from starvation. They described finding tins of food at some campsites and on the one abandoned ship that was later discovered. Some of this food was very good, described as meat laced with fat (probably pork or corned beef). Other tins contained only "white man's snow" (flour or salt), which was of no use to them (Burwash, 72).

The native traditions suggest that Crozier's men did not all follow the simple script indicated on the Victory Point record. Many of the stragglers broke into small parties and wandered off; some simply fell down and died on the march, while others at the limit of their strength, refused to leave camp.

Some oral traditions have been selectively used by historians. Those that seem to accord with the idea of a single retreat are accepted, while those that are at variance with Crozier's intentions are disbelieved. One of those that is accepted is a very detailed account relating how four native families met forty of Franklin's men walking along the shore of Washington Bay. After a short time together the Inuit abandoned the white men to their fate, and the bodies of these men were found scattered along the shore the next year. This story, originally told by the participants themselves, contains so many corroborative details that there has never been any doubt that it describes a real encounter (Hall, Book 38). Even so, most historians selectively filter out the most significant details remembered by the Inuit. Unable to believe that only forty percent of Crozier's men could have reached the southern shore, many commentators doubt the description of the party. The natives were quite specific that they met the party in the late summer when the ice was breaking up. Since Crozier's record indicated that the ships had been abandoned in April, many have wondered at this. Even more surprising was the fact that the natives claimed to have seen these men in 1850, a full two years after Crozier and his men first left the ships. Most commentators have concluded that the native account is wrong in both season and year. The Inuit remembered that the leader told them the party was headed for Iwillik, or Repulse Bay. As the Crozier record indicates that the Back River was his destination, this too is disbelieved.

Another troubling Inuit tradition deals with the discovery of one abandoned ship at a place called Ootjoolik, hundreds of miles south of where Franklin's ships were abandoned (Gilder, 78). When the ship arrived at Ootjoolik the Inuit believed that they saw men aboard and were afraid to approach it. Many months later, when they were sure the crew had left, they found evidence of their presence. There was a gangplank from the deck to the newly formed ice. This brings into question the widely held theory that the ship drifted at the mercy of ice and tide for over one hundred miles. Near the main hatch a pile of deck sweepings was found which appeared to be only a few days old. The ship was locked from the outside and yet, when the natives broke in, they found the body of a white man in a bunk near the stern. Efforts to explain this as remembrance of a painting hanging in the cabin (or even a figurehead!) are complicated by the explicit statement that the body "smelled bad." Even more telling was the discovery of the tracks of three white men and a dog which were found on the nearby shore.

Traditions of a ship manned by few survivors are incompatible with the idea of a single disastrous retreat. Historians have again discounted these Inuit tales and refused to countenance the clear implication that some of Franklin's men must have returned to the ships after the 1848 abandonment.

It must be admitted that there are several factors which temper a too-ready acceptance of Inuit tales. Inuktitut is a very difficult language to master, and the various dialects often posed problems for interpreters. The natives were very reticent among strangers, and quickly learned that their interviewers were not entirely pleased with what they were being told.

The Inuit were perhaps the most observant witnesses on earth, and they faithfully preserved their traditions, in amazing detail, for generations. Their remembrances showed that they could often recall elements that allowed a reconstruction of the events that inspired their stories. This attention to detail could often be used to tease the facts from otherwise inexplicable tales. Quite often we find that "garbled" stories are easily understood in light of modern evidence. In certain stories we can see how Victorian historians have misinterpreted what they were told, either as a result of ambiguous translation or preconceived ideas of what happened to the expedition.

When Knud Rasmussen interviewed the grandchildren of the hunters who had seen Franklin's men on the march, he found that they had preserved an amazing amount of detail (Rasmussen, 121–129). When Rasmussen's accounts are compared to those collected two generations earlier by Hall (who had interviewed the participants themselves), we find almost complete agreement. Even today many of the older people recall the stories told by their parents although there is evidence that with the intrusion of a modern lifestyle the strength of the oral tradition is fading.

When the stories concerning strangers are examined carefully, and those known to deal with other expeditions filtered out, those that remain tell a remarkable tale. We learn of a two-year interaction between a few Inuit hunters and two ships full of white men, years in which they conducted a massive caribou hunt together and repeatedly visited each other. The tales also tell in detail that it is hard to ignore or explain, of the dramatic sinking of one ship and the struggles of the survivors.

Most historians state that the Inuit could not have visited Franklin and Crozier simply because the Victory Point record makes no mention of it. They point to the disinterest of the Inuit in the northwest coast of King William Island as corroboration that the natives knew nothing of the presence of the expedition in their country. It is true that the natives did not know that the expedition first came ashore in the north. Most of their stories are focused to the south at Erebus Bay. They tell that the ships were first seen here, a detail which supports the supposition that some of Franklin's crew returned to their ships after an abortive 1848 journey. Here the natives tell that survivors lived at least two and probably three years longer than is usually thought. They left memories of their activities among their hosts that would survive unrecognized for over a century.

I do not believe that we have yet reached the end of the investigation into the Franklin saga. After the passage of 150 years there is little evidence remaining on the surface that can be of much use, but perhaps the most significant relics do not lie on the surface at all.

The last decade has seen a renewed interest in searching for clues. In the 1980s Dr. Owen Beattie searched the coast of King William Island and excavated the well-preserved remains of three of Franklin's men from their graves at Beechey Island (Beattie, 1987, 122). In 1992 a magnetometer survey of the area indicated as the site of the Ootjoolik wreck was conducted. Three of the most promising "targets" were investigated by sonar the next year, without result (Woodman, 1993). Last year an expedition conducted by the Royal Canadian Geographical Society commenced a search for the "cemented vaults" spoken of by the natives; another field season is planned for this year, 1995 (Woodman, 1995). [Between symposium and publication this expedition completed the survey of the northwest coast between Cape Felix and Victory Point; it identified one new Franklin era campsite but did not find traces of the vaults spoken of by the Inuit.] Barry Ranford has conducted yearly investigations in Erebus Bay, while others have recently taken the search for artifacts as far afield as Prince of Wales Island (Ranford, 1994; Bertulli, 1995).

The Franklin disaster is like a giant jigsaw puzzle. We have only half of the original pieces, and some of these have been cut or deformed by earlier players and cannot be made to fit. Pieces from other puzzles have been mixed in—somehow we have five corners—and some pieces, when assembled, are so incongruous and out of place as to defy analysis. Perhaps this uncertainty is why the story still exercises a strange fascination on us more than a century later. The loss of 129 men was tragic, but greater and more immediate tragedies have overtaken us since. None of the participants in the events were prominent figures, with the possible exception of Franklin. Even so there is something compelling about the image of a small party of men, thousands of miles from home, hunched in the traces as they drag sledges through the snow. They faced challenges and hardships that are difficult for us to imagine and they should not be judged harshly for having been overcome by them. Their story deserves to be remembered; we should avoid distortions wherever possible, and all of the evidence should be used. By turning Franklin's men into bumbling Victorian caricatures who could not learn the lessons of survival, and by portraying the Inuit themselves as savage and ignorant people who did not know what was happening in their own land, we demean both parties. As always, the reality, still not completely illuminated, was both more complex, and more interesting, than that.

WORKS CITED

Beattie, Owen. "Forensic Sciences Applied to Historical Problems: The Franklin Expedition." Cultures in Contact: McMaster Anthropology Society Annual Symposium. Hamilton: McMaster University, Ontario, 1992.

Beattie, Owen, and John Geiger. *Frozen in Time: Unlocking the Secrets of the Franklin Expedition*. Saskatoon: Western Producer Prairie Books, 1987.

Bertulli, Margaret. *Survey of Cape Felix, King William Island, June 1995*. Yellowknife: Prince of Wales Northern Heritage Centre, 1995.

Burwash, L. T. *Canada's Western Arctic*. Ottawa: King's Printer, 1831.

Cyriax, Richard J. "The Two Franklin Expedition Records Found on King William Island." *Mariner's Mirror* 44 (1958): 179–189.

Cyriax, Richard J. "Adam Beck and the Franklin Search." *Mariner's Mirror* 48 (1962): 38–40.

Cyriax, Richard J., and A. G. E. Jones. "The Papers in Possession of Harry Peglar, Captain of the Foretop, *H.M.S. Terror*, 1845." *Mariner's Mirror* 40 (1954): 186–195.

Dickens, Charles. "The Lost Arctic Voyagers." *Household Words* 32 (Nov. 1854).

Franklin, John. *Narrative of a Journey to the Shores of the Polar Sea, in the Years 1819, 20, 21, and 22*. London: John Murray, 1823. New York: Greenwood, 1969.

———. *Narrative of a Second Expedition to the Shores of the Polar Sea in the Years 1825, 1826, and 1827*. London: John Murray, 1828. Edmonton: M. G. Hurtig, 1971.

Gilder, W. *Schwatka's Search*. New York: Scribner's Sons, 1881.

Hall, Charles Francis. Hall Collection. Washington: Smithsonian Institution. Document 58914, 8 December 1864. 218. Fieldnotes, Book no. 31. Document 58931, Book no. 38.

McClintock, Francis Leopold. *The Voyage of the "Fox" in the Arctic Seas. A Narrative of the Discovery of the Fate of Sir John Franklin and His Companions.* Philadelphia: Porter and Coates, 1859. Edmonton: Hurtig Publishers, 1972.

Rae, John. "Rae on the Eskimos." *Beaver* 284 (March 1954).

Ranford, Barry. "Bones of Contention." *Equinox* 13, 74 (Spring 1994): 69–87.

Rasmussen, Knud. *The Netsilik Eskimos.* Reprint. New York: AMS Press, 1976.

Woodman, David C. *Unravelling the Franklin Mystery: Inuit Testimony.* McGill-Queen's Native and Northern Series. Kingston: McGill-Queen's University Press, 1991.

———. "Project Ootjoolik." *Sentinel* 29: 2 (April/May 1993).

———. "Probing the Franklin Mystery. *Canadian Geographic* 15: 2 (March/April 1995).

Wright, Noel. *Quest for Franklin.* London: Heinemann, 1959.

Science as Poetic and Visual Narrative: J. Dewey Soper (1893–1982)

CONSTANCE MARTIN

In John Buchan's *Sick Heart River* the hero has been diagnosed with a probably fatal disease, tuberculosis. He can stay home in Britain and wait to die or he can accept an assignment to cross the ocean and search in the Far North for a missing man, the Canadian husband of a friend, lured by the secrets of a hidden place, an apparently lifeless area at the source of the Sick Heart River. Only the Hare Indians, who fear its power, know where it is. In the end Leithen, the hero, goes, finds what he is looking for, is cured of his disease, and, by his own wish, spends the rest of his life in the Arctic helping the Hare Indians, who have become his friends.[1]

For J. Dewey Soper, the natural scientist, explorer, writer and artist born in 1893, there are haunting similarities in Buchan's novel to his own real experience in the Far North. Soper was drawn to the Arctic in his early teens by reading the many books available at the time: the stories of the early Vikings, and of British and American explorers such as Frobisher, Baffin, Franklin, Parry, Ross, Kane, McClintock, and Hall were familiar to him. So too were the explorations in our own century of Nansen, Amundsen, Sverdrup, and Peary. Among the books that excited him were John Richardson's *Arctic Search Expedition*, Fridtjof Nansen's *In Northern Mists*, and Vilhjalmur Stefansson's *Hunters of the Great North*. In his own book, *Canadian Arctic Recollections*, written at the end of his long and productive career exploring the vast unmapped areas of southern Baffin Island and searching for the nesting grounds of the blue goose, he writes, "I seem to have been born with this longing for boreal latitudes" (Soper, 1981, xii).

In his late twenties, while studying biology and English at the University of Alberta and already with a few ornithological publications to his credit, Soper longed for opportunity to reach the Far North. This materialized when he was offered a summer assignment with the Victoria Memorial Museum (now known as the Canadian Museum of Nature) to travel on the government's annual patrol boat to the Arctic. His instructions were to gather specimens of birds and plants for the museum's collection. This was the beginning of Soper's favourite time in his long career. Leaving the University to learn on the job, Soper spent between 1923–1931, a total of eight years, exploring over 30,000 miles of southern Baffin Island on four separate expeditions of one and two years duration. After 1931 his work with the government in the natural sciences continued, but he was never able to return to the Far North—a disappointment that he addressed late in life, in his seventies and eighties, by gathering together his logs, field notes, and photographs and writing *Canadian Arctic Recollections,* as well as by painting over two hundred watercolours of the Inuit and his Arctic adventures. Written and rendered in tranquility, the two studies look back with a mixture of scientific fact and romantic nostalgia on the most treasured experience of his life.

Soper was well prepared for work in the North. From the age of thirteen, he tells us in his unpublished autobiography, he developed a "very pronounced yearning for a knowledge of wildlife . . . an insistent desire to know more and more about native birds and mammals—a love for these things that was never to be extinguished . . . it was like a divine excitement in the blood" (1969, 5). He grew up roaming the woods near his family's farm in rural Ontario, learning to identify the wildlife of the area. One might say he was a natural natural scientist, for beginning with these years, he kept meticulous records of his observations, a habit which in his lifetime yielded over one hundred publications on the flora, fauna, and especially the bird life of Canada.

The Arctic of the 1920s was still a land with vast tracts of unmapped territory and Inuit people following the traditions and customs of centuries of forebears. It was a time of tupiks, dog sledding, and igloos. It was also a time of wearing caribou-skin clothing and carefully storing supplies in caches. In many ways it seemed the land depicted in the beautiful illustrated narratives of the nineteenth- and early twentieth-century explorers, a place to try the hardiness of the adventurous and fire the imagination of young men from the south.

Southern Baffin Island, especially the interior and much of the rugged west coast, was unknown at the time to white men. But neither exploring nor collecting a wide variety of specimens for the museum were Soper's primary goals. More important was the specific scientific quest to find the breeding grounds of the blue goose, "one of the leading enigmas of North American ornithology" (1942, 142).[2] Like Baffin's search for gold, or the many voyages in search of a northwest passage, or the search which continues today, to find the *Erebus* and the *Terror,* or the search for the source of the fictitious *Sick Heart River,* the search for the blue goose was Soper's star in the heavens, drawing him farther and farther into the northern regions: a quest he completed when, aided by the Inuit, he recorded the site of the blue goose nesting grounds at Bowman Bay in the spring of 1929. [3]

Soper described in prose and watercolour many high points of his four expeditions. The first voyage, in 1923, aboard the Canadian patrol ship *Arctic,* under the command of Captain Joseph Bernier, sailed up the west coast of Greenland to Melville Bay and north to within eleven degrees of the Pole, where Soper was astonished to find blooming flowers such as mountain avens and arctic poppies. Stopped by ice, the ship turned south toward Cape Sabine, entering Lancaster Sound and stopping briefly at Cornwallis Island and then Beechey, where Soper saw the Arctic's best known landmark, the graves from the Franklin expedition of 1845. At Pond Inlet and other stops along the way Soper collected specimens for the museum and made his initial observations of Inuit life. Finally, before returning home, the ship visited Pangnirtung in Cumberland Sound. It was here at Pangnirtung that Soper was to be quartered with the Hudson's Bay Company during his next assignment from 1924–1926. Except for the fall seasons, Soper spent most of his time away from his Pangnirtung base on extended treks with Inuit guides, exploring and collecting specimens for the museum. Living close to an old and established Inuit village, Soper made friends and began to learn the rudiments of the Inuit language. He was an outsider who willingly recognized his need to be taught as much as possible of the Inuit's hunting, dog sledding, and survival skills.

In *Arctic Recollections* he describes the Arctic on his arrival at Pangnirtung in July 1924, at the height of the brief summer, as a heavenly place, a "veritable Paradise of warm sunny days, blue skies, and sparkling waters, which attracted wild fowl in multitudes. . . . Against the background of austere terrain . . . one may . . . watch the careless flight of bumble bees and butterflies and gaze on gaudy beds of small exquisite Arctic flowers that exist only in polar lands" (1981, 13). By contrast there are his descriptions of the hell of winter, especially the extremes of the inland cold.

One such journey of five months with a party of six Inuit, several sledges and seventy dogs explored the south of Nettilling Lake and Foxe Basin. On another, during the winter of 1926, Soper and his party traversed the island from Cumberland Sound to Foxe Channel. This was the most intense cold Soper had ever experienced. In his day journal he wrote:

> The whole day has been an unceasing battle with the cold. It is positively forbidding, savage, and sinister in its intensity—quite unlike the more moderate cold of the eastern seaboard. The dog harness

is frozen stiff even in use, while the rawhide traces are hard and brittle and rather easily broken. The like of this had never come into my life before. The hours seemed interminable with the tramp, tramp, tramp of many feet and the endless fight to keep warm freezing was a serious factor. (67)

Though accompanied by Inuit on his travels and a seasoned and hardy outdoor man himself, he wrote that the Arctic was rarely hospitable, "except during the summer." Understandably he found Stefansson's book *The Friendly Arctic* unrealistic, his thesis a myth. "There is altogether too much hardship, suffering, slow starvation and death most of the year to believe that such a 'friendly' land could exist in the high latitudes. Lesser or greater misadventures will continue to threaten man at times as long as these 'lands forlorn remain'" (21).

The blue goose search took Soper and his Inuit assistants thousands of miles, but it was not until August 1926, just before Soper's return to Ottawa, that there was a crack in the mystery. An old Inuit hunter from the Tikoot Islands, off the southwest coast of Baffin, told them that they would find the blue goose in Bowman Bay—northeast of Foxe Peninsula. Too late to confirm the information that year, Soper had to wait until a return voyage in 1928. This time based on the southwest coast of Baffin Island at Cape Dorset, Soper met an Nuwata Inuk named Salia who drew him a free-hand map pointing again to Bowman Bay (Salia, 15).[4] This remarkable document, like many of the Cumberland Sound area preserved from the 1880s by the eminent anthropologist, Franz Boas, was an example of the native people's deep knowledge of the land (Boas, 236–238).[5] Done without surveying skills or measurement, it nonetheless recorded every bay and inlet of the intricate multi-islanded west coast. This treasure resides in the University of Alberta archives.

Using Saila's map, Soper in mid-May, with a party of five Inuit and sledges pulled by forty-two dogs, set out for Bowman Bay to confirm the information. Camping near the bank of a stream, they awaited. On June 2, a single flock of mixed snow and blue geese flew honking over the camp, and, on June 6, flock after flock winged their way into the district, birds by the thousands. Soper wrote, "Spring had come at last. My Eskimo informers were proved right and I blessed them for it" (91).

Soper and his party remained at Bowman Bay through July, recording in field notes and photographs every stage of the blue goose migration, from their arrival to the hatching of the goslings. The thrill of discovery is best reflected in a simple watercolour of a blue goose nest Soper painted over forty years later (Ipellie, 37). Worthy of John Ruskin, it is rendered with an intensity of observation, in delicate fine lines of colour, that calls to mind the beautiful nature studies in Arctic books Soper read in his youth.

His mission completed, Soper boarded a ship for home in early August of 1929; the news of the discovery of the blue goose nesting ground was broadcast over the air waves, bringing him international recognition among ornithologists and bird-lovers. Many honours were to follow in his long and full career, including an honorary LL.D. but the one Soper most prized was the Canadian government's decision in 1957 to set aside Bowman Bay as a bird sanctuary. Soper made one more trip to Baffin Island in 1930–1931 accompanied by his wife, a nurse, and his two-year-old son, Roly. He writes that he would have gladly returned again and again; but his assignments for the rest of his career were closer to home in areas such as Wood Buffalo Park.

Though Soper, unlike Leithen in *Sick Heart River*, had to leave the Arctic, his longing for "the Far North" became the inspiration for *Canadian Arctic Recollections*. It was a way to return. Its narrative style, like his watercolours, is sensitive and often poetic. In fact Soper's often romantic turn of phrase, even in official reports, was a bit of a thorn to his peers, whose perceptions tended to be more literal. Here is Soper discussing the search for the blue goose in a paper for the *Canadian Field-Naturalist*:

> Any object savoring of the unknown especially stimulates speculation and curiosity. The mystery, therefore, which previously surrounded the Blue Goose nesting grounds was well calculated to arouse the interest of biologists in general and particularly those having opportunity for travel in the regions of the Canadian Arctic Archipelago and the Mainland immediately to the south. Where in this vast area it nested was unknown, to hazard a guess . . . brought the truth no nearer. Decades and generations passed, even centuries, since the first coming of the white man, yet the eternal solitude of the Arctic still claimed its secret. (*CFN*, 2)

This longing for the "eternal solitude of the Arctic" continued to the end of his life and found expression not only in his book but in the over two hundred watercolours he painted based on his Arctic photographs (2).

These paintings, like "the nest of the blue Goose" discussed above (Ipellie, 37),[6] were the only watercolours he ever rendered. They depict scenes and events from his four Baffin Island expeditions. Although Soper was a trained natural scientist and therefore adept at the visual recording of his observations, he was not a trained fine artist. Yet his sense of colour, form, and composition enabled him to create charming naive images of the land, the ice, the people, and the wildlife and provide us with an added dimension to his story. More than his precise drawings for official records, and in surprisingly strong colour, they are nostalgic remembrances of his time in the Arctic. They are beautifully commensurate with his book, which he originally hoped they would illustrate. One might speculate that like his prose their embellishments were perhaps less objective than his peers could accept. The publisher instead used his literal on-the-spot pen and ink drawings.

Without diminishing the wealth of factual information that Soper relays in his writings, it is nevertheless the descriptive power of his memoirs and the charm of his paintings that together bring us a deeper understanding of the mysterious hold the "... boreal altitudes"[7] held for a remarkable natural scientist (1981, xii). J. Dewey Soper apparently found what he was looking for.

NOTES

1.   John Buchan, Lord Tweedsmuir of Elsfield, governor general of Canada from 1934 until his death in 1940. *Sick Heart River* was first published after his death in 1941, after being serialized in *Blackwood's Magazine.* Buchan traveled extensively in the Northwest Territories and wrote many novels, a series of adventure thrillers, or "shockers" as he called them. Among these was *The Thirty-Nine Steps,* later made into a popular movie.
2.   Soper's interest in the blue goose was inspired by the work of Bernhard Hantzsch, the German ornithologist who died of trichinosis while exploring the west coast of Baffin Island. His journals were saved by his Eskimo companions. See: L. H. Neatby, ed., *My Life Among the Eskimos, The Baffinland Journals of Bernhard Adolh Hantzsch 1909–1911.* (Saskatoon: University of Saskatchewan, 1977).
3.   Since Soper's study of the blue goose, stimulated by his observations, knowledge has greatly advanced. Today we know that the blue goose is a phase of the snow goose, not a separate species. The snow goose, including its blue phase, has steadily increased in population. With this growth in numbers, the geese have selected many other nesting sites, expanding from Baffin Island into several other areas of the Arctic. See: Ray T. Alisauskas and Hugh Boyd, "Previously Unrecorded Colonies of Ross and Lesser Snow Geese in the Queen Maud Gulf Bird Sanctuary," *Arctic,* 47, 1 (March 1994): 69.
4.   Soper added place names and notes to the face of the map, such as the following: "This map was drawn by the Eskimo 'Saila' in the fall of 1928, as the breeding grounds of the Blue Goose were discovered by J. Dewey Soper in June, 1929, with the help of Cape Dorset, B. I. Eskimos."
5.   Through his reading Soper had a deep knowledge of the history of Arctic exploration as well as the work of scientists such as the pioneer anthropolgist of the Arctic, Franz Boas. Boas's study includes the following Inuit maps drawn in 1883–1884. "figure 154, Cumberland Sound and Frobisher Bay, drawn by Itu, a Nugumio (original in the Museum fur Volkerkunde, Berlin)"; "fig. 155, Cumberland Sound and Frobisher Bay, drawn by Sunapignang, an Oqomio"; "fig. 156, Cumberland Sound, drawn by Itu, a Nugumi": "fig. 157, Peninsula of Qivtung, drawn by Angutuqdjaq, a Padlimio."
6.   Other Soper watercolours are reproduced in Constance Martin, *Search for the Blue Goose: J. Dewey Soper —The Arctic Adventures of a Canadian Naturalist,* (Calgary: Bayeux Arts, In Press, Summer, 1995).
7.   *Ibid.*

WORKS CITED

Alisauskas, Ray T., and Hugh Boyd. "Previously Unrecorded Colonies of Ross and Lesser Snow Geese in the Queen Maud Gulf Bird Sanctuary". *Arctic,* 47, 1 (March 1994).

Amundsen, Roald. *The Northwest Passage: Being a Record of a Voyage of Exploration of the Ship Gjoa, 1907.* New York: Dutton, 1908.

Boas, Franz. *The Central Eskimo.* Lincoln: University of Nebraska Press, 1964. Reprint of Smithsonian Institution edition, 1888.

Buchan, John. *Sick Heart River.* Loanhead, Midlothian: Macdonald Pub. 1981.

Franklin, John. *Narrative of a Journey to the Shores of the Polar Sea in the Years 1819, 20, 21, and 22.* London: John Murray, 1823. Reprint, New York: Greenwood, 1969.

Hall, Charles Francis. *My Five Years with the Eskimeaux.* New York: Harper and Brothers, 1865.

Ipellie, Alootook, Peter White, and Constance Martin. *Recollecting: J. Dewey Soper's Arctic Watercolours.* Exhibition Catalogue. The Nickle Arts Museum, University of Calgary. Calgary, 1955.

Kane, Elisha Kent. *Arctic Explorations: Second Grinnell Expedition in Search of . . . Franklin, 1853, 54, 55.* Philadelphia: Childs and Peterson, 1856.

Loomis, Chauncey, *Weird and Tragic Shores.* New York: Knopf, 1971. Reprint: Lincoln, University of Nebraska Press, 1991.

———. "The Arctic Sublime", *Nature and the Victorian Imagination,* ed. U. C. Knoepflmacher and G. B. Tennyson, Berkeley: University of California Press, 1977.

Martin, Constance. "Toward No Earthly Pole: The Search for Franklin in Nineteenth Century Art" in Sutherland, P. ed., *The Franklin Era in Canadian Arctic History.* Ottawa: National Museums of Canada, 1985.

———. *Search for the Blue Goose: J. Dewey Soper — The Arctic Adventures of a Canadian Naturalist.* Calgary: Bayeux Arts, 1996.

Nansen, Fridtjof. *In Northern Mists: Arctic Exploration in Early Times.* 2 vols. New York: Frederick A. Stokes Company, 1911.

Neatby, L. H. *My Life Among the Eskimos: The Baffinland Journals of Bernhard Adolph Hantzsch, 1909–1911.* Saskatoon: University of Saskatchewan Press, 1977.

Parry, William Edward. *Second Voyage for Discovery of the Northwest Passage from the Atlantic to the Pacific, 1821, 22, 23.* London: John Murray, 1824.

Peary, Robert E. *The North Pole.* London: Hodder and Stoughton, 1910.

Richardson, John. *Arctic Search Expedition: A Journal of a Boat-Voyage through Rupertsland and the Arctic Sea . . .* London: Longman, 1851.

Ross, John. *Narrative of a Second Voyage in Search of a Northwest Passage 1829–1833.* London: A. W. Webster, 1835.

Salia of Nuwata. *Native Map of Foxe Land, NWT.* University of Alberta Archives. In Alootook Ipellie, Peter White, and Constance Martin, *Recollecting: J. Dewey Soper's Arctic Watercolours.* Ex. Cat., The Nickle Arts Museum, University of Calgary, 1995.

Soper, J. Dewey. "Discovery of the Breeding Grounds of the Blue Goose." *The Canadian Field-Naturalist.* Ottawa, Canada, XLIV, 1 (Janauary, 1930): 2–11.

———. "Life History of the Blue Goose."*Proceedings of the Boston Society of Natural History,* vol. 42: 2 (November, 1942).

———. "Dr. Joseph Dewey Soper—An Autobiography." Unpublished with family, 1969.

———. *Canadian Arctic Recollections, Baffin Island 1923–1931.* Mawdsley Memoir 4. Saskatoon: Institute for Northern Studies, University of Saskachwan, 1981.

Stefansson, Vilhjalmur, *The Friendly Arctic.* New York: Macmillan, 1921.

———. *Hunters of the Great North.* New York: Harcourt Brace, 1992.

Sverdrup, Otto. *New Land.* 2 vol. London: Longmans, Green and Co., 1904.

On Making History

WAYNE GRADY

Ask what is history, how is history made?

JOHN MOSS, *Enduring Dreams.*

We belong where we live; everywhere else is myth.

KRISTJANA GUNNARS.

I have been thinking lately about polar opposites. There is a line in Philip Rahv's book *The Myth and the Powerhouse* that has long intrigued me: "The mythic," he writes, "is the polar opposite of what we mean by the historical." Until I went north, I believed it. History, in Rahv's view, stands for process, mutability; it is, he says, "that powerhouse of change which destroys custom and tradition." Myth, on the contrary, "is reassuring in its stability." But myths can be powerhouses of change—and history can be stable and constant, if not downright repetitive. In the north, myth and history are often yoked together, sometimes by violence, and nowhere is the fusion of myth and history more dynamic than at the North Pole. I like the concept of polar opposites, for it is at the Pole that opposites meet and merge, just as all lines of longitude, all national boundaries, all time zones, fuse at that mythical and historical, utterly real and imaginary spot, the North Pole.

The North Pole, like the object of all quests, is both a mythical and an historical place, like Glastonbury. Farley Mowat calls it "the chimerical Pole," and John Moss refers to it as "a singular zero, an algebraic integer or geometric dot . . . sheer essence, a swirl of white quite still upon the shifting ice cap, upon the spinning globe." It is Eliot's "still point" at the turning centre, Rudy Wiebe's "motionlessness."

I was there on August 22 of last year. It doesn't look any different than any other spot on the ice. A seeming infinitude of light, infused with blue. A tumbled geometry of frozen fire. You can't take your mind off the ice. You stand on it, as far from the ship as you can get, and you listen to it sing—wind over hard snow. You scrape away the snow with your boot, or thrust the point of an ice chisel into it, and the hole glows with an intense blue light, as though from a gigantic blue ember in some vast, cosmic fire. Fire and ice, polar opposites. The snow is dry, it feels like crushed glass under your boots. When you come to a melt pond, you see the blue glowing up from the bottom, the wind-rippled surface creating another illusion of heat. When you kneel to drink, the water is warm and distantly salty, like tears.

We had come on two icebreakers—the Canadian Coast Guard Ship *Louis S. St. Laurent* and the United States Coast Guard Cutter *Polar Sea* —up through Bering Strait, across 1200 nautical miles of ice. We were two hundred crew members, sixty-four scientists, two Inuit guides, two painters, a filmmaker and a writer. Our goal was to spend as much time in the western half of the Arctic Ocean as daylight and marine diesel fuel allowed, between the Canadian archipelago and the North Pole, doing science in a vast reach of the ocean sea to which no surface vessel had been before. We were to work our way north by a route determined by the three science leaders, the two captains, and the ice, with the ultimate goal of reaching the North Pole from the Canadian side.

Other surface vessels had been to the Pole—the first was the Russian nuclear-powered icebreaker *Arktika* in 1977, and the Swedish ship *Oden* and the German research vessel *Polarstern* had been there in 1991– but they had all taken the eastern approach, sailing up through Fram Strait, between Greenland and Iceland, or from the Barents and Siberian Seas. The captains of these vessels will forgive me for saying so, but there's not much ice on that side of the Pole: the ice edge in the Greenland Sea begins at about 86 degrees in July. North of Alaska, in the Chukchi Sea, we entered the ice at 72 degrees—an extra eight hundred miles of ice. The Russian ship *Yamal* routinely plies between Murmansk and the North Pole along the 35th meridian. It takes the *Yamal* three and a half days, and for $28,000 you can go with it. When we got to the Pole the *Yamal* was already there for the third time that year, with a boat-load of school children who were dancing and singing around a giant apple that opened up to form a stage on the ice; their performance was being broadcast live via Russian satellite television to mark the International Year of the Family.

But the western route is different. No vessel has even attempted the Pole from the Bering Strait side since the *Jeannette's* disastrous voyage in 1879. The *Jeannette's* captain, George Washington De Long, was testing the hypothesis that the warm Japanese Current flowed through Bering Strait into the Arctic, creating an ice-free passage to the Pole. The open polar sea proved to be a myth: the *Jeannette's* true mission was to create copy for the ship's owner, James Gordon Bennett, who also owned the New York *Herald* —four years earlier, Bennett had sent Stanley to Africa to find Livingstone; now he was sending De Long to the Arctic to find the North Pole. The *Jeannette* was crushed by ice in the East Siberian Sea in 1881, but parts of her drifted with the ice across the Arctic to turn up, eight hundred days later, on the southern coast of Greenland, inspiring Nansen's attempt to drift the *Fram* across in 1893. It was not Stefansson's intent, when he and Robert Bartlett took the *Karluk* north through Bering Strait in 1913, to make an attempt on the Pole. Stefansson pretended to believe there might be a continent north of Canada—the fabled Wrangel Land posited by August Petermann in the 1860s, that joined Wrangel Island with the northern tip of Greenland—but both De Long and Nansen had proven that Wrangel Land was another Arctic dream, and either Cook or Peary, if either of their accounts is to be believed, had proven it again just four years previously: Stefansson just wanted to see how far north North America went.

The only other polar attempt by ship from the Canadian side was a paper one: that of Canadian sea captain Joseph Elzéar Bernier, whose plan was to sail through Bering Strait and put his ship, the *Arctic,* into the ice three hundred miles east of where the *Jeannette* went down and, like Nansen, let it drift over the North Pole. This plan was an improvement on—and may have anticipated—that of Nansen, but it was 1904 before Bernier had his ship ready, and at the last minute the Department of Marine and Fisheries scuttled Bernier's dream and sent him instead to Hudson Bay to stop American entrepreneurs from selling liquor to the Inuit. It wasn't until 1913, with Stefansson's Canadian Arctic Expedition, that the Canadian government began its flag-waving references to "our destiny in the North."

So we had the historical field pretty much to ourselves. The scientific field was also open: a few Soviet ice camps, one or two ice islands, a clandestine submarine or two were our only predecessors north of about 80 degrees. There were no charts. There were very few soundings. Our bathymetric maps had been compiled by guesswork and satellites. Columbus may have had a better idea of where he was going than we did. We were entering the last ocean basin on Earth where no hydrography or geology had ever been done.

Our sailing orders were: science first, the Pole second—first history, then myth. In fact, the chances of our reaching the Pole were considered pretty slim: David Johns, then the Coast Guard's chief of northern operations, told me before we left that they were about fifty-fifty, but that it didn't matter because we were going primarily to do science. The stated purpose of our journey, what some might term the funding basis of the expedition, was to find the extent to which Global Warming had already affected the Arctic—i.e., is the ice melting, is the water warming?—or was likely to affect it in the future—i.e. how fast? And to identify the various industrial contaminants present in the water, ice and air, and to trace, if possible, their sources, rates of entry, and residency times. Now, there are few better examples of the complex interconnectedness of myth and history than can be found in the highly contentious but no less speculative debates

over climate change and global pollution. Our expedition was to provide
the beginnings of a data base that would put those debates into some kind
of realistic perspective; to bring myth and history a little closer together.

But we had few illusions about our ability to do that. Textured
within these admirable objectives was a deeper, in some ways more urgent,
desire—one that has been luring explorers to the Arctic since England's
first merchant-mariners came pretending to be looking for the Northwest
Passage, sailing west to get east. This is the desire to explore an unknown
part of the world, to see what is out there, to experience the sense of wonder that has always linked science with art and magic and religion. To get
to the North Pole. There are very good scientific reasons for getting to the
Pole, of course, since it is the remotest in an uncompassable sea of remote
points. Getting there was important: to find Livingstone, Stanley had to
enter the heart of darkness; getting to the North Pole for us meant penetrating to the heart of illumination, entering what Aritha van Herk in a
beautiful phrase calls the ocean of liquid light. As we neared the Pole,
Eddy Carmack, the chief scientist aboard the *Louis,* began to give us his
version of Heisenberg's Uncertainty Principle: the closer we get to a thing,
the less likely we are to reach it.

But as the degrees dropped away, as history blended into myth, we
seemed to be more and more drawn to the idea of the Pole—our eyes
looked less frequently downward, and turned more and more often northward. But at the same time, the Pole seemed to us to be becoming more
and more illusive. It was like approaching a mirage. A mirage that was not
only floating above oases of ice; it was also floating with the ice.

Let me give you a mundane example, something from a Grade
Three arithmetic textbook that suddenly veers off into meta-geography.
Driving to Ottawa one day, I experienced a version of the same phenomenon I am trying to assign to the North Pole. At one point along Highway
16, which connects Ottawa with the 401, I passed a sign that read: "Ottawa
80 kilometres." I set my trip odometer to zero, and thought when the
odometer reads 80, I'll be in Ottawa. Fifteen minutes later, I passed a second sign, this one reading: Ottawa 45 kilometres. Ah, I said, my odometer
must now read thirty-five. But when I looked at the odometer, it said
thirty-three. Now, thirty-three and forty-five add up to seventy-eight, not
eighty, and so something, somewhere, had gone wrong: my rational mind
told me that either one of the signs or my odometer was inaccurate. But
as a science writer, I had to consider a third hypothesis: that the city of
Ottawa was moving south at the rate of eight kilometres an hour—a rate
which, I calculated, would have the nation's capital crossing the American
border at approximately 1:35 the next morning, which was sooner than
even Brian Mulroney had anticipated. Of course, the probability is that
the city is not moving anywhere—but isn't it tempting, just as a matter of
principle, to believe the signs?

When you're approaching the North Pole, there are no probabilities. The Pole is a spot on the ice four thousand metres above the ocean floor. The ice is drifting at a rate of about 1.5 metres per minute. The ship is moving. The maps are unreliable. The compasses are useless. The satellites have all crashed. The sea is one huge margin of error. When the numbers refuse to add up, you don't know which of them are wrong, and your rational mind has to consider all the variables: the instruments are true but are also malfunctioning, the maps are accurate and wrong, and the Pole is both still and moving.

The bicameral mind has a great deal of difficulty with the concept of polar opposites, perhaps because the left half of the brain is constantly trying to rationalize what the right half sees, and when polar opposites appear to exist as a single phenomenon, synapses explode. Various explorers have tried to separate the two halves of the paradox and have come out with some startling solutions. Let's look at how four narratives deal with a single totally familiar problem: you know you are at the North Pole, but you cannot get your instruments to read 90 degrees.

The first is Robert Peary's account, from his book *The North Pole:*

> The last march northward ended at ten o'clock on the forenoon of April 6 . . . After the usual arrangements for going into camp, at approximate local noon, of the Columbia meridian, I made the first observation at our polar camp. It indicated our position as 89°57'.

Peary is three miles from the Pole: what does he do? Does he press on to realize his ambition of the past thirty years? No, he sets up his tent and goes to sleep: "I was actually too exhausted to realize at the moment that my life's purpose had been achieved." Well, in fact, it hadn't been achieved. When he wakes up two hours later, he takes a reading, then loads a sleigh with his instruments—a sextant and an artificial horizon—and sets out with two of his Inuit companions. After a while he stops and takes a second reading: "These observations," he writes, "indicated that our position was then beyond the Pole." Peary then concludes that he has passed over the Pole. He turns his team around and goes back, passing, as he imagines, over the Pole again. He does this thirteen times, criss-crossing back and forth over an area of ten square miles within which he thinks the Pole is located: "In traversing the ice in these various directions as I had done," he concludes, "I had allowed approximately ten miles for possible errors in my observations, and at some moment during these marches and countermarches, I had passed over or very near the point where north and south and east and west blend into one."

In a footnote to this account, Peary anticipates the ensuing controversy. "No one," he writes,

> except those entirely ignorant of such matters has imagined for a moment that I was able to determine with my instruments the precise position of the Pole, but after having determined its position approximately, then setting an arbitrary allowance of about ten miles for possible errors of the intruments and myself as an observer, and then crossing and recrossing that ten-mile area in various directions, no one except the most ignorant will have any doubt but what, at some time, I had passed close to the precise point, and had, perhaps, actually passed over it.

By Peary's own admission, then, he doesn't have the slightest idea whether he was at the North Pole or not. I may be entirely ignorant of such matters, but when I hear words like "approximate," "arbitrary ," "about ten miles," "at some time," and "perhaps," my eyebrow can't help but rise. Imagine what Monty Python would have made of it. Can you hear Sir Galahad saying to King Arthur: "Well, yes, I did find the Holy Grail, that is, I had it approximately within my grasp, after making an arbitrary assumption that I was in the right county. I mean, I actually several times passed the precise castle where I reckoned the Grail perhaps was, and may possibly have actually picked it up at some time, or come very close to picking it up."

Wally Herbert doesn't believe Peary made it. In his book *The Wreath of Laurels,* in which he ridicules both Cook's and Peary's claims, Herbert points out dozens of places in Peary's account that don't stand up to scrutiny. The only part he doesn't tear to shreds is Peary's confession that he never actually measured 90 degrees. Could this be because, when Herbert himself arrived at the Pole on April 5, 1969, he never measured 90 degrees either? Here is his narrative from *Across the Top of the World.*

First Herbert prepares us, as Peary had, by explaining how difficult it is to calculate position at the Pole (he was using a theodolite rather than a sextant, but the problems are similar): "If your calculation of the longitude is slightly out," he writes, "then the time at which the sun crosses your meridian—in other words, the time at which the sun is due north—is wrong, and so you head in the wrong direction." The sun is due north? Eventually, he continues, "you increase your errors progressively until you spiral into almost a complete circle. This is what happened to us on this particular day." Herbert and his companions, seven miles from the Pole, three weeks behind schedule, and having already radioed a message to Queen Elizabeth that they had made it on April 5, suddenly realized they hadn't the slightest hope of finding anything they could confidently call the North Pole. Herbert's language now becomes familiar:

> In desperation, we off-loaded the sledges, laid a depot and took on with us only the barest essentials, just enough for one night's camp. . . . With the lighter sledges we made faster progress, and

after about three hours estimated that we must surely be at the Pole, possibly even beyond it. So we stopped, set up our tents, and did a final fix which put us at 89°59' N, one mile south of the North Pole on longitude 180. In other words, we'd crossed the Pole about a mile back along our tracks. But the drift was now with us, so we must surely cross the Pole a second time as we drifted overnight. We got into our sleeping-bags and fell asleep.

The third narrative is that of Ikaksak Amagoalik, one of the Inuk guides who travelled with us on the *Louis*. Ikaksak had already been to the North Pole four times. He told me about one of his trips while we were standing together at the starboard rail of the *Louis*, looking out over the expanse of shadowed ice, broken like teeth by its own internal pressure. He had been guiding two Norwegians, who were attempting to get to the North Pole by snowmobile. Here is Ikaksak's story:

When we got close to the Pole, maybe above 87 degrees, there were lots of places where the ice had piled up on top of itself. Ridges. Some of them were fifteen feet high. We had to cut our way through them. Usually it would take six hours to cut through a ridge, because we had to get everything down smooth enough for the Skidoos. All we had to cut with was a chisel I had made out of a 1–inch steel bar. It was about 7 feet long and flattened at one end, very sharp. I had to be careful not to cut myself with it. One day we travelled for 12 hours and made only 5 miles.

I think we missed the Pole by half a mile, but I'm not sure. The satellite didn't work that well so close to the Pole. The Norwegians wanted to go farther, to make sure, but I said no, this is close enough—I didn't want to go on the Russian side. So we headed back south—well, up there it was south everywhere — but we had to go back through Norway. It was already May, and the ice was breaking up. We were going very slowly, because we had to wait for a floe to come up sclose to the floe we were on, so we could get the Skidoos across. After a while I could see we weren't going to make it, so we called on the radio for a Twin Otter to come to get us from Spitsbergen. I had to find a landing place for it. I knew it needed two feet of ice, and about 500 metres to land. I found one, and when the plane landed we had to leave a lot of stuff behind. Two Skidoos, the sled, lots of food and gasoline. We left it all on the ice. All we took with us was one Skidoo. To put in the museum.

The fourth narrative is my own.

I don't know what I was expecting. Certainly not an actual pole; but I suppose I had imagined a place I could look at and say, if there were a pole, this is where it would be. I thought there would be a place I could describe, or photograph, and say later, this is the North Pole. I have such a photograph, of course—so did Robert Peary, so does Wally Herbert, so do some three thousand other polar revenants. Friends look at it and ask, Is the ice miles thick? No, I say, ice can't get more than sixteen feet thick. It grows from the bottom, and sixteen feet below the surface, the water isn't cold enough to freeze. Oh, they say, but I can tell they're disappointed. They want canyons of ice, they want ship-crushing jaws of ice, they want polar bears reaching down to pluck sailors off the mizzen mast, they want Gustave Doré and *The Rime of the Ancient Mariner.* They want myth. I give them history.

Toward the end of the fourteenth century, an Oxford friar travelled to the North Pole and discovered there a continent which, he said, he measured all around with his astrolabe. His description was incorporated by Neogeorgus Thomas Mercator, the sixteenth-century card maker, onto the map of the world. Thomas Best, the writer who was to Martin Frobisher more or less what I was to the *Louis St. Laurent,* included the friar's description of the Pole in his account of Frobisher's 1576 voyage. According to Best, the North Pole was one of the most habitable places on Earth. It received twenty-four hours of sunlight a day for six months of the year—and even during its six months of darkness, the high mountain located directly at the Pole afforded exposure to the sun's horizontal rays for those who lived on its slopes. Here was dominion. *Terra Septentrionalis.* The continent, however, was cut through by four great "guts," or channels—one each at 110 degrees longitude, 190 degrees, 280 degrees, and at the meridian of the Fortunate Isles. According to Best, "these channels deliver themselves into a monstrous cavern with such violence that any ship that enters one is doomed. It cannot be held back by the force of even the greatest wind, but is swept headlong into that monstrous receptacle, and thence into the bowels of the earth." In the 16th century, this was not myth, it was geography; it is what Frobisher knew about the Arctic when he set sail: no wonder he turned back when he felt a strong current pulling him farther into Frobisher Strait.

I want my own narrative to be as accurate as the friar's, as honest as Ikaksak's:

> At 3 o'clock in the morning of August 22, the sun is low behind us. The temperature is exactly zero. The only ice maps we have are two weeks old, and show 10/10ths coverage of multi-year ice, braided by pressure ridges that form impenetrable sinews of ice nearly forty feet thick. To go around them has taken days: at one point it took us four hours to make a single ship length. The ridges seem to be guarding the Pole, as in some Arctic dream of Snow White. The ship rides up on a multi-year floe, the floe does not

crack, and the ship slides back into its own wake like an exhausted whale.

Mike Hemeon, the chief officer, stands at the GPS read-out and calls our position to the captain. "89:55:662, we're losing latitude fast, captain. Now it's 89:55:642."

Captain Grandy and his helmsman, Les Drake, are singing the ancient antiphonary of the sea:

Twenty degrees starboard, Les.

Twenty starboard.

Hard a-starboard.

Hard a-starboard.

What's our reading now, Mike?

89:55:659, coming up slowly.

Continue working to starboard, Les.

Working to starboard.

She's starting to jump up good now, captain: she's at 89:56, four miles from the Pole.

Steady as she goes, Les.

Steady as she goes.

We have all come up to crowd the bridge, and stand silently against the wooden railing, staring ahead through the glass. Time contracts. We are 1.58 miles from the Pole. We can all see it, each of us is looking at a different spot on the ice.

How far now, calls the captain?

Half a cable.

Goddamn it, the length of the ship!

These are hard floes, Captain.

Play snooker with 'em, Les!

We're 150 feet from the Pole, Captain, half a ship's length.

The GPS says 89:59:970. Our bow rides up on a floe, pauses for a long instant, and slides off to starboard. The captain reverses the engines and charges the floe again. The Pole is at its dead centre. Again we slide away from it. The captain shouts: "Once you find it, it's gone!"

Eddy Carmack has been watching calmly. Now he turns to the captain and says: "You know, theoretically it's impossible to reach the Pole." The captain looks at him as though at a madman. Mike Hemeon nearly shouts at Eddy: "No it isn't!" And he runs to the port side of the bridge, behind the line of watchers at the rail, runs across a hundred collapsed meridians and through seven time zones, and points down to the ice, to a spot 20 feet off our port beam: "That's it there," he says. "That's where we'll put the North Pole!"

And he is as right as anyone in history has ever been.

WORKS CITED

Wayne Grady would prefer not to supply notes. All references within his text may readily be discovered by the reader, should the reader wish to discover them.

Creating Willem Barentsz; Piloting North

ARITHA VAN HERK

Narratives of the Arctic, however much they may attempt to display some essentialist Canadian configuration, are polyvocal, even global alchemies. I have lent ear to many such stories and my own refuses to follow their directive, although my discourse engages a version of Arctic story, as well it should. There exists a perpetual complicity between narrative form and ideology, a complicity that late twentieth-century narratives of the Arctic, in their focus on adventure and destination, product rather than process, are tempted and usurped by. This necrophiliac ambition is reflected by often repeated narrative tropes: a ship struggling through an ice-choked sea, an albatross flung dead on a heaving deck, and, not least, the oh-so-heroic visitations of death (icily afire) embraced or withstood by stalwart heroes. From my anhistorical position, as pilot or guide and hence interested in journey for its own sake, Canadian narratives of the Arctic are driven by archaeologies of destination, and by the heavy-lidded view that Canada alone is Arctic, that Canada has the only Arctic, that Canada owns its Arctic. Such enstoried presumption reflects ignorance more than hubris. The Arctic, let me say to you, in this anti-narrative that I promise to thread, is a mirage of land and water, an ice-shape beyond political declension. The farthest reaches of the north are a configuration of the imagination, a transgressive act for those who dream of a nirvana beyond ice. In any physical geography, Ellesmere has more in common with Spitsbergen than with Ottawa on the Rideau.

But who am I to speak, and wherefore comes my narrative? My name is Willem Barentsz, and, in my time, that Canada so much tossed into the configurative conversational and cartographical air does not exist. I was born on the island of Tershelling, probably (records were scant) in 1560, and I died in 1597 on an ice-floe in the sea which now bears my name. I am not incapable of irony. I could cite you the sources for such brief ascribements of time, but they are easily available in any compendium of northern exploration. From 1560 to 1597 is a short life, but for all that, a life of process, a changing story. You will note that I am not Canadian. You would ascribe my nationality as Dutch, but like many others who followed the drifting compass, I am merely northern, a cipher in the great region that the world points to and calls Arctic, yet can never know. Mine is a sepulchral (but not sequacious) voice, working a different language and a different time, ready to narrate for you a strangely skewed story, a story drifting with the compass that cannot point toward true north once it is close to that north. But let me first engage with one of the more famous representations of polar climes, made companion to a gothic disquisition.

To Mrs. Saville, England

St. Peterburgh, Dec. 11, 17—

. . . I am already far north of London, and as I walk in the streets of Petersburgh, I feel a cold northern breeze play upon my cheeks, which braces my nerves and fills me with delight. Do you understand this feeling? This breeze, which has travelled from the regions towards which I am advancing, gives me a foretaste of those icyclimes. Inspirited by this wind of promise, my daydreams become more fervent and vivid. I try in vain to be persuaded that the pole is the seat of frost and desolation; it ever presents itself to my imagination as the region of beauty and delight. There . . . the sun is forever visible, its broad disk just skirting the horizon and diffusing a perpetual splendour. There . . . snow and frost are banished; and, sailing over a calm sea, we may be wafted to a land surpassing in wonders and in beauty every region hitherto discovered on the habitable globe. Its productions and features may be without example, as the phenomena of the heavenly bodies undoubtedly are in those undiscovered solitudes. What may not be expected in a country of eternal light? I may there discover the wondrous power which attracts the needle and may regulate a thousand celestial observations that require only this voyage to render their seeming eccentricities consistent forever. I shall satiate my ardent curiosity with the sight of a part of the world never before visited, and may tread a land never before imprinted by the foot of man. These are my enticements, and they are sufficient to conquer all fear of danger or death and to induce me to commence this laborious voyage with the joy a child feels when he embarks in a little boat, with his holiday mates, on an expedition of discovery up his native river. But supposing all these conjectures to be false, you cannot contest the inestimable benefit which I shall confer on all mankind, to the last generation, by discovering a passage near the pole to those countries, to reach which at present so many months are requisite; or by ascertaining the secret of the magnet, which, if at all possible, can only be effected by an undertaking such as mine. (Shelley, 1–2)

Recognize this narrative? Alas, poor Walton, we know him well. His is the vision of every nineteenth-century explorer imagining an Arctic, repining an Arioch of sublimity refracted through the prism of a sensibility beyond space, as remote from the Forest of Arden as is possible and yet, in peculiar ways, metaphored by that verdant glade. A forest treed by ice, skyed by snow, contiguous to a rolling ocean black and cold as no imagination can conjure. Walton is not Canadian, but he will discover, oh yes, he will be forced to hear an unimaginable story and its ground sea swelling past the portals of the land of wonder and beauty that he so optimistically imagines.

Poor Walton. But 1818 factually and fictionally precedes by some years 1845 or 1847, whichever date—disappearance or death—affixes itself to the romanticized narrative of that most repeated and repeated and repeated mantra of Canadian Arctic failure, Sir John, ahem, Franklin. Please forgive my lack of sympathy; remember, I am Dutch rather than Canadian, and having lived some three hundred years before the nineteenth century, I am not so awed by that era's unwise dyings, its necrophiliac gropings and sentimental measurements.

Surrounded by mountains of ice which threaten to crush his vessel, a fictional Walton writes to his fictional sister in England the chilling fictional tale recounted to him by a fictional Frankenstein, a tale initiated by the toll of justificatory words; when asked why "he had come so far upon the ice in so strange a vehicle" (11), Frankenstein answers, "'to seek one who fled from me'" (11). A fictional seeking of a fictional progeny, the monster offspring of hubristic creation, or the seeking of a story, a tale with which to wile away a winter's night? A tale that literarily configures the south's metaphor of the Arctic.

To seek one who fled. The impetus of Arctic narrative is spoken there in an unCanadian but Canadian voice. A fleeing and its follow, a series of re-visitations, themselves modelled on the quixotic jest and quest of grand adventure, the destinationed script of finding, dis/covering and its betrayals, a marked narrative closured before telling, and all for the ransacking magnification that is the near-sighted work of post-exploration, its fetishism of the remaindered document: journal, letter, report, survey, chart, grave, bones, boat.

Let me introduce myself again. My name is Willem Barentsz and I am most definitely not Canadian—could not be Canadian, for Canada as nation did not exist yet while I lived. When Frankenstein, via the scribe familiar of Walton, via Walton's listening sister, via the gothic pen of one Mary Shelley, daughter of Mary Wollstonecraft and William Godwin, wife of Percy Bysshe Shelley, subsequently revising, in 1831, with the same pen the same novel, prefacing the revision as follows: "I bid my hideous progeny go forth and prosper" (xxvi)—when Frankenstein recounts his tale, he is, to the best of all possible geographical estimations, on a ship cradled in the ice-choked Barents Sea. Named after me, the sea where I expired, where I breathed one last shallow intake of thin and eerie air before I died, having made no less than three voyages to the Arctic, three voyages as a pilot, a *loods,* one trained to conduct ships through difficult waters.

My death is not important and I am not about to toil toward its closure. My journey and its process is worthy of better attention. Unlike the English, the Dutch were then and are still (perhaps excessively) pragmatic. The Northeast Passage was for us a commercial more than an heroic disputation. After Brunel sailed eastward from Archangel but was unable to break through the ice of Pet Straight, his backers were reluctant to invest in such uneasy returns, and wanted to stop all such exploratory journeys. It was against that reluctance that I persuaded a group of Amsterdam merchants to outfit strong ships and to let me try again for what I knew would be the ocean current to Cathay. What convinced them? My chartbook of the Mediterranean, which set the standard for all future pilot guides? Manuscript chartbooks of the Mediterranean, from that time, resemble my printed atlas in a manner that can only be considered striking. Yes, I was a good mapmaker. Or was it my name as a hydrographer and cartographer, made on those portolan charts? After 1595, I was somewhat famous. Why? Perhaps it was the way that the ships puffed wind in their sails in the frontispiece to the chartbook, the way that the roads meander so clearly up the Genovese hills. But by then, the date that my *Description of the Mediterranean Sea* was published, it was already 1599 and I was well and truly dead. Having been first proclaimed, in 1595, on a wall map declensioned by those Dutch masters of map, Hondius and Kaerius, as having been the first European pilot to reach the latitude of 78 degrees North. Which is easy to verify if you can find a facsimile of that map. You see how process and its record works? Death becomes irrelevant.

So it is with maps, with courses and coastal profiles, with the corollaries of charts. They are made to be copied, repeated, pored over as gestures of combined guidance and exquisitely embellished falsehood. The same can be said for my map of the Northern Seas, those seas I rode into my own oblivion, a map in polar stereographic projection, published in 1598, also after my death. I was on my way to fame, not for my death but for my chartings, amongst pilots who knew that I tried to make transparent the shoals and courses of both oceans and coastlines.

I was defeated by ice, ice that was neither Canadian nor Russian nor Danish. Merely Arctic ice.

Do you insist on my credentials? I am a pilot, in my own language, a *loods*. I am Dutch. I "discovered" Spitsbergen, or so the books say, but again I beg to note not the discovery but the passage. I had no grandiose intentions. I was merely a marine pilot under the command of Jacob van Heemskerk, who trusted me to navigate while he controlled his ship and his men. They were my men too, by the end of that long winter: we were a strange family who knew one another through an ongoing baptism of cold and terror. And who, I hasten to assert, survived. Yes, **survived.** Disappointed, are you? Such a Canadian reaction—and no, I do not intend to make reference to the way that you have permitted yourselves to be narrated by a Frygian critic of nature and its entextment. Let me repeat the bare bones of the story; this group of men (or at least most of them) who overwintered at 78 degrees North in 1597, lived to tell their tale. No romance, no slanting ship masts ground by ice into disappearance (although our ship was utterly destroyed), no cannibalism, no inter-racial love affairs, no cryptic bones left to be disinterred and measured for their poisons. We met no Inuit people.

I was convinced that the true path to the east lay to the north of Novaya Zemlya, and so we—there were two ships, one commanded by Ryp and one by van Heemskerk—set out, on that third, always fateful voyage. Three voyages seem to argue the measure of the north, like three strikes, or the trinity, a triptych of beginning, middle, and end, man's threefold occupation of body, mind, and spirit, while the world is a thrice-carved configuration of earth, air, and sea, the kingdoms of nature animal, vegetable, and mineral, synchronicity fitting for the Arctic's celestial mark. I would add another element to this elaboration, namely, the kingdom of ice, which could be deemed mineral but is a different substance altogether, monomineralic crystalline, solid yet mutable, stubbornly itself yet capable of far more than mineral, vegetable, or animal, so tenaciously does it resist the blandishments of both skill and desire. Not for nothing does Frankenstein speak of the most learned philosophers having "partially unveiled the face of Nature, but her immortal lineaments were still a wonder and a mystery" to them (25). But my third voyage was no Frankensteinian or Franklinesque cabaret. It was—how unCanadian—a triumph.

I was pilot and cartographer for van Heemskerk, and I had no time to keep a journal. But my comrade, Gerrit de Veer, wrote everything down, making ink from charcoal and bear fat and keeping his jottings as faithfully as if they would guarantee him eternal life. As they have, they have in a most unCanadian way. The full title of his account is enough to précis the narrative that I had a role within. Listen: *"The True and Perfect Description of Three Voyages, so strange and woonderfull, that the like hath never been heard of before: Done and performed three yeares, one after the other, by Ships of Holland and Zeeland, on the North sides of Norway, Muscouia, and Tartaria, towards the Kingdomes of Cathia and China; shewing the discouerie of the*

Straightes of Weigates, Noua Zembla, and the countrie lying under 80 degrees; which is thought to be Greenland: where neuer any man had bin before: with the cruell Beares, and other Monsters of the Sea, and the unsupportable and extreame cold that is found in those places. And how in that last Voyage, the Shippe was so inclosed by the Ice, that it was left there, whereby the men were forced to build a house in the cold and desart Countrie of Noua Zembla, wherein they continued 10 monthes togeather, and never saw nor heard of any man in, most great cold and extreame miserie; and how after that, to saue their lives, they were contrained to sayle aboue 350 Dutch miles, which is aboue 1000 English [which is 1600 Canadian 'miles,' although there is no such thing anymore. So much for the tyranny of measurement], *in little open Boates, along and ouer the Maine Seas, in most great daunger, and with extreame labour, unspeakable troubles, and great hunger"* (Mirsky, 35).

Could that possibly be a Canadian account? I ask you. The cruel bears and the unsupportable cold sound familiar, as does the hunger. But that trip in little open boats, 1600 units of measure, back to more predictable elements, until they reached the golden-age centre of wealth and urbanity, Amsterdam, is no Canadian construction. Of course, in 1597 Canada did not yet exist; besides its original peoples, only Frobisher and Davis had touched its northward shape. But Ice Haven, the site of that first over-wintering, does exist, as does de Veer's narrative, and most of the crew, who lived, and who "as long as they lived were called on by eager listeners to 'rehearse' their journey" (43).

So here attends my version, which you are free to check against de Veer's.

In 1596 we sailed straight north instead of tracing the Scandinavian coast, and early in June, sighted a small, steep-sided island where we landed and killed a large white bear, naming the place Bear Island. Had I known how their spirits would follow our winter, I would never have allowed that first animal to be killed. But we learn only by living, another narrative without conclusion. We continued northward, through fog and drizzle, until we again saw land, which I mistakenly thought was Greenland, and which I now know was the northwestern tip of Spitsbergen. But although we tried to push onward, we encountered heavy ice, and we turned back to Bear Island, where it was decided that Ryp would return home and van Heemskerk, with me as pilot, would sail on toward Novaya Zemlya.

I began, in those months of dodging clots and plates and rafts of ice, to think of ice as a mutable coastline, mercilessly chameleonic in its shiftings. We advanced and retreated, dodged and zigzagged and retreated and then advanced again a little way at a time, twisting and writhing in a path that thirsted for open water, the black lead of a navigable element. But the ice closed tighter and tighter, choking us, and although we sailed around the northern tip of Novaya Zemlya, we were finally ground to a halt by the heavy resistance of that crystalline opacity that refused to remain water and became instead a mass stronger and more imperious than any land. At the end of August we tried to find shelter in a harbour that we called Ice Haven, on the northeast coast of Novaya Zemlya; and there we were witness to the absolute implacability of moving ice and its grip. That ice took our ship, for all its size and strength, in its jaws, and shook the sturdy wooden vessel, squeezing it, smashing it into splinters before our eyes, a spectacle that "'made all the hairs of our heads to rise upright with fear'" (39). Do not forget that this was 1596 and we were not Canadians, but Dutchmen who had lived with benevolently sweet water all our optimistic lives. Even the North Sea was lamblike in comparison to this bristling terror.

We were, unquestionably, undoubtably, stuck fast, and we determined to use the few passable days to construct a sort of shelter for ourselves. No trees grew on that rocky land, but there was a good supply of driftwood. "'That wood served us not only to build our house, but also to burn and serve us all the winter long, otherwise without all doubt we had died there miserably with extreme cold'" (39). We were not, you see, Canadians. But while we tried to build a shed, our carpenter died, and "'it froze so hard that as we put a nail in our mouths, there would ice hang thereon when we took it out again, and made the blood follow'" (39). And then there were the snow bears, those great white beasts awesome as the ice they walked and swam between, effortlessly shifting from solid element to liquid. Accustomed to the report of exploding ice, they merely lifted their heads when muskets were fired at them, they tore great slabs of meat from beached whales, their knife-like claws ripped every substance as if it were a sack. They loomed as large as the driftwood house we constructed, although at last it stood, "thirty-two feet long by twenty feet wide and with a chimney" (39–40). We set up our Dutch clock from the captain's cabin, and heard it striking the proceeding hours with mixed anguish and relief. We made a bathtub out of an empty wine cask; we melted bear fat to burn in the lamp. We were Dutch. We washed our shirts, "'but it was so cold that when we had washed and wrung them, they presently froze so stiff that, although we laid them by a great fire, the side that lay next the fire thawed, but the other side was frozen hard'" (40). Again and again, we shot at the great bears that came toward us, unafraid, noses erect to our scent. Muskets were futile against their enormous weight; we fired and fired into their thick pelts with hopeless repetition. One that we killed was "'nine feet long and seven feet broad'" (41); we took at least a hundred pounds of fat from her belly.

Beyond the cold rested the darkness, its weight as iron as the cold's nails driven into our hope. One night we conceived of making our little abode completely airtight. We stuffed every crack, every leak, the tiny fissures around the chimney and the door, and shifted toward sleep at last faintly warm. But a strange dizziness beset us, and the strongest struggled to the door, tearing it open to fall "'groaning upon the snow'" (Mirsky 41), the cold again accomplice to our senses. A Canadian would call that experience carbon monoxide poisoning. To us it was the trickery of geography, mischievous as the foxes which scattered our drift woodpile and ran inquisitively across our roof. But we were not Canadians.

Sickness and death. I admit my hubris, my belief in the sweet currents of water that led me to imagine I could outthink ice. I know that I ought to repent, I know that I have blood on my soul, that I am accountable for these men, I should have urged them to return with Ryp, back to the *kacheltjes* and the perils of nothing more than cobbled streets and purse-thefts in the stews of Amsterdam, back to the meek water of rain and canals, water that nourishes, that encourages growth and green. But the clock ticked minutes, days, months, in a slow parade. "It was so extremely cold that the fire cast almost no heat; for as we put our feet to the fire, we burnt our hose before we could feel the heat, so that we had constantly enough work to do to patch it. And what is more, if we had not sooner smelt than felt them, we should have burnt them quite away ere we had known it'" (41). The hose that is; we could neither burn nor patch our spirits, which grew dull and listless from the lack of light, from the creeping certainty of death.

And then, on January 27, from that netherworld of eternal darkness, the sun, having withheld itself for months, crept a little above the horizon. It was, by my calculations, twelve days earlier than expected, divine intervention sent to give us heart, although a Canadian would call that strange looming a solar mirage, the sun "still 5 degrees below the horizon, its rays bent towards [us] by a refractive condition in the atmosphere," (Lopez, 24) Novaya Zemlya images, a Frankensteinian temptation to rejoice.

Slowly, the light grew longer, and we could see around us, the wondrous arrogance of ice: "'the ice was in such wonderful manner risen and piled up one upon the other that it was as if there had been whole towns made of ice with towers and bulwarks round about them'" (Mirsky, 42). But that same ice had ground our ship to splinters. Our only hope of return was to buttress our small boats and yawl. We worked at the small boats to strengthen them, all the while watchful against the hungry bears, who came "'as if they had smelt that we would be gone, and that therefore they desired first to have a taste of us'" (42). But by June the boats were ready.

I kept no journal. But before we left Ice Haven, I wrote three letters. I was not a Canadian, but I was a thorough man. One I left in the chimney of the shelter where we had spent that winter; one was given to each boat so that there would be some record of our hardships and our triumphs. I was ill, sick with the scurvy that ate into flesh and strength alike, but I could not let my comrades see my impending death, and we set out on June 13, in fine weather over open water. As we rounded the point of Novaya Zemlya, I said to Gerrit de Veer, he whose account would be published under its long-winded and most unCanadian title, "'Gerrit, if we are near Ice Point, just lift me up again. I must see that Point once more.' And when Heemskerck asked how [I] felt, 'Quite well, mate. I still hope to be able to run about before we get to Vardo'" (42–43). And when a gale lashed at us, and the ice floes again ground their edges against the sides of the boat, I suggested that we pull the boats onto a large floe, to ride that bucking ice as if it were the ship we had relied upon and lost. There, on an ice pan, on June 20, as the solid water began to relent, streaking a black path toward spring, did I, Willem Barentsz, pilot, first of the Europeans to spend a winter at degree 78 North, die, not a product but a process, and happily I might add, since I could believe that the men I had taken into the perilous Arctic reaches with me were strong enough to survive, to reach Vaygach and Kola. Which they did, navigating with sail and oars, against wind and ice, some 1600 miles in small open boats over an ice-choked sea.

And so mine is no Canadian narrative, of buried bones and fierce unearthings. I was a practical man. Stay warm, eat bear fat, chant the beauty of the Song of Songs against the darkness, and it might be possible to navigate one's way to a version of harbour. But I am Dutch, pure and simple.

No other European reached 78 degrees North until some three hundred years later. So much for Franklin and his romantic perishings, that man who created the monster of the romantic northern search, and all its voyages of recovery. The search for Franklin's bones persists into the ludicrous, while the search for me has become a happy narrative. In 1871, Elling Carlsen, a well-equipped Norwegian sealing captain, set out to follow our earlier voyage and found our little hut in Ice Haven—yes, three hundred years later—perfectly preserved. "Protected from decay, guarded from prowling destructive foxes and bears by a thick layer of ice that hermetically sealed the house, were the books, instruments, clothes, tools, engravings, utensils, used by Barents's men. . . . There were found the clock, the muskets, a flute, the small shoes of the ship's boy who had died there, and the letter Barents put in the chimney for safekeeping" (43). So goes the story, not a Canadian story, bred for survivalist and data-infected scholars munching on the Frygian theories of Atwood and the cannibalism of survival. Mine is a Dutch story, perhaps also a fiction reminding every careful listener to heed the end of Shelley's *Frankenstein*, when the poor monster springs from the cabin window onto an ice floe, and is "borne away by the waves and lost in darkness and distance" (Shelley, 206). To search for that dreaming monster is futile: he merely disappears over broken ice into the north, site of all disappearing, Frankenstein, Franklin, the apparatus of magnifying glass inspection and recovery a chimera only too like the chimera that led poor Frankenstein to imagine that he could replicate the power of creation. To die upon an ice floe is a stroke of both remembrance and forgetting. What is yet to be discovered is what ought to be remembered and what ought to be forgotten. But I am not Canadian; I am merely a Dutch pilot who wintered in an Arctic that chose to narrate me. As others will, I have no doubt, seek to narrate my brief voyage on earth.

And here follows a third person version of my death, as if I were a cautionary narrative.

* * *

Novaya Zemlya, 1597

Willem Barentsz lies in the bottom of the open boat's frail shell and tries to control the shivering that rakes his frame. His body is one terrible green and yellow bruise, his joints race with fire. Although he is but thirty-seven-years old, he has not long to live. He knows that fact as implacably as he has lessoned all the other failures that he manifests now, a physical metaphor for his optimistic search and its revision. The Straits of Anian, the northeast passage, the wealth of Cathay, are a mirage that he does not willingly close his eyes against, even here, on the choppy, ice-clogged Arctic sea. A pilot, he has been trained to conduct ships through difficult waters. He would laugh at this irony if the tiny boat did not wallow so wretchedly and if his mouth and gums did not ache, but his lips are swollen like crusted bladders and he cannot speak.

de Veer, who has been set to watch him, is making cryptic marks in his journal. Gerrit de Veer is determined that he will live to publish his account under the title, *The True and Perfect Description of Three Voyages so Strange and Wonderful that the Like Has Never Been Heard of Before.* Barentsz would like to suggest to him that the words "true and perfect" are dangerous, but de Veer is not interested in editorial emendations. He manages to keep tallow and charcoal mixed with a little sea water liquid enough to jot his abbreviated words, his determination to record as fierce as Barentsz' earlier determination to push farther, past one more ice-floe, one more tempting island to the imagined open space beyond.

Barentsz knows that he ought to repent, for he has been wrong, wrong about many supposedly irrefutable facts, their impenetrable mysteries now swirling around him in this terrible pitch and toss of wooden boat against water. The fact of water is one example. He thought water was water, but these northern seas contain water beyond imagining. As penetratingly metallic as rock, this water is iron cold, ready to erupt with monstrous beasts and sea lions. The fact of beasts is another example, and none more awesome than the white bears tumbling and wrestling one another over enormous cake pans of ice. Hugely unafraid, accustomed to the report of exploding ice, they merely lift their heads when muskets are fired at them, they tear great slabs of meat from beached whale skeletons, their knife-like claws rip men and sacks of supplies open with equal swiftness. They appeared silently, looming on padded feet, larger than the driftwood hut the men built at Ice Haven, stranded there at the island's tip for the entire darkness of what seemed like months more than winter. The bears killed, for their pleasure it seemed, two sailors who had wandered a few steps away to crouch in the snow and relieve themselves. Barentsz, dreaming that he does not dream, hears their screams still, screams that almost tore light out of the darkness. Until they were stunned silent by a paw's backhand blow.

Yes, he has blood on his soul, if he is to be held accountable for taking these young men with him, across the Kara Sea from Spitsbergen— his discovery, Spitsbergen, that outcrop of fingered land indecipherable from ice. He should have urged them to return to Amsterdam when Ryp, who piloted the second ship, turned back, back to foot-warming stoves beneath skirts settled in wooden pews, back to the perils of nothing more than uneven cobblestones and purse-thefts in the stews, back to the meek water of rain and canals, water that follows a pre-ordained path. There is green here on the open waves, too, but it is the green of ice rather than vegetation, reflecting a black, nacreous shine, that of depth and finned sea mammoths. Barentsz, he chides himself, you have been a Dutch pilot for years, you know there are no sea monsters, only stories of sea monsters. But he can see one now, riding the waves just to the left of their fragile craft, its nostrils distended above the surface of the water, its scales lashing in swim. He is dreaming, dreaming as surely as he dreamed of the spices of Cathay, of matching geography to his greedy imagination.

He has told the men to throw him overboard when he dies. They will make better progress without a stiff, water-logged body to hamper their tossing journey. They are afraid to do so, afraid that they will be accused of murder, if they reach Amsterdam again, without him. For all that his facts have been so brutally amended, he does not mind the idea of a watery grave. He has travelled this ice-bound twilight and its dawn three times, he has navigated the threaded selvedge of pack ice enough to feel that it reserves itself as destiny for him. Three times he sailed past the edges of warning, returning twice from the shrivelling cold triumphant, full of boastful adventures and a desire to push farther. And now, this third venture, he will not return, he will succumb to the scurvy that eats his wiry, compact body. It will be a miracle if any of them return, they have dragged this slender vessel, hammered together of the leftover splinters of their ship, over ice ridges and opens leads, they have tried to row against the battering waves. It is sixteen hundred "miles" to the Kola peninsula and they are only half-way there.

He tries to shift, to prop his head against the gunwale, but can find no comfortable position. He is wet from the waves that sweep this open boat, this subsidiary boat they reinforced and refurbished, using what they could of the shredded hull of the ship. His ship—he thinks of it always as his own—its smooth beautiful lines ground to a pulp by the ice, this ice that crushes all it rubs against. They stood helpless outside the hut in the half-twilight and watched from the shore, listening to the scream of ice gouging wood, the trim masts pitching, askew, the ship's prow staved in by one berg slamming it against another as if those icefloats were vindictive animals. Beside his crew, Barentsz knew their hair crawled with horror, felt his own lift from the back of his neck. They were then, with the ship's destruction, trapped there, on the north shore of that desolate and indifferent island, Novaya Zemlya. Another of his discoveries, Willem Barentsz the intrepid explorer, not afraid of the mysterious north, believing in the high black rock of the North Pole, a lodestone for his dreams of passage. For all that he wanted to find a shorter way to get there, he has never sailed to Cathay. And now he never will.

He hopes that Gerrit de Veer will remember to write about the sun's miraculous rise, twelve days earlier than they had calculated it should appear. The long darkness was worse than the cold, its unbreakable depth sometimes lit by eerie shadows, ice and snow crawling under a heavy moon. And the taunting lights that curtained the sky, unfurling delicate streams of colour, miraged sails fluttering. The aurora crackled like canvas lifting wind, although he knows those lights are illusion, too, another polar mystery that he cannot factualize.

The cold is fact beyond articulation, impossible to describe how it entered their very souls and cast itself solid within them. The fire that they fed with driftwood and polar bear fat burned and burned but seemed unable to cast heat; two feet from the fire, ice on the floor of the hut refused to melt. But the darkness, the absence of sun, was fact enough to negate all others. Light withheld itself as if to trifle with their belief in the concept of day, and they trembled with fear that the sun would never return, that they had been tricked into entering a netherworld of eternal darkness. They read the Bible, searching for references to the sun lost and re-risen.

"Who is this who looks out like the dawn, beautiful as the moon, bright as the sun?" Now Barentsz understands the Song of Songs, its dazzling radiance.

The sun came twelve days earlier than he had calculated, divine intervention sent to give them heart, to let them know that they might withstand their adversities. Looming, he called it, a trick of the light on the shelves of ice, a refractive mirage. But now he is too ill to approach that insight scientifically, and even if he could speak, he suspects that de Veer would not wish to write his observations down. Gerrit de Veer will fashion his own version, just as future cartographers will feel they must embellish Barentsz's plain and serviceable maps. *Polus Arcticus* will ride only too neatly in the compassed middle, and Baptista van Doetechum will add charming sketches of whales and seals frolicking in benign waves on the margins.

Still, his charts will survive. Will he?

No. His body is finished, he knows that, he is eager for the pain to end. But will he be remembered? Willem Barentsz, leader of the party that survived the first winter ever spent by Europeans in the extreme Arctic, discoverer of Spitsbergen and Novaya Zemlya, the man who penetrated the ice-choked reaches of the Kara Sea—78 degrees North—farther than anyone will reach until the nineteenth century, before the British and the Spanish and the whole scurvy race of northern passage hunters, of that grail later called Arctic exploration. He, Willem Barentsz, even dying in this open boat of scurvy, of an overfondness for facts, is a Dutchman, pure and simple.

* * *

Another narrative attributing me to myself:

At the end of *Frankenstein,* Walton writes to his sister telling her that Frankenstein has "corrected and augmented" (195) Walton's notes of his history. They are, he reports, "still surrounded by mountains of ice, still in imminent danger of being crushed in their conflict. The cold is excessive, and many of my unfortunate comrades have already found a grave amidst this scene of desolation" (196). I, Willem Barentsz, found my grave. But it was a happy enough grave for one intrepid Dutchmen, and I settled for sending with my men the strength of my spirit, so that, by hugging the coast of Novaya Zemlya, they would reach Vaygach, so that they could make their way along the Russian coast to Kola, so that they could reunite with Ryp and sail to Amsterdam, a triumphant return. Which they did, they did.

In Westminster Abbey in the great city of London is a bust of Franklin, and an inscription round its base. *Not here; the white north has thy bones; and thou, heroic sailor-soul, art passing on thine happier voyage now toward no earthly pole.* A pretty sentiment, a sustainment of that thirst for destination, even if a heavenly destination has replaced the earthly. So does the monster/traveller disappear into his or her process, remain within his or her narration; question then, the destination that palimpsests its artifactual conclusions onto an undefinable place that occupies the imaginations of those who dare to imagine.

But who am I to speak, and wherefore comes my narrative? My name is Willem Barentsz. I am merely northern, and I merely died. All I can say in my own defense, or suggest to those who would read the Arctic, is that the north is a configuration of narrative imagination, without nation, without destination, and without inherent motivation. It is a geography only traceable by an eye willing to abandon its prescribed latitude and longitude. The Arctic lives within us all.

So, here is my advice: learn from Frankenstein and be not so determinedly Canadian.

NOTES AND WORKS CITED

1.   Shelley, Mary. *Frankenstein.* New York: Bantam, 1981.
2.   Mirsky, Jeannette. *To the Arctic!* London & New York: Allan Wingate, 1949. Mirsky quotes at length from de Veer's narrative. I have employed her quotes because I have been unable to access de Veer's text. So are such narratives narrativized and passed on.
3.   Lopez, Barry. *Arctic Dreams.* New York: Scribners, 1986.

Thirsty for Life:
A Nomad Learns to Write
and Draw

ALOOTOOK IPELLIE

I don't know what it is about this day and age, but wherever I go in this world, I always end up being surrounded by so many Qallunaat of all persuasions. This reality usually gives me a strange feeling, and I get a little scared at times. How did this ever happen to an innocent Eskimo such as I?

I do not mean to offend any of my Qallunaat friends here, but perhaps you will understand better why I feel a little apprehensive standing and speaking in front of you. A trailblazer I am not, but at least allow me to be a great pretender.

Let me speak, for a moment, of my fellow Inuit of the recent past, who were rendered by outside forces a fated people thrown collectively for a loop into an uncertain future. Their long history as a nomadic people living in one of the world's largest deep freezers has now proven their traditional culture and heritage were destined for a wholesale change. This change left behind, in its wake, victims whose sense of Eskimo reality was irreversibly altered by cultural upheaval.

As a people, when the first wave of settlers came to their domain, they did not have any immunity to an infection not unlike the flesh-eating disease, streptococcus A bacteria. This disease, fatal as it can sometimes be, was somehow prevented from doing further gorging on the already minuscule Inuit population. However, even at this late hour, the fall-out from the recent cultural explosion is still vibrating through the lives of four generations of Inuit. And what was their devious crime? Just being culturally different with a distinct ideology far removed from those of the settlers. Whoever thought curiosity didn't come with a price has gone the way of Franklin and his forlorn men. None of us are deaf, dumb, and blind to the fact that if there is a buck to be made, the salesman will be at your door with a brand new deep freezer in hand, or for that matter, the eternally infamous, and the latest edition, of a vacuum cleaner. What wondrous technological, and engineering, achievements these are! The Eskimo will love 'em. The latest blue millionaire is born. Never mind that the salesman also happened to be a huckster working for a blue-blooded descendant from the former British Empire.

I well remember the heady days when me and my family slowly got up early each morning in the dark dampness of the igloo, our eyelids still stuck shut with the fluid that had soured and become pasty during the night. The fluid had actually been teardrops left over from the previous day's loss of an animal we should have since devoured to help replenish our bodies, and therefore, our minds.

Each day was a struggle full of hope that bounty was waiting for us in one of those seal breathing holes on the vast sea ice. Our dogged determination to survive will never be understood by those who did not keep company with us when out stomachs yearned for their latest salvation. Not even the greatest of Arctic narrators, I believe, will ever come close to interpreting the anguish we nomads felt when each day dawned and darkness fell at the end of the day. Our only saving grace was to continue dreaming about the feast that had once again eluded us.

I have read many good Arctic yarns spun out by the so-called giants of Canadian Lit., such as Farley Mowat, who, despite his deep earnestness as an Arctic narrator, was inadvertently trapped into Arctic folklore as a writer some Inuit are fond of referring to—in friendly Eskimo terms, of course—as "Farley Mowat, Hardly Knowit." Do not despair, my fellow interpreter of the imagination, even after living in Ottawa for nearly thirty years, the Qallunaat still earnestly call me, "Alootook Ipellie Hardlyknowit." What a vile civilization we live in. Aside from this harsh reality, I have been waiting, all these years, for another of Farley's incredible recipes for those delectable Barren Lands Mice. I am still in culinary heaven, ever since I first tried his recipe for "Creamed Mice." Except in my case, I substituted Tundra Lemmings.

One of our godfathers of Canadian Lit., Pierre Berton, undoubtedly toiled, long and hard, into many a late "Arctic" night, retelling the trials and tribulations of both the heroic and infamous in his book, *The Arctic Grail*. Even after coming out with an incredible narrative of Arctic lore, Peeta has always been an enigma in the very Arctic he has written about. Is it only me, or are there others out there, who have never heard of him actually setting foot onto the Arctic tundra? If this is the case, my speculation is his trademark bow tie may have rendered him an illegal alien in the land of the fur-clad Eskimos. If Douglas Adams can write *The Hitchhiker's Guide to the Galaxy*, then Peeta is a welcome addition to a band of Arctic narrators from the alien galaxy of the Qallanaaq. Beam me up, Scotty.

Some years ago, after reading the Preface to "The Collected Poems of Al Purdy," I was happy to learn Al and I had several things in common. One, is our first name, since I usually introduce myself as "Al" to the Qallunaat who are, quite literally, incapable of speaking in a guttural voice like so many of us Inuit are wont to do. Second, we both like to write poems. Third, we share a mutual enjoyment of a beer or two, although, at this point in my life, I can only claim to have filled a mid-sized lake in southern Baffin Island. Not to worry, Attikuluk (my name-sake), I will soon be able to boast to one and all that I, too, will not be able to ever see the shore again from my rowboat from all the beer I have drunk in my lifetime.

"Hello, Margaret Atwood!"

Upon opening Rudy Wiebe's, *Playing Dead: A Contemplation Concerning the Arctic,* there is a map of Canada entitled, "Inuit View to the South," showing how the south appears when viewed from the North Pole. The map throws your sense of equilibrium out the door after being so used to looking at a so-called "upright" map of Canada, as seen by Qallunaat from the south. I immediately thought of Rudy as a genius for having come up with an aptly titled book (although, in his case, the title derives from an Inuit legend). What a revelation! The south really does look like that when you are very dead and looking at the world below from your little perch in Heaven. I had better get used to looking at this "Inuit view to the South" in readiness for whenever I am destined to meet the Divinity. What an optimistic Eskimo I am. But, to me, Rudy will forever be a diviner. He travelled to the Arctic and foresaw the future.

John Moss. Here is a writer who certainly will never be referred to as a "mossback" as far as interpretation of the Arctic landscape is concerned. Mr. Moss has certainly travelled the ruggedness, as well as the plainness, of the Arctic landscape. He has done it over a time span of many moons in the moonless Arctic summers, and for that matter, in daylight that refused to retire for days on end. He has also done it on the backs of so many others who travelled the Arctic landscape before him. Oh, how their mighty words drew his curiosity and he, too, had to find out how it felt to be reincarnated as an Inummariq, a real Inuk. The ghosts of the previous Arctic, explored, were visible everywhere he went. The well-trodden trails snake their way in the valleys, over countless hills, and along numerous beaches. The Arctic seas echo still with the wailing cries of once proud men who were swallowed by the mighty Arctic seas. They were certainly defiant to their last breath, only to surrender to the almightiness of nature; all humble men. Mr. Moss, who possesses enduring Arctic dreams, has lemmings in his pants that want to go along with the next voyage of discovery. And up to this day, he has covered only the first leg of his long Arctic journey ahead. We envy you, sir. However, let me take you back to your Katannilik Journals for Wednesday, July 29, 1992 ("It's hard to make love on the tundra . . ."). Without pretending macho, I have had similar experiences over the years. I am not saying that I am an expert in such predicaments, but perhaps we can at least compare notes and learn from one another.

And so, there are countless other Arctic narrators who have all been, more or less, intellectually lured by the incredible Arctic and its hardy and resourceful people, the Inuit who were made to settle down. The myth and mystique of the polar lands has summoned countless men from far-off lands, some of whom came to their unfortunate final end on what turned out to be such an unforgiving land. No living generation of Arctic narrators will ever get enough satisfaction out of spinning yarns about the Arctic and its cast of thousands, from the bygone days to this very moment. I am standing here in front of you to announce, unfortunately, that none of us will ever live long enough to finally complete the elusive final book on the Arctic and its people, or any facsimile of them. The Great White Arctic will remain an unfinished story to the very end of human habitation on planet Earth. How sad.

However, it is this very reality that keeps those of us who spin yarns about the Arctic and its people full of adrenalin—infects us with a chronic frothing-in-the-mouth disease which, to this very day, is incurable.

I am, while pursuing other professions, a little-known Inuk cartoonist, in possession of a slightly warped mind like so many of my colleagues. It is for this reason that I am often saddened by the thought that there aren't more people like us in this world. God was not very kind to humanity for creating so few cartoonists among a sea of blockheads overpopulating this planet. Shame. Shame. You and I know we will never tire of being entertained by social satirists, who are among the best interpreters of this world-wide human tragicomedy.

I once drew a cartoon of a very friendly Inuk, and I cannot emphasize this too lightly, as a sandwich man walking smack in the middle of a very busy intersection in a large Canadian city. On both sides of the sign-board was written:

> I'm Nanook from the Far North. I've come here to dig up somebody's grandfather to find out what an interesting life people used to live in Toronto. Have a nice day!

On either sidewalk are Qallunaat walking to and fro, perplexity splashed all over their faces, and a question mark over their brains. "What the hell is this Eskimo crackpot doing in our civilized world?"; they seem cannonading vermin beside the poor Eskimo urban anthropologist. The cartoon did give me a chuckle after completing it. Except that, horror of horrors, it was also the very week that my own grandfather, Inutsiaq—famous for

his childbirth carvings—was being dissected by a redoubtable anthropological team just outside Iqaluit. No, no, just kidding. . . .

I will not apologize for being in possession of a slightly warped
mind . . .

I have a clipping of a cartoon which appeared in a newspaper
about ten years ago. It is a depiction of a landing by three crew members
of an exploration ship, not unlike the *Santa Maria*. They are garbed in
attire from Columbus's time. One of them is holding what probably is the
conquering nation's flag, one knee to the ground, the other arm sweeping
over the great land, proudly boasting: "Behold! A new land . . . where
every man can forge his own future, be free to pursue happiness in an
atmosphere of justice and equality for all humanity! . . . Get rid of the
locals and we'll be all set." The name of the cartoon? "Bizarro." Indeed.

Gary Larsen, please, for the continued retention of my fragile san-
ity, un-retire!

Over the years I have drawn hundreds of cartoons about my people and their relationships with the so-called "civilized" world. One, in particular, is memorable, not only because *The Globe and Mail* reprinted it in
its edition of January 11, 1982. The cartoon was aptly captioned: "Cartoon
in recent edition of *Inuit Today* shows Pierre Trudeau gorging himself on
seal depicting aboriginal rights." Further down the column three paragraphs read:

> Mr Trudeau has been roundly caricatured by political car-
> toonists during his 14 years in power, but perhaps never quite so
> viciously as in the recent edition of *Inuit Today*, the bi-monthly pub-
> lication of Inuit Tapirisat of Canada.
>
> The centrepiece cartoon, under the name Alootook Ipellie,
> the Ottawa-based editor of the magazine, shows a tuxedoed Prime
> Minister gorging himself on an upturned seal depicting aboriginal
> rights "celebrating the occasion of finally bringing home the consti-
> tution." Blood and guts drip from Mr. Trudeau's knife, fork and
> mouth.
>
> What is also surprising about the virulence of the caricature
> is that the ITC has been the most moderate of the major native
> groups throughout the constitutional battle and supported the
> project, at least tacitly, at various stages while others were off lobby-
> ing the British.

It felt good, with a restrained inner elation, to see a cartoon of
mine published in "Canada's National Newspaper." A colleague at ITC
broke the news to me that wonderful day. It had indeed been published
without my knowledge. "Those buggers," I thought to myself as I admired
the image opposite me in the office washroom mirror. "Here I am, a

world-renowned cartoonist and those nerds didn't even ask for my permission? How insensitive!"

Over the years, since that fateful day, I've had nightmares about "sins of omission or commission." So, today, I am inclined to ask a great favour from any Torontonian to do the impossible by volunteering to visit the good editor of "Canada's National Newspaper" and ask for a belated apology. And make sure this apology is sweetened by an appropriate commission that was, and is, due me; with interest added, of course. Is there any good Torontonian whose Draconian methods are a little rusty and in need of some honing?

These recollections give me pause to ponder a little cut of my personal past. It has been an incredible journey so far. It is as if I were catapulted to this very room straight from a lonely hunting camp on the northern shores of Frobisher Bay where I was brought into this world, in the year of our Lord, nineteen hundred and fifty one. Where has the time gone, my friends? And where will it take me from here and, therefore, each of you?

In the Introduction to my book *Arctic Dreams and Nightmares,* the first paragraph reads in part:

> I was often in awe of the extraordinary abilities of my elders to understand the seasons, in knowing the behaviour of all Arctic animal species, and to co-exist with their fellow Inuit in a common goal to survive as a collective. In the Arctic's harsh environment, one mistake or a lapse in judgement could spell certain disaster. By observing, listening and practising what my elders did, I was instilled with the will to survive for the moment and go on for another day. Being a young man exposed to such mentality, I learned to be thirsty for life. Today, this same thirst is firmly placed in my heart and mind.

Going back to my roots—I had a difficult childhood and upbringing. I blame some of my early struggles on the difficult days of living off the land, the cultural upheaval that came so close to victimizing me—while other of my childhood friends did not make it through—and the physical abuse I received from a family member's alcoholism. I well remember feeling total helplessness; the utter hunger that was often so prevalent in our home; the sleepless nights walking the town because I had no place to sleep. Now you can better understand why I would write, many years later, the words in the Introduction to my book: "I learned to be thirsty for life."

When I was still a student here in Ottawa in 1967 I went to a therapist at the Royal Ottawa a number of times, although not of my own volition. A wild rumour had started spinning at my Northern Affairs counsellor's office that I was somehow mentally ill because I was so quiet and shy. I hardly ever spoke to my teachers or to the people I was boarding with. So, I went to the R.O. every day after school for an hour session with this woman who would end up doing all the talking between the two of us.

One day, I handed her an excerpt of a story later serialized in *Inuit Today* magazine, chronicling my experiences of growing up in Iqaluit during the cultural transition of my people. She was most surprised by the part where I wrote about being locked out if I did not get home before my family went to sleep. Locking up was a common practice in Iqaluit at the time, since there were so many drunken Inuit walking around after the local bar closed or after a drinking party at someone's house. The serialized stories, then called "Those Were the Days," were a way of coming to terms with the demons of my past. They were my real therapist.

And, come to think of it, any sensible, prospective publisher out there would be a little mental not to take on a completed manuscript based on those serialized stories, now re-named, "Iqalummiut: the People of Iqaluit."

I have been pleasantly surprised by a positive critical and public reaction to *Arctic Dreams and Nightmares*. Aside from the fact some of the drawings offended a few feminists, who berated me and accused me of being insensitive to their gender by saying I was portraying women in a sexist way, I also had scores of people who came to me, hand extended, with perfect Cheshire cat grins, which made my many a day. Shortly after the book came out, I exhibited ten of the original drawings in a local Ottawa pub. A friend of mine thought that it might be good to have a guest book for people's reactions to those particular drawings.

Some comments:

> "Incredible technique!" "Excellent work—very 'awe' inspiring." "I want to come back for a closer look." "'Crisp' dream landscapes are *beautiful*." "Powerful messages, deep meanings, works of true art." "I said I'd be here." "May the circle of your life and mythologies continue to grow." "Great pub, great beer, good service, however, 'Hunting For Skins and Fur' was violent in its portrayal of women. In light of the violence against women in society, perhaps a better choice of artwork could be selected!" "I find the idea of someone hunting me for my skin and 'fur' very degrading." "Horrific and funny." "Re: the above comments . . . You can't fight the first amendment!!! Thanx. Another pint please!"

The four years it took me to complete approximately forty drawings were a full smorgasbord of emotions which I will most certainly bring to my deathbed. What is an artist or a writer who does not practise his beloved profession with emotion, whether it is with exasperation or exultation?

I well remember a great sigh of relief after the last stroke of my pen completed each perfect piece of artwork.

As I told one interviewer who wrote an article about my book: "The drawings came out by themselves. I really didn't have any control over what happened to the final product of that image. You let the darn thing interpret itself. Otherwise, it doesn't work out. If you are struggling with it, then it doesn't deserve to come out."

I suppose I can say this is also true of the written word.

Fear of failure. It's a great equalizer in both man and beast. Personally speaking, it has been a driving force ever since I can remember as a small child in that cold land with its warm people, to this very day, where I have to contend with awful humidity and at times a hostile population. Now you can better understand why I said earlier that I sometimes feel a little strange, and a little scared, whenever I am surrounded by so many Qallunaat. I can only thank my astonishing human instinct to keep me well away whenever I detect any scent of human animalism round me.

One of the driving forces behind any of my writing or artwork is the incredible challenge of interpreting the mixture of the two, very different cultures I live with on a daily basis, by no choice of my own. This is the crux of my motivation whenever the planet Earth somehow rotates into the shine of the sun on our part of the world. Each day is not always successful but the hope of tomorrow draws me vigorously forward, dreaming about creating perfectly connected words, sentences that happily marry one another, and paragraphs that become good neighbours in a greater hope that a good yarn will be spun to entertain hundreds and thousands of bored human minds out there in the real world. And as an artist, other parts of my human instincts come into play when I go after the all-too-rare beautiful strokes of luck on a drawing board.

I am the luckiest person in the world, even if there are some naysayers in this room who know themselves that they, too, are the luckiest among all of us. We all know a little clashing of opinions, when appropriate, can't hurt once in a while. It is a human trait that acts as a defensive mechanism which can only be good for our respective minds, fragile as these always are, from moment to moment.

I once read an obscure book which made the incredible claim: "The meek shall inherit the Earth." But let me say it doesn't hurt to be a little aggressive once in a Blue Moon when making one's point about the unravelling of human events in this cruel world. This is our sacred duty as writers and/or artists. We sometimes have to play the part of "Alarm Bells" in order to help humanity wake up from its ugly lethargy in a lifetime that cannot end too soon. I speak of the prevalence of endless human poverty, the human slaughterhouse of useless wars, and the mindless abuse of our one and only lifeline, the planet Earth; not to mention the slow deterioration of the fragile Arctic ecosystem, which all of us should help preserve, whatever way we can.

I am well aware of my place in the Inuit community. I have worked hard for a lifetime to help put a recognizable "face," as well as a united "voice," to our people's long struggle for political recognition and respect from the powers-that-be in this huge country. For this, I am eternally grateful for having been given even a small chance. And I have never treated this opportunity as anything less than an incredible privilege for someone who started out so humbly.

As we all know, the sum of any person's grit is the combined experiences of his or her life to the end of each succeeding day. For a nomad who learned to write and draw, it has been a roller coaster of a ride, writing and depicting my people's songs of sorrow and joy. The "Arctic Narrator" within me has not come easily. It is not now easy. And I expect it will never become easier as I look to the future. Contemplating my lifelong experiences, I like to think of myself as having been driven to become a mad, nomadic locomotor, gone wild, living in a society that tries so hard to appear, feel, taste, sound and smell "civilized."

In conclusion, I want to quote a passage I wrote close to three years ago as part of an editorial entitled, "If the Mind Could Speak," in *Kivioq, Inuit Fiction Magazine,* which is now stuck in limbo due to a lack of funding, and of which I am still editor:

> Let us write passages that will sway the centuries-old impressions that others have about our true colours. Let us put, without a moment's hesitation, a voice in the mouth of our silent mind. Let us help breathe out the songs that want to be sung. Let us free ourselves from the chains that shackle our imagination and explore the unknown world that is within us. Let us help our silent mind speak through the beauty of the written word. Let us help to release it from Hell's world of pure silence. Let us dream forever and write.

Speech Habits and Inuit Ethos

HAROLD HORWOOD

When I decided to attend this symposium the first thing I did was re-read my own Arctic narratives—not the biography of Captain Bob Bartlett, which concerns white explorers almost exclusively, and the Inuit only marginally, but the novel *White Eskimo,* and the short stories in the collection *Only the Gods Speak,* which include native people as principal characters. I then looked at Arctic narratives by other Canadian writers, and made a curious discovery, namely, that in few instances had there been any attempt to record actual dialogue either among Inuit people themselves, or between Inuit and visiting whites. The actual flavour of speech by native people of the north occurs hardly at all in Canadian fiction, and yet this flavour of speech is so important an element that I think we should call attention to it, and make an effort to record it, before it vanishes from the world.

My novel *White Eskimo* belongs to the first half of this century, as even its title makes clear: We do not refer, now, to Inuit as Eskimo, as even the Inuit themselves did until the 1970s, and as they are still named in the United States. My short stories "Men Like Summer Snow" and "Love in a Very Cold Climate" belong to the early 1970s. Comparing the people and the conditions I wrote about then with the youthful crop of Inuit leaders that I met a few years later, during the James Bay development controversy, has led me to the conclusion that I wrote about a society, an ethos, a people that have all but vanished.

The Inuit leaders, women and men of the Tapirisat, whom I met while they were negotiating land claims with Canada and the province of Quebec, were truly delightful people, sitting in centrally heated rooms, on furniture upholstered in white leather, sipping rare and expensive varieties of coffee. They bore no apparent relationship to the hunters with whom I had hunted seals and caribou just a few years earlier, crouching around a kettle of boiling tea and complaining about the cold.

For one thing, women were filling a new role. When I was travelling in Labrador in the 1940s and 1950s, first as a politician, then as a journalist, finally as a researcher into native life in the late days of the fur trade, women and men filled very restricted roles firmly delineated by tradition. Men were hunters, travellers, workers for the white establishment, guides for the rare visitor. Women were "keepers of the lamp" and experts in such skills as sewing sealskin and caribou hide. They often accompanied men on their travels, as children did, too, but always as cooks, seamstresses, makers and repairers of tents and clothing—jobs they did with great finesse. Then, overnight, women were representing the native people in negotiations with the white establishment, were sometimes sent to Ottawa or to Quebec City as spokespersons for the Tapirisat, or for some group within it. There was no traditional prohibition against women taking on political roles, or roles as traders, for that matter, because in traditional native life no such roles existed.

The Inuit had no political structure of any kind, even the most rudimentary—not so much as a clan chief from one end of the Arctic to the other. So when the need for a political structure emerged it was open to anyone with the necessary education, especially the ability to speak fluent English (though not French, incidentally; during the James Bay negotiations, which I covered for *The Reader's Digest,* I did not meet a single French-speaking Inuk or argna.)

Until 1970 the Inuit ethos was more or less intact. Sex roles were defined. Hunters were honoured. The supernatural world was everywhere present. Children were treated with unfailing kindness, and the environment, rather than a set of rules, created the discipline that they needed to become effective adults. The one discernable change, perhaps, was that the missionaries, who had been stating their case for more that two centuries, were losing their influence.

In the 1980s a new breed of missionaries arrived—white feminists who wished to change the status of native women, and to reform sexual relationships that, until then, had been totally permissive and without regulation. Their radical idea of puritan sex or none at all was henceforth to be imposed on the Arctic, and is now being imposed with the help of the RCMP, the perhaps reluctant co-operation of some Inuit women, and one or two willing volunteers who were sent south for re-education, then brought north again to spread the gospel. A prophecy of this state of affairs, of heavy-handed white meddling in native sexual mores, is contained in my short story "Love in a Very Cold Climate," written in 1973 and published in 1979. This story, perhaps the most socially significant one I have written, has been totally ignored, while another of mine, written at the same time, "Men Like Summer Snow," has been republished in places as distant as Denmark and the People's Republic of China.

In all these narratives I attempted to reproduce Inuit habits of speech. In "Men Like Summer Snow" the story is carried entirely by dialogue between two young Inuit hunters, and I tried to show them talking as they really do talk, not translating their conversation into literary English, as nearly all writers do, even Inuit writers when they write in our language.

Inuktituk, and spoken English, when used by the Inuit, are full of conventional and polite qualifiers. Such words as "maybe" and "perhaps" and "I suppose" keep cropping up. Impersonal pronouns are used even more widely than they are in French. Instead of saying, "Let's go seal hunting," an Inuk will say, "It might be a good day to go looking for seals, should anyone wish to do so." Crossing the caribou barrens with a black bank of cloud to windward and little doubt that a blizzard is imminent, a hunter will say to his companion, "Snow coming bye and bye, maybe." If you take the trouble to read "Men Like Summer Snow" you will find such turns of speech on every page, even though the speakers are absolute equals, two young hunters just reaching manhood.

I noticed by the mid-seventies that these turns of speech were used far less by the white-educated men and women of the Tapirisat than they had been a few years earlier, by the men with whom I hunted caribou and seals. This new breed seemed to be speaking and thinking much like the white people with whom they had to deal.

More, perhaps, than is generally realized, forms of speech reveal character, ethos, a whole attitude toward life. In this case it shows a polite, tentative, indirect approach, rather like that of the fisherman who said to Farley Mowat: "We don't be takin' nothin' from the sea. We has to sneak up on what we wants, and wiggle it away." Among the Inuit, you don't even wiggle it away. Meat is always regarded as a gift from the animals, or their spirits.

Inuit are not only tentative and indirect when addressing other people, but even when speaking of the animals, or addressing the "game lords" as the anthropologists like to call the animal spirits. The bear is "the great one." The caribou is "the wanderer." The otter is "the playful one." And so on. Really typical are the concluding lines of the hunter's song in *Cycle of the Sun*:

> So I sit here brewing tea at the door of my tent,
> and sing you this song, Old Man of the Caribou,
> that your heart might be glad,
> and my belly may be full.

If the game lord is pleased with this song, the hunter will get his meat.

Perhaps none of this will matter to the future, but will be relevant only in depicting a way of life that is past, or passing. The speech of the future, in the Arctic as in other places, will be taught by videotape and picture tube and satellite, and will express realities far more brutal than those of the past:

> Some of the shamans have become
> schoolteachers, priests in collars, angekoks
> denying the gifts of song and fire and drum,
> dreaming and prophecy. So we await
> new revelations of the Kabloonait:
> Tobacco, tea and marijuana,
> moonshine, gasoline and glue
> have served us in their turn; the spirit masks
> beckon us into worlds we never knew.

This speech is a long way from that of the young hunter, explaining to his friend: "If one wishes to kill a seal, one lies still, and pretends to be part of the ice."

And here are a few examples from *White Eskimo:* Stormbound at Kiglapaite Cove in a small boat, the Inuit pilot says, "The wind will die out, I suppose, pretty soon. It might be a good time to start for Port Manvers, if anybody wished to get there before dark." Abel Shiwak, after three days sheltering in a snowdrift, looks at the clearing sky and says: "Oho! One could travel tonight, if it should happen that someone had the urge to do so." And the White Eskimo, Gillingham, makes a typical Inuit speech: He was lucky, he said, and had stumbled on a part of the country where one had to drive the foxes away from one's door with a stick. He was but a poor trapper, if the truth were known, and if he had to hunt in the same country as Abel Shiwak, he would starve. As for his converse with the world of the spirits, he received only rarely a poor and meaningless dream that he did not know how to interpret, while he had heard that the people of this coast commanded vast powers over the spirits of nature.

Perhaps we should try to preserve, when we write about former times in the Arctic, a little of those old patterns of speech that revealed attitudes now past or passing, before the people of the Arctic were imprinted forever with our ways of speech and thought, and were taught to accept the values that serve us so badly in the cities of the south.

Farley Mowat, Harold Horwood: Conversations

EDITED BY ANGELA ROBBESON

R\ OBBESON: We are very pleased and honoured to welcome now to the panel Farley Mowat, who will join Harold Horwood and Alootook Ipellie. Harold Horwood has been described as something of a Renaissance man; his career has included politics and art. He was a member of the Newfoundland House of Assembly from 1949 to 1951 and he is the author of such books as *White Eskimo, Bartlett the Great Canadian Explorer,* and *Only the Gods Speak: Ten Tales from the Tropic and Seven Pieces from the North.* He has also written numerous essays and articles that touch on Arctic and sub-Arctic matters.

Farley Mowat requires very little introduction to any of us and indeed to the reading public of the nation as a whole. He has been called, quite rightly, "Canada's Storyteller," and his many books about the Arctic include the Arctic Trilogy—that is, *Ordeal by Ice, Polar Passion,* and *Tundra*—as well as *People of the Deer, The Desperate People, The Snow Walker,* and *Never Cry Wolf.* He will discuss some topics on the Arctic and the creation of Arctic narrative. John Moss will mediate. So I will turn these proceedings over to those three people and invite them up to the front.

MOSS: I think I'll moderate; I'm not going to mediate.

MOWAT: That might be necessary, too, you know.

HORWOOD: Considering the people involved!

I want to make a brief statement separate from my paper, then give Farley a chance. I didn't realize, it might surprise you, those of you who have read *White Eskimo*—and this book was published so long ago that I suppose most of you haven't, even though it was a national best seller for seventeen weeks at the time it was published, but that was back in the Dark Ages—I didn't realize until after I'd written this book, until after it had appeared in print, that what I'd produced was an indictment of

Canadian imperialism within Canada, in the Canadian Arctic. And it was only when a television interviewer pointed this out to me and asked me to comment on it that I realized that it was exactly what had happened.

MOSS: Since Harold's had his turn, Farley, would you like to speak from the lectern?

MOWAT: All right. I can't resist a podium. Especially one that has been hallowed by my fellow speakers. I feel inspirited—but of course I have nothing to say. This has been one of my great strengths as a writer. I am not here as Farley Mowat; I am here in my proper alter-ego: Hardly-Knowit, well-known Arctic entrepreneur. The other day somebody sent me a copy of a new magazine called *Yeast*—something like that—and it has a comic strip in it, and the comic strip has "Hardly-Knowit." Hardly-Knowit is in the Arctic; he's standing on an ice floe, and there is a gum-chewing, white man standing beside him and Hardly is saying, "Can I borrow your mutt?" and the guy has a dog which might be a husky, but, you know, it's just a dog, and the guy says "Okay." So, "Will you take my picture with your mutt?" "Okay." "I'll grab this thing—what is it?—and hold it in my hand." "The thing you've just grabbed is an ice-spear." "Okay. I'll grab that. Now take the picture." So, he takes the picture, and the next frame shows the latest product of Hardly-Knowit: "How I Lived My Life in the Arctic as a Spearman, with My Trusty Tame Wolf."

I was tempted just for about thirty seconds to tear the thing up, wad it into the toilet bowl, and ram it down with my feet. And then I thought no, this is the true accolade; I have become a tradition, a mythic tradition, in my own country. I am now, as Harold was pointing out, the kind of person that the Inuit had lots of, and have lost most of. I have become the same sort of imaginary mythic person to our society and our culture. So I have that to solace me in my older days.

I have nothing serious to say to you today because I am too old to be serious about anything. But I have something that approaches seriousness. I am deeply concerned with what is happening to the last few vestiges of human animals on this planet, people who recognize their animality, who know what they really bloody well are: part and parcel of animate creation. And what is happening to them, as we all know, is that we are being divorced, weaned, perverted away from our convictions of who we are. We are beginning to believe more and more that we are some sort of a creation of our own minds, our own intellect, of the reasonable aspect of humanity, of logic. We are becoming aliens on our own planet. We are becoming aliens in the whole bloody web of life. And this is the thing that concerns me most. And when I see the people—and I didn't know the Inuit very well; they knew me a hell of a lot better than I knew them. I came amongst them as a stranger and they could evaluate me quickly. I came as a white man who didn't know much and made some wrong conclusions, but what the hell.

However, the point that I wanted to make is that *they had that ability* I'm talking about. The other native peoples that I have known—I knew some as a kid in the west, Crees on a reservation near Saskatoon—they all, in retrospect at least, seemed to have been people who were fully aware of their animality. They knew that they were good animals. They didn't reject that concept. They didn't think that was demeaning. They didn't think it was in some way a derogation of their marvellous humanity. That was their strength, it was their power, it was theirs, to endure. I see it going, now. And listening to you this afternoon, Alootook, I suspect that this is one of the things that concerns you—the need to hang on to this conviction and this belief, this knowledge that you're one, you're part and parcel of the whole of the animate world. But, in most cases it's disappearing.

I think it's time that we stop thinking about who we are and consider feeling what we are, put our trust in our feelings, in our emotions, be subjective. We're animals. We're either good animals or bad animals. It looks as if, at the moment, we're pretty bloody bad animals. If so, then we've had the biscuit. But if we think of ourselves in true animality, we can perhaps recover the ability to be good animals.

Short, sweet message; there you are.

MOSS: It is such a delight in this age, in this country, and especially in this city, to hear someone speak off the top of his head in whole sentences, and indeed in whole paragraphs. It's a rare thing in Ottawa, to have such a phenomenon. I think what I'll do is simply open things up to questions.

MOWAT: What are we questioning?

MOSS: We are questioning Harold Horwood and Farley Mowat. What I want—and I'm sure there are people who have things to say—is people to open up any line of discussion related to the Arctic, Arctic narrative, your own writing, or your responses to Arctic writing in general.

FIRST QUESTION: Yes; I'd like to ask the panel about the ersatz igloo at the Museum of Civilization that is so highly offensive . . . a plastic bunch of bladders stuck together.

MOWAT: Where is it?

QUESTIONER: In the Museum of Civilization.

HORWOOD: It's right here, in Ottawa?

QUESTIONER: Yes.

HORWOOD: Well, they couldn't make it out of real snow, could they?

MOWAT: The first one of these was built by a guy by the name of R. A. J. Phillips with the Department of Indian Affairs in 1963.

QUESTIONER: Yeah?

MOWAT: He built it in the back of his marvellous suburban luxurious home up on the edge of town here somewhere, and then he invited us all to come up and see what the solution was to Eskimo housing. It was built with an early plastic. He had got an Inuit to show him how to make the right cuts, to shape the thing and put it together. He had a celebration that night, and we fired off roman candles to celebrate the solution to modern Inuit housing. One of the roman candles hit this thing and it went off like the bomb that just blew Oklahoma all to hell—WHUMP!—like that. There were no more. You've heard of those?

IPELLIE: It happened in Cape Dorset, also.

MOWAT: It did, eh?

IPELLIE: Yeah. They built—

MOWAT: It actually did?! Oh my God—

IPELLIE: —plastic igloos in Cape Dorset.

MOWAT: Uh huh.

HORWOOD: They shipped the plastic there?

IPELLIE: Yeah.

HORWOOD: And built snow houses out of it?

MOWAT: I see, yes.

HORWOOD: Well my daughter attempted to build a real snow house in Nova Scotia, and succeeded in doing it, but it wasn't long before the roof fell in—which would have happened here in Ottawa too if you'd built them out of snow.

MOWAT: Anyway, down with phony igloos, right?

HORWOOD: Yes.

MOSS: Yes?

SECOND QUESTION: I wanted to ask both Farley Mowat and Harold Horwood about your stand on appropriation of voice and, particularly Harold Horwood, about your decision to write from an Inuit perspective.

HORWOOD: Well, I never have written from an Inuit perspective. I wrote from the perspective of a recorder who recorded the conversation of two young Inuit and the hunting expedition in my story "Men Like Summer Snow." The "men like summer snow" are the white people, of course, who've gone north and who are going to vanish like summer snow when the time comes. In this story I'm not writing from anybody's point of view except the point of view of a person recording dialogue.

My feeling about appropriation of voice is that it's a lot of damn nonsense, to be perfectly frank with you. I think a man can write from a woman's point of view, and a woman from a man's point of view. But you don't forget when you are reading these things that you are indeed reading a narrative written by somebody who's not writing from his own standpoint. D. H. Lawrence, for instance, wrote a great deal from a woman's point of view.

But there's a big difference between this kind of thing and the sort of journalistic structure which I used in "Men Like Summer Snow," where what you're doing is recording dialogue as though you're standing back listening to two people speaking it. I wouldn't attempt to write a first person narrative from the point of view of any culture other than my own;

and although I do have Inuit people among my ancestors, that doesn't give me the the right to write from an Inuit standpoint because culturally I'm by no means a Labradorman. I've spent a lot of time in Labrador but culturally I'm a white Newfoundlander.

MOWAT: I don't think there's any such thing as appropriation of voice. I think it's a line of bullshit, to be quite frank with you. I've never read a good story in my life that didn't impinge upon somebody else's experience, somebody else's culture, somebody else's background, somebody else's ethnic or racial differences—that's storytelling, it's par for the course. This, I think, is largely an invention of people who feel inadequate as storytellers so they want to protect their territory. So, I don't buy it.

HORWOOD: Someone's clapping. It must be a writer!

THIRD QUESTION: I know this is supposed to be directed to the panel but I was just wondering if maybe we can get Aritha van Herk into the dialogue because she has said writing is an act of appropriation. How do you feel about this discussion we've just been having on writing and appropriation and in light of the paper you just gave, appropriating the voice of Willem Barentsz? Do you have any comments?

VAN HERK: No, no I don't.

QUESTIONER: Okay.

VAN HERK: If you want to know what I think about it, read the first essay in *In Visible Ink.*

MOWAT: (to van Herk) Would you feel that there is any validity in the restraints that some people are trying to impose on us about appropriation of voice?

VAN HERK: Farley, I'm not in this dialogue.

MOWAT: I can't get you in?

VAN HERK: I think you should ask Alootook; I think perhaps he has an opinion.

MOWAT: Sure. Fine. (to Ipellie) What's your opinion about this?

IPELLIE: My opinion is also very similar to yours because I'm a writer, too. I write about my own people's experiences and also about the experiences of other people here in the south, because I've related to both societies for so long. I think a writer has to have that freedom to express their own creativity, imagination, in what they're putting on paper. You have to have that freedom. I have a problem with only one thing: if someone relates stories from the Inuit people and then puts it into their own work without even mentioning the source, then I would have a problem with that. And otherwise—

HORWOOD: That's theft. I must say that when I wrote *White Eskimo* back in the 1960s, there were no Inuit people writing, or at least very, very little attempt by the Inuit people to do any writing at the time. I certainly looked forward to when they would be writing their own stories, but meantime I felt that the only people who could interpret the Arctic at all for Canadians at large were people who went down and visited it. I also looked forward to the time when they would take over their own political affairs, and indeed at the very end of the novel *White Eskimo* a character who appears as a minor character in the novel turns out to be the head of the Division of Northern Labrador Services. I didn't mention it in the novel but this was a division that I personally created.

Anyway, the thing is that I was writing in a transition period and I'm very happy to have seen native peoples, all the various native peoples, begin telling their own stories now, not only for themselves, not only around their fires, but telling stories for general consumption and creating all sorts of other works of art, too, for general consumption.

MOSS: Mary? Mary Carpenter?

CARPENTER: Hi, Farley, how's it going?

MOWAT: Hi, Mary, how's the girl?

CARPENTER: Well, I'd like to tell you all that I'm very concerned about this appropriation of voice. I think no one should have to second-guess their thoughts when they write. I think you should write what you want to write in any gender and in any race because nobody can own you, or own your power to write or tell stories.

MOWAT: Amen.

MOSS: A good note on which to end an all too-brief sesssion. Thanks to everyone.

Approaches of White Regret: John Steffler's *The Afterlife of George Cartwright* and Harold Horwood's *White Eskimo*

JOAN STRONG

"**W**ho, if not God, is to blame for making monsters like me?" (268). With these words John Steffler's George Cartwright arrives finally at the question central to his maker's text and more broadly to postcolonial ruminations in our times. Steffler constructs a fictional Cartwright based on journals written by the eighteenth-century British explorer, and this assembled creature suffers the horror of his own resurrection as surely as any Frankensteinian production. Cartwright's self-awareness is made possible through the unflinching gaze of his travel companion, housekeeper, partner and lover, Mrs. Selby. From her extremely limited appearances in the original journals she springs in Steffler's text fully formed to confront Cartwright's ambitions, functioning in the novel as the moral disciplinary assessor of Cartwright's achievements. Comparing Cartwright to the Inuit—her use of the term "Inuit" identifying her as representative of our age, unlike Cartwright who in the journals fumbles between the terms "Indian" and "Eskimo"—Selby calls Cartwright "more of a savage . . . than any of them" (10). Selby's representation of Cartwright is one which our century, through Steffler, has created. She asserts our condemnation of imperialism and the terrors it rained on aboriginal peoples in this country, and she condemns Cartwright for his part in it. Her views are written lucidly and with conviction, and we are invariably in agreement with her. Yet, the complexities which arise from Steffler's use of Mrs. Selby reveal our own uncomfortable posturing in the face of Cartwright's guilt. Mrs. Selby's easy rebuke of Cartwright's enterprises distances him from us. In her view, and her view becomes ours, he is a monster whose actions we deplore and whose victims we pity. But in this view we recognize neither the difficulty of self-analysis within one's own cultural matrix, nor the difficulty of locating the colonizer-creature

within ourselves. Steffler's Cartwright leaves us easily outside such questions and in knowledgeable contempt outside the horror that Cartwright's
needs and guilt are not always so easily distinguished but are born out,
often invisibly, in our own survival.

Harold Horwood's *White Eskimo* also chooses the vehicle of historical fiction to examine relationships between the white and the Inuit and,
ultimately, to expose with regret the lust for power that fuels exploration
and exploitation. Yet, the framed story-within-a-story strategy of Horwood's work refuses to explicate race relations in museum-like text, where
one century meets the casting of another. Instead, *White Eskimo*'s narrative invites the reader to seek cultural difference in actual landscape
unknown, language untried, and narrative possibilities untold. Here we
may see an alignment of the text to the Inuit "idea of a story" which has
nothing to do with "what we [Euro-narrators] mean by being objective"
(27). This is most clearly revealed by Horwood with a narrator's narrator,
Ed Hamilton, who tells us his version of the events of the life of Esau Gillingham. To do this, he must preface the tale with a warning of the uncer-
tainties encoded in its telling through the Inuit teller from whom he first
heard the tale:

> [The Inuit] idea of a story isn't at all the same thing as ours.
> They tell better stories, but have no idea of what we mean by being
> objective. The world of spirits and magic is always getting mixed up
> with ordinary affairs of life in their accounts. . . . They've grown up
> with the habit of distilling literal meaning out of a mass of imagery,
> some of it highly fanciful, and making allowances for the polite
> conventions of exaggeration, understatement, and so forth. But it
> doesn't do for us, of course, with our literal minds, our habit of
> expecting narrative to mean exactly what it says. So to fill in this
> next part of Gillingham's story I have to give you my own version of
> what I heard from Abel Shiwak. This isn't the way he told it though.
> (27)

Here Horwood urges that his narrative must be understood as the Inuit
understand it: as a vehicle conveying sensibility, rapport, possibility, and
webs of culture rather than definition, authority, linear history, and
exclusion.

Horwood's work stands in marked contrast to Steffler's version of
Cartwright's journals. Steffler establishes Cartwright as a ghost living con-
currently in the eighteenth and twentieth centuries and materializes the
explorer's life through Cartwright's longing backward gaze—a gaze both
enriched and blinkered by Steffler's substantial augmentation to Cartwright's actual papers. Cartwright, a man who lived by his wits and physical
strength in an environment that demanded blood and sacrifice for daily

survival, is inflated in narrative detail yet diminished through Steffler's characterization of him as merely crude and sport hungry. Where Horwood denies access to the most significant details of the protagonist's life and supplies various possible versions of the outcome of the historical tale, Steffler pins down Cartwright's every vulnerability—real and imagined. Where Horwood's Gillingham disappears into the landscape, provoking and denying the reader and his or her need to conquer story and cultural knowledge, Steffler provides the reader more than all, projecting safety for the reader through omnipotence in the revelation of Cartwright's flaws.

Setting the agenda in Steffler's work are the overt manipulations of Cartwright's original journal in order to cast Cartwright and his culture's impact on the Inuit as simply unconscionable. On a trip to England with Cartwright, for example, Cartwright's closest Inuit companion is horrified to discover human bones one evening at the home of John Hunter, a surgeon and anatomist:

> Attuiock left the table to visit the privy, then almost immediately rushed back into the room, his face rigid with fear. Ignoring the company, he rounded the table to where Cartwright was rising to meet him, gripped Cartwright's arm, and spoke close to his ear. 'They plan to eat us here! I have seen the bones! Inuit bones. I know whose they are.'
>
> He tugged Cartwright into the hall, into Hunter's study. There were human skeletons in glass cases on two of the walls. (211–212)

Steffler's conclusion here is both abrupt and damning. Cartwright's ensuing silence may be taken for acknowledgment of the anthropological cannibalism which his companion implies. Yet the original journal offers a version of events which grants Cartwright greater credit:

> Being on a dining visit, with that excellent surgeon and anatomist, the ingenious John Hunter, in the afternoon Attuiock walked out of the room by himself but presently returned with such evident marks of terror, that we were all greatly alarmed, fearing some accident had happened to him; or, that he had met with an insult from one of the servants. He seized hold of my hand, and eagerly pressed me to go along with him. I asked the cause of his emotion, but could get nothing more from him than 'Come along, come along with me,' and he hastily led me into a room in the yard, in which stood a glass case containing many human bones. 'Look there,' says he, with more horror and consternation in his countenance, than I ever beheld in that of man before, 'are those the bones of Esquimaux whom Mr. Hunter has killed and eaten?

Are we to be killed? Will he eat us, and put our bones there?' As the whole company followed, the other Indians had also taken the alarm before the old priest had finished his interrogatories; nor did any of them seem more at ease, by the rest of us breaking out into a sudden and hearty laugh, till I explained to them that these were the bones of our own people, who had been executed for certain crimes committed by them, and were preserved there, that Mr. Hunter might better know how to set those of the living, in case any of them should chance to be broken; which often happened in so populous a country. They were then perfectly satisfied, and approved of the practice; but Attuiock's nerves had received too great a shock to enable him to resume his usual tranquillity, til he found himself safe in my house again. (Cartwright in Townsend, 126)

In Cartwright's version he is compassionate to his companion's needs as one might be to the fears of a distressed child. Initial laughter gives way to gentle explanation and reassurance, followed by a clear acknowledgment of Attuiock's lingering shock and an understanding of the safety of a friend's home.

Cartwright's self-description in no way alleviates grievances rightly lodged against his imperialist ways but it does lend fuller complexity to the issue of colonial enterprise. He is not without good intentions, gentleness, and affection towards his guests, but Steffler's diminution of these attributes places the created Cartwright merely in an exhibition of contempt. Steffler establishes this setting early in the text, perhaps too easily conveying Cartwright's plans for the Inuit:

Cartwright could see his success . . . the Inuit would bring him renown, audiences with curious grandees, people of influence—perhaps even the King himself. . . . Tall doors opening everywhere to admit the adventurer-gentleman back from the Empire's outposts with proofs of supremacy. . . . He wanted to show [the Inuit] . . . the true proportion of things, arrange them, make them willing subjects of his rule. . . . He pictured himself in London walking his wolf cub on a leash, carrying his eagle, escorted by Inuit, and felt the power they gave him. . . . They proclaimed what he'd always harboured inside himself. (8–9)

Further, Steffler belittles Cartwright, even in imagining the sexual prowess of an imperialist:

Cartwright and Mrs. Selby had no children together largely because of Cartwright's use of a sheath. . . . The operation of extracting a sheath from its jar of preservative, drying it, and fitting it on was an interruption in the natural process of love-making that Cartwright overcame to an extent through the practised adroitness and the air of playful ceremony with which he carried the actions out. 'To your battle stations, men!' he'd exclaim, leaping out of bed when the time had come, imitating the sound of the drum or the bugle. 'Powder! Wadding! Rammer! Shot! ... Take aim! ... Take better aim!'. ...

When the sheaths he'd brought with him to Labrador had worn out, Cartwright fashioned his own using the mesentery of the animals he killed. ... He softened his pouches with butter and preserved them with rum. Their odour was festive, but Mrs. Selby complained that they smarted. ...

He experimented with tissue from various animals and would hesitate before the half-dozen jars that lined one of their bedroom shelves. 'What about otter?' he'd say. 'A tireless swimmer.' Or he'd snort tossing his head, 'what about ... caribou?'

'Stop it, Cartwright,' Mrs. Selby finally said. ...

He persisted with his pouches and sheaths, and Mrs. Selby accepted them, in the same hardy spirit of self-reliance they brought to all their endeavours in Labrador. (163–164)

As critic Russell Smith succinctly puts it, in this novel "the protagonist is ... often more ridiculous than evil" (22). Steffler's Cartwright adds to this summation: "my appetites and my ingenuity are a kind of stupidity, the infancy of intelligence, perhaps ... mentally, I have barely learned to toddle and talk. I am at the stage of trying to break whatever I pick up, or of putting it in my mouth" (268).

What are we to make of this kind of re-evaluation of our country's history? Critic Larry Mathews muses:

Is *The Afterlife of George Cartwright* an exercise in white liberal self-flagellation? Not really. It's more like a sophisticated contribution to a complicated debate which is, just possibly, more likely to be clarified by the literary imagination than by the polemical skills of politicians and academics. Cartwright's more spectacular spiritual descendants include the likes of Peter Pocklington and Frank Stronack, but what he represents has also, like it or not, become a component of our collective psyche. Until we're ready to confront that fact, we may be doomed to re-experience Cartwright's ultimate disappointment. (30)

Yet I contend that Mrs. Selby's existence in this text along with Steffler's manipulations of Cartwright's journals prevents any possible analysis of complexity or confrontation and also prevents the recognition of "spiritual descent," particularly within ourselves.

Narratives like Steffler's may be seen merely to distance us from the mistakes of our past rather than to encourage association with them: hence our repeated doom looms large if we accept Selby's voice and vision solely. Cartwright's journals do not depict a fool or madman. As Patrick O'Flaherty has written:

> . . . Cartwright must not be judged harshly. By 1778 he had become accustomed to scarcity, to making a living by slow accumulation and dogged effort. . . . The Labrador peninsula in the 1770's was no place to nurture a tender conscience. Cartwright had to be ruthless to survive. . . . And yet, for all his severity, there was a compassionate and even a courtly side to Cartwright which one is surprised to see surviving in a man following his pursuits. This emerges particularly in his relationships with the Eskimos, whom he treated on the whole with courtesy and decency. (38–39)

Examples of such courtesy abound in Cartwright's journals. In them, for instance, Cartwright is able to convey the surprise he experiences at the ease with which Caubvick, an Inuit, returns to her own way of life after journeying to England with him: "I found Caubvick along with this [Eskimo] family, and wondered at her taking so cordially to her former way of living, after the comfort and luxury to which she had lately been used, and which she seemed most heartily to enjoy" (Cartwright in Townsend, 140). He defers to her experience and seems bemused that he had ever thought it would be otherwise.

Yet Steffler tells a different story in his narrative of political agenda:

> [Caubvick] . . . had changed since coming to England. Whereas before she had been a normal sweet-tempered Eskimo woman, different from the rest only in her exceptional neatness and charm, now she was openly at odds with her family in everything. Eskimo clothes were ugly, she said, Eskimo food was unclean. [And after she shortly contracted smallpox it] . . . occurred to me then that my influence, my country's influence on her, and on all of them, was likely to be much greater than I had imagined, and more terrible. (230–231)

Without doubt Cartwright's country's influence was terrible, but Steffler reduces the origins of horrors possible in the exchanges of cultural exploration to simplistic terms. Steffler's Cartwright destroys all he touches because he is stupid, he is greedy, and he is power-hungry. We see

Cartwright as emotionally needy, confused, and weak. Mrs. Selby, described by Smith as the "moral control" of the text, "a faceless feminist anti-colonialist to give voice to 20th century hindsight" (22), tells us how easy it is to locate and confront the Cartwrights behind and around us. In this identification Cartwright and others like him are hermetically sealed off from us: we are wiser now, more socially aware than the primitive Cartwright before us.

Selby leads the post-mortem on Cartwright's era, yet as Mathews notes, "These opinions are so consistently politically correct by late 20th century standards that one's credulity is strained" (30). Mathews suggests that: "the real . . . subject of this novel [is] . . . the extent to which Cartwright remains alive in the mentality that we as a society (for 'we' read 'white middle class') bring to bear in our dealings with aboriginal peoples, with the land and more broadly, within our collective sense of self as inheritors of liberal individualistic tradition" (29–30). If this is so, then the novel fails to sustain that inheritance, that approach of regret towards the past. For Mrs. Selby's indictment of Cartwright is complete—she excises his evil, but his likeness to us as well, and we, with her, walk cleanly away from his subsequent torturous demise.

Horwood's Gillingham, in contrast, refuses to lie down for the kill. In fact, before the conclusion of the text Gillingham has already disappeared. In the telling of the tale of Gillingham, *White Eskimo* is a deliberate confrontation of the question of narration and the role of the narrator (as I have written elsewhere: Strong, 69–74). Throughout the novel Horwood's various narrators take on the task of mythologizing or discrediting Gillingham—it is key to an understanding of the novel that the reader never meets Gillingham directly, but must piece him together inconclusively as various narratives are assembled. This is one of the greatest strengths of the novel, in spite of the fact that some reviewers claim "more encumbrance than otherwise is a story-within-a-story framework" ("Review," *Booklist*, 275).

The "encumbrance" that Horwood creates is a kind of archaeology of culture: the reader must approach the text as artifact and develop his or her own interpretation of findings while recognizing that the essence of the history, Gillingham, has long since slipped away through time, past the fingers of those knowledge seekers who wish to pin him down. This further illuminates the differences of culture that Horwood sketches between the Eskimo and the colonizer. Oral tradition cannot be explicated in museum silence; instead the Eskimo culture must be preserved through living memory and encounter, and this denies the very medium in which Horwood works. His awareness of this tension is demonstrated in his narrative strategy, where colonizers who attempt to imprison and destroy Gillingham—and the independence for which he stands—have no more power over him than does the reader for whom the novel's tale of murder and intrigue is left unresolved. The breakdown of linear narrative and the eventual non-existence of the central character within the text create an instability of construction in the novel which reflects tellingly on the instability of white culture as it attempts to overpower and narrate the culture and experience of the Eskimo. Hence the novel succeeds in urging the reader not only to seek out living cultures as representative of their own experience, but more importantly urges the reader to accept and respect the autonomy of such cultures before their disappearance.

White Eskimo opens in the lounge of the *S.S. Kyle* amidst a poker game and allusions to the Conradian trip to face one's own interior—the desire to conquer and gain, as generated by a heart of darkness—are difficult to miss. Horwood does not name himself as first narrator until the conclusion of the novel, but at that point the narrative intention is wittily confirmed. Horwood steps unnamed into his own novel at the opening, handing the tale over to the accomplished trader of both goods and yarns at the Hudson's Bay post, Ed Hamilton. Within Hamilton's tale other stories are told and this series of puzzle boxes—and narrative empires—reveals at bottom both that the protagonist who is chased by the reader has ceased to exist and that the author has fictionalized himself. The interweaving of these points of view creates a web of possible cultural encounters.

By the conclusion of the novel the reader is linked and enfolded in this web and is directly implicated in assumed responsibility for judgments made and actions taken on the basis of stories told. The reader as well as the author must accept heavy responsibility for the community of narrative created and the power of stories both permitted and enforced. Like Conrad's Kurtz, Horwood's Gillingham turns narrative outward until, through the turning, we see our own responsibility to the past in horror descending relentlessly upon us.

Horwood is clear in showing us that we all create stories, legends, and laws in order to assert our own survival and our own rightness, regardless of the cost to others. Horwood's Finnian, departed from the police force, is self-condemning as he remembers that "In remote stations like this we were expected to sort of make up our own laws" (6). Manfred Kosh, the missionary, interprets an Eskimo party as a siege on his own fort remembering "the lurid tales he must have read in his church histories and martyrologies, hearing all night long the weird chanting in a musical scale unlike anything he knew, sounding 'barbarous' to his ears . . ." (65). The court system, too, is shown to be entangled in prejudicial cultural mayhem with the Eskimos. Gillingham's attorney seizes on judicial disregard of them to defend his clients: "Gillingham's defense attorney . . . was able to show that an 'Eskimo' as repeatedly mentioned in various laws, was, in fact, indefinable—that nobody could actually be shown in court to an 'Eskimo', and that consequently all laws referring to Eskimos were, in that particular, meaningless" (186). Similarly, Horwood frees Gillingham from the confines of narrative enclosure at the end of the text—there are no clues as to whether Gillingham is guilty or innocent of murder charges, or whether he lives or dies. We are left with the fictionalized Horwood on a journey to the Labrador, which, like Kurtz's jungle, whispers to us to "come and find out" what would be drawn out of us there.

Horwood's text continually reminds us of our own responsibility in detailing the cultural landscape: exploration must be an individual journey webbed by the possible mythologies of others. Steffler, on the other hand, allows us complacence in the judgments we pass on his foolhardy and foolish Cartwright. It is easy—far too easy—to distance ourselves from the sadly greedy, over-sexed and pitifully unsatisfied "hero." We can sagely deduce that Cartwright's eternal purgatory is of his own doing. Worse than despising his bloodthirsty nature, we pity and overlook it as the product of his times. In this, we absolve ourselves as rightful heirs to his need to survive, explore, and conquer, as well as the guilt attending, although each of these attributes marks our beginnings in this country. As Horwood heaps challenge and responsibility on readers to recognize our own struggle for survival in cultural exploration, both then and now, Steffler's seductive writing, like Cartwright's own seductions, is safely sheathed from procreative transference. Cartwright's story leaves us with regret for him alone. It is a white, clean, sterile regret, unlike Horwood's webs of narrative which draw us to sticky inevitable conclusions.

WORKS CITED

Cartwright, George. *A Journal of transactions and events, during a residence of nearly sixteen years on the coast of Labrador, containing many interesting particulars, both of the country and its inhabitants, not hitherto known by George Cartwright.* 3 vol. Newark, England: Allin and Ridge, 1792.

———. *Captain Cartwright and his Labrador Journal,* ed. Charles Wendell Townsend. Boston: Dana Estes and Company, 1911.

Horwood, Harold. *White Eskimo.* Toronto: Doubleday, 1972.

Mathews, Larry. "Review of *The Afterlife of George Cartwright.*" *Canadian Forum* 71 (September 1992): 29–30.

O'Flaherty, Patrick. *The Rock Observed: Studies in the Literature of Newfoundland.* Toronto: University of Toronto Press, 1979.

———. "Review of *White Eskimo* by Harold Horwood." *Booklist* 69 (15 November 1972): 275.

Smith, Russell. "Review of *The Afterlife of George Cartwright.*" *Quill and Quire* 58 (May 1992): 20–22.

Steffler, John. *The Afterlife of George Cartwright.* Toronto: McClelland and Stewart Inc., 1992.

Strong, Joan. *Acts of Brief Authority: A Critical Assessment of Selected Twentieth-Century Newfoundland Novels.* St. John's: Breakwater, 1994.

Places of Spirit, Spirits of Place: The Northern Contemplations of Rudy Wiebe, Aritha van Herk, and John Moss

ARON SENKPIEL

In the last six years, three unusual books have been published about the Canadian north. Part literary theory, part personal narrative, part philosophical reflection, Rudy Wiebe's *Playing Dead* (1989), Aritha van Herk's *Places Far from Ellesmere* (1990), and John Moss's *Enduring Dreams* (1994) are "explorations" or, to use Wiebe's word, "contemplations" of the relationship amongst writer, literary text, and northern landscape. Each writer affirms that the Arctic—in its vastness, its stubborn silence, its apparent indifference to the writer—asserts, somehow, something we might call "actuality." The Arctic reminds us, willfully, of what simply is.

Out of these three writers' recognition of this comes a shift in perception and valuation which, notwithstanding its simplicity, is of great importance. Instead of measuring what they see and experience in the North against text and tradition, they measure text and tradition against what they see and experience. Each writer discovers that it is tradition, not landscape, that must be rewritten, reformed. This shift in emphasis is similar to that which has been noted in prairie writing (later we'll need to talk about the similarity between prairie and northern landscapes, between prairie and northern imaginings. In one of her essays about the prairies, van Herk writes of ". . . the landscape now not written upon but permitted to write, to cry out its own naming ("Prairie as Flat as . . .," 134). The result is a north that is not just imaginatively rich, but a north that is "true" to experience. Together, these three works suggest that a radical rethinking, a remapping of sorts, of the literary landscape of the North is underway within mainstream Canadian literature. It is this rethinking, this remapping, which this paper explores.

Each of these works has been described, by turns, as eccentric and complex. This is understandable. Wiebe subtitles his a "contemplation," van Herk subtitles hers a "geografictione," and Moss subtitles his an "exploration." Then, in each we face, often head on, the conceptually difficult. Working from the linguistics of Raymond Gagné, for example, Wiebe examines the difference between the "areal" and the "linear"—a distinction I have badly muddled at least once ("From Wild West to the Far North," 141). And Aritha van Herk, as if "geografictione" isn't modern enough, uses the square bracket, parentheses, and the slash as though she were a mathematician. As for Moss, his restless, excited writing in *Enduring Dreams* skips back and forth between Bellrock, Lake Chapala, and the Canadian High Arctic as though they were adjoining streets in an Ottawa suburb; and I have read at least one rather complex critical exposition on the complexity of his thinking (Ross). Indeed, to the reader's initial bewilderment, each seems to offer, to quote a statement about Wiebe's *Playing Dead* which Moss makes in the final pages of *Enduring Dreams* (which is, itself, a reiteration of an earlier statement (49): ". . . an archipelago of random thoughts, quotations, observations, exhortations, mediations, meditations, documentary excerpts, judgements, visions, memories, and dreams" (156).

That being said, once reading has begun, the works quickly become refreshingly direct, even simple. Each reads like an extended personal essay; that is, each "behaves" as though it is a non-fictional narrative made interesting and, at times, circuitous by illustration, anecdote, and aside. And, notwithstanding van Herk's use of the second person, we equate the voice of each work with its author. This is supported by the plethora of accurate biographical data each author supplies, including numerous references to places of origin and habitation that, while not necessarily part of all Canadians' experience, are factual extensions of it: places like Edberg and Calgary and Edmonton and Bellrock.

Each work is also the "story" of an individual—the writer—walking through/into the northern landscape and thinking about what she sees and does and examining this in the light of what she has previously thought, read, and done. Moss is I think only partly right when he says Wiebe, in his *Playing Dead*, uses "personality as a narrative device" (49); rather, the story line of *Playing Dead* is the same as that of *Places* and *Enduring Dreams*: each is the story of a person thinking about the North or, to capture some of the three works' postmodernist tendencies, thinking about thinking about the North. This story subsumes, then, in the case of Moss and Wiebe, their many visits, the many personal narratives they could have written but have chosen not to write as many others have.

Interestingly, Moss says near the end of *Enduring Dreams* "Wordsworth is an absence in the Arctic" (147). But it is in Wordsworth's method of composition—as he described it in his 1802 Preface to the *Lyrical Ballads*—that I find a compelling description for what these writers do. They walk (or, in Moss's case on occasion, run), they look, they think. They "recollect in tranquility" and they write. This familiar explanation of the creative process helps us understand these three works' contemplative quality. It also helps us better understand Moss's description of Wiebe's *Playing Dead* as "an archipelago of random thoughts . . ." as well as his own "plan for an Arctic book" (26) which is to be "a Möbius loop of endless contemplation." It even clarifies van Herk's notion of *Places* as a series of archaeological "site explorations" and her description of the final segment of *Places* as a "record of reading *Anna Karenin* on Ellesmere" (83).

Appropriately, then, the books' rhythms are the very human, even humble rhythms of walking and looking and thinking. In each we sense the natural ebb and flow, the endless questioning and uncertainty, the humility and doubt, the circling about, of human thought. This is not at all like the staged movement of a troop of British naval officers walking to the Arctic coast or a convoy of Airstreams heading for Alaska. Nor is it the headlong rush of the single explorer trying to beat winter or evade "hostile locals." It is an altogether more leisurely kind of movement, one that fits the landscape and, by extension, is far more in keeping with traditional, that is to say, successful ways of moving in the North. "And now," says Moss, "the writer is explorer; not the other way around" (129). Or, as van Herk notes about reading: "reading is a new act here, not introverted and possessive but exploratory, the text a new body of self, the self a new reading of place" (113).

Structurally, it is useful to compare the three works with J. Michael Yates's "The Hunter Who Loses His Human Scent." First published in *Man in the Glass Octopus* (1968), this story recently reappeared in *Arctic of Words* (1993), a special issue of *Canadian Fiction Magazine*. It concludes the issue which begins, interestingly, with what was to become the second section of Moss's *Enduring Dreams* (28–52). Yates's story records the efforts of a "hunter" to throw off the "impediments" of the south (53)—preconceptions, prejudices, beliefs perhaps—and move north. In time, he does so. The always troublesome separation of subject and object is resolved and the "hunter" vanishes into the landscape, becomes one with it.

Yates's story is complete abstraction; it offers a formula of sorts. Its variables are defined, but no specific values are given. Our three narratives can, I suggest, be usefully thought of as specific manipulations or tests of Yates's formula. Each is a highly individual recounting of the search for what Wiebe calls "true NORTH" (114). These three writers realize, it seems to me, what Yates imagines. In their different ways, each announces that one of the principal impediments to their explorations of the North are earlier literary mappings or geographies of it. T. S. Eliot would have found ample corroboration for his thesis that "the difference between the present and the past is that conscious present is an awareness of the past in a way and to an extent which the past's awareness of itself cannot show" (39).

Of the three, it is the critic, John Moss, who looks most comprehensively at the written record of northern exploration, both ancient and modern. Indeed, he provides in *Enduring Dreams* what may be the most useful critique yet written about the northern historical/literary tradition, noting both its enormous imaginative power and its frequently and, for some, disturbingly inauthentic representations. He notes, for example, that this tradition is an imaginative one often quite unconnected to the place it purportedly describes:

> The Arctic of outsiders is a landscape of the mind, shaped more in the imagination by reading than by experience and perception. . . . For those who have never been to the Arctic, this is the only northern reality they know, this world gleaned in fragments from narrative accounts by explorers and adventurers, scientists and artists. . . . (28)

Moss also fairly assesses the extraordinary power of this tradition. For example, he says:

> Every venture into Arctic landscape, recorded to extend knowledge of the known world and impose meaning on the unknown, participates in a text of infinite complexity. From the fabulous accounts of Pythias to frenetic press releases by the beleaguered Weber-Malakhov Expedition of 1992, Arctic narrative has displaced actuality in the search to connect with other narratives, as each encounter with the Arctic enters an extensive verbal construct, the reality of print. Measured and named, the landscape has become geography; written into narrative, it is history. (93–94)
>
> When you enter Arctic narrative, you enter every narrative of the Arctic ever written. When you enter the Arctic in person, you become part of the extended text. When you write the Arctic to affirm your presence in the world, you become in writing an imaginative creation. You could imagine anything and write it down and it would seem real forever. (105)

In and of itself, the enormous imaginative power of what Alison Mitcham has misleadingly called "the northern imagination" isn't bad. It is, after all, a measure of the tradition's artistic power and aesthetic accomplishments. Yet, as Moss notes, this isn't just a matter of art:

> Government policies on the north are made in consequence of how outsiders imagine it to be. Legislation affecting land claims, ecology, and human welfare is enacted on the basis of an Arctic written into the imaginations of legislators whose own experience of the north is often limited to, and always shaped by, what others write of it. (31)

Given this "authority" of the historical/literary record, what then, we might ask, are the consequences when what is written isn't accurate? What if what is imagined as "northern" is, to use an old-fashioned word, dishonest to what is experienced? Moss notes that this is the dilemma presented by works like Theriault's *Agaguk*:

> The problem, then, is how to reconcile our appreciation of the novel's inherent aesthetic value with our revulsion at the mendacity of its falsely realistic vision. I'm not sure, but I suspect that the only solution is the evasive and irresponsible notion of art for art's sake, in which case no reconciliation is necessary. (86)

The northerner who reads this—written, surprisingly it seems, by a critic who writes from his study in Bellrock—cannot help but be excited, cannot help but ask whether Moss will go the next step. Will he follow his argument to its necessary but, to some, heretical conclusion, one which will put him at odds with much of what has been written about the North? He does:

> But if misappropriation occurs in the course of writing another's life, if the lines running through the text between writer and reader, between textual reality and actuality, limit or distort that other's world, then such a work should be treated with the same contempt in which we hold the mindless tracts of misogynists, racists, and religious fanatics. When another's world is turned into metaphor, to give meaning to the writer's own, its metamorphosis denies the original of intrinsic worth. (86)

Much later in *Enduring Dreams* Moss returns to much the same point, although in a lighter vein, when he questions the value of the plethora of "I found myself in the North" books. Speaking specifically of Robert Perkins's *Great Solitude: An Arctic Journey*, he writes:

> The Perkins book, wrapped in a jacket with a full-moon spaceshot superimposed on a black stripe over a monochromatic blue icescape, is called *Into the Great Solitude: An Arctic Journey*. For Perkins, who names his canoe and travels with seven different hats, the Barrens offer a sort of fecund austerity in which to explore the experience of being himself, on his own, although he intersects several times with a film crew and also films himself in attitudes of profound contemplation and postures of ordinary survival. It is a fascinating book, deconstructing in almost every studied passage.
>   More self-consciously than most, Robert Perkins addresses other texts as he writes, intersecting with the words of Warburton Pike, shaping his course across the tundra among passages from

George Back's *Narrative of the Arctic Land Expedition to the Mouth of the Great Fish River, 1833, 1834, and 1835.* Like other contemporary adventure-writers, he turns the Arctic of dreams, the Arctic of terror, into the Arctic of personal fulfilment and the escape from personality. These are not explorers of the soul, who share the land, but men whose books lean rakishly against one another on library shelves. Read Perkins, or James Raffan, or M.T. Kelly and you encounter again and again, in words from the past, the Douglas brothers, Hanbury, the Tyrrell brothers, Warburton Pike, George Back, Richardson, Franklin, Samuel Hearne. Each provides a gloss on those preceding. . . . Text echoes text. From intertextual adventuring we conceive the Arctic wilderness a place where stories happen, written down, in effect, to articulate terrain like the lines of a topographical map. Narrative writes narrative. The rest is empty; solipsism is endemic. (143)

The library shelves, Moss seems to suggest, are bent under the weight of such books. Something else is wanted.

When Wiebe, van Herk, and Moss go north and enter the landscape, all strongly sense the disjunction between where they are and what they have read. In "Exercising Reflection," the first section of *Playing Dead*, Wiebe examines Franklin's 1819–1822 expedition north of present-day Yellowknife. Instead of evaluating it according to some European notion of heroism, he evaluates it in light of what he knows about Inuit life in the North. He writes: "In startling contrast to the difficulty even the strongest white men have with living in the Arctic, the Inuit—both men and women, infants and elderly—have lived there happily for at least eight thousand years" (15). When he actually enters the landscape, the historical record seems quite inadequate:

> But when one personally goes to the Mackenzie Delta, Franklin and Richardson seem amazingly irrelevant. There they appear little more than the typical wilfully blind or at best only partially seeing men who will force themselves upon a landscape, will try to bulldoze their way through whatever confronts them and who, when this deliberate blindness kills their companions and, eventually, themselves, will become heroes to be forever memorialized. (43)

And, in the following pages, it becomes clear that Wiebe's preference is to enter the northern landscape and seek its secrets firsthand.

In *Places Far from Ellesmere* the examination of tradition takes a somewhat different turn. First of all, "reading" has both literal and metaphorical meaning for van Herk. With this in mind, we can recognize in the following quote a recognition similar to Wiebe's: "Reading in this clear green light [is] an act different from reading south under the sanctimonious permission of fluorescent and incandescent fixtures" (123). At first, the point of friction in her "readings" seems to be gender, not geography. The final section of *Places*—"Ellesmere, woman as island" (77–143)—is more an angry re/reading of Tolstoy's *Anna Karenin* than an account of a trip in the extreme north. Yet, on her way to Ellesmere, flying over places with names like "Cornwallis Island" and "Wellington Channel" and "Lancaster Sound" and "Devon Island" and "Grinnell Peninsula" and "Arthur Fjord," van Herk forcefully connects gender and geography:

> These names, every mapped configuration male/lineated. Is this the answer to Tolstoy's question, "What then, can we do?" Name, name, leave names on everything, on every physical abutment, leave behind one's father's name, the names of other men, the names of absent and abstracted/ideal women. (88)

The male writer's appropriation of "woman" is likened to the male cartographer's appropriation of landscape. Such acts must, of course, be challenged. Connecting with Anna means getting past Tolstoy; connecting with the landscape means getting past the old "male" maps. To re/read, re/write Anna is to re/discover, re/create "her island," Ellesmere.

John Moss's experience is similar to Wiebe's. He is struck by the apparent unconnectedness of what he has read and what he sees. Note the exceptional particularity of time and place:

> Mackenzie River, the summer of 1989. In the late evenings by the light of the midnight sun, from Fort Simpson to the Beaufort Sea, Virginia and I read aloud the accounts of others who have camped on these ice-scarred shores before us. We read Mackenzie's journal, Franklin, Gary and Joanie McGuffin. But there is little to connect the places we read about and the terrain we are travelling through. The textual world is real enough, yet it seems to exist in parallel and not to intersect with our experience on the Deh Cho. Somehow, in being here, we have reached beyond words; through the rhythm of exhausted muscles, we have become part of northern landscape in the ways no text, apparently, can apprehend. (41–42)
>
> Travelling in the eastern Arctic, we have found the same discrepancy between apparently authentic renderings of landscape and the world perceived. (42)
>
> Until we journey through the landscape literally with books in hand, we are unable to escape the world as text, aware only of unease between remembered readings of the Arctic and our own experience there. (43)

At some point, then, the experience of the place forces these three writers to re-evaluate what they've read and how they've read. Confidence is shaken; doubt enters. Moss writes that "the more time I spend in the Arctic, the less sure I am about what I imagine it to be, even on the best authority" (41).

I recognize such doubt, this critical point of arrival and departure. During the past fifteen years, I have found the North that I have lived in, experienced on a daily basis, has been fundamentally at odds with the North that I have read about. This goes far beyond such simple differences in geography as the fact, for example, that I live off in the far northwest, while most writers, situated as they are in central Canada, travel in the eastern Arctic. It has to do with the difference between writing about "a trip there" and writing about "life here."

I very clearly remember when I first became aware of this. It was a fall day in 1980. Al Purdy and I were walking the small road that circles the Whitehorse subdivision in which my wife and I still live. On one side of us were houses, on the other bush. Looking over his right shoulder at the houses, Al drawled, "Hell, it could be Mississauga." "You'd be right," I said, a bit defensively perhaps, "if it weren't for one important difference. Look the other way. That's east. I figure if you were to walk that way you'd cross just three, maybe four roads before you hit Hudson Bay."

But Purdy's point, quite literally, struck home. Where we were bore no resemblance to the rich, marvellous and distant place he had written about in his *North of Summer.* And my "north" was somehow diminished.

In the following years I often thought about that conversation, about the discrepancy or disjunction that we had, together, stumbled over. So conscious did I become of this disjunction, so uncertain did I become about where I was, that, seven years into my stay in the North, I wrote:

> The only time I confidently knew what the Yukon was was before my wife and I set out on the long journey here, when I reread Jack London's *Call of the Wild* and Service's "Spell of the Yukon" and poured over three-colour pictures of sunsets over the Ogilvies and Dall Sheep feeding on the windswept slopes of Kluane. Since then, I have travelled . . . over much of the territory. I have watched as the image of the North given me during my school years has been roughly pushed aside by a confusing jumble of often contradictory images and experiences. ("Of Kiwi Fruit and Moosemeat," 77)

What I went on to describe in that article was the confrontation of my very romantic notions of the North, with my immediate apprehension, my firsthand experience, of it. What I went on to write about in the following years was, at least in part, an attempt to explain this gap between what I had read about and imagined as "North" and what I had found in the North ("From the Wild West to the Far North").

The questioning of authority is, as we all know, artistically liberating. Wiebe's discovery of Franklin's and Richardson's "irrelevance" when he finds himself confronted by the Mackenzie Delta allows him to shift his and his readers' attention elsewhere (43): to the thoughts and actions of individuals who have, until recently, been inconsequential bit players in the Franklin story. As I noted in a 1989 review of *Playing Dead* :

> When he describes Franklin and his men's arduous trek to the Arctic in 1820–21, [Wiebe] almost ignores Franklin. Instead we get cherished glimpses of stalwart ordinary seaman John Hepburn and of Green Stockings, the Yellowknife woman whom the young Back and Hood squabble over. ("Review of *Playing Dead,*" 141–142)

On Ellesmere, says van Herk, she finds herself "free to un/read [her]self, home, Anna, the rest of Canada, all possible text" (91). Elsewhere she writes:

> Free here of the graspings of most of [ ]man's impositions, his history or fiction or implacable des/cribement, [wo]men either real or invented. You can walk, sleep, read, within this pristine novel, waiting to be read, pleasure yourself in its open spine. This geografictione, this Ellesmere. You have read farther than there are pages, travelled farther than there are fictions. (113)
>
> In a never/read text, you lose the text of your usual fictions. Words speak a different weight. Your feet resemble only faintly the feet you walk in Calgary, that walked from Edberg to Edmonton and on, despite their mileage, despite their obvious physical connexion to you. Ellesmere un/reading. (121)

Clearly, in Wiebe's refocussing of the public's attention on lesser known participants in the Franklin story, in van Herk's heated attacks on Tolstoy and her efforts to "re/read" Anna, in Moss's at times mischievous digs at Robert Perkins and his spiritual forebears, we see three writers consciously distance themselves from received notions of the North and refocus on their immediate apprehension of it. In van Herk, this distancing comes from her metaphorical linking of Anna and Ellesmere, of male writer and male cartographer, and of her refusal to accept "male" ways of perceiving and exploring (exploiting?) the Arctic. In Wiebe and Moss the matter is not quite so complex: they simply say that what they see doesn't fit with what they've read.

With this shift from myth and convention to the particularity of experience comes a change in language. Gone is the masculine, heroic language of exploration. Gone is its masculine arrogance. In its place is an altogether more human, more colloquial, humbler language—a new openness. It is a language of many questions and few answers. It makes a new type of northern narrative seem possible.

What then do these writers see/record as they approach the North with eyes open? Emptiness? Remoteness? Absence? Silence? Certainly these are mentioned repeatedly by all three. van Herk, for example, writes:

> And Ellesmere is a happy island, happy in its strange remoteness, its inaccessibility. Unaltered much by [ ]man. . . ." (105)
>
> You are at Ellesmere . . . her island, tabula rasa, awayness so thoroughly truant you have cut all connexion to all places far from Ellesmere. (77)
>
> Ellesmere is absence, a hesitation where you can pretend there are no telephones in the world. . . . (77)

But our writers' eyes adjust. Instead of looking into the distance, their eyes shift towards the foreground. Detail becomes important. They begin to look differently. There is, in all three, the loving attention to the interesting, engaging detail that comes from leisurely walking and looking about in a spare landscape. To see better, van Herk kneels:

> Cushion plant tundra this must be called, these plants visible only when you drop to your knees. From standing height, it seems as if you walk across a ground cover of desolation, shards of rock, sand, the occasional clump of purple sagafrass, a sudden yellow dotting of Arctic poppies. (105–106)
>
> Not only the Arctic poppies yellowing the mornings but the steady wind and the rustle of the creeks braiding their paths down from the glaciers. Even hauling water is magnified pleasure, to kneel so at the edge of a rocky stream and clatter your small plastic bucket against the stones worn down by the very coldness of the water, and the water swirling to fill it so icy it hurts the teeth, the nose, the forehead when you drink. These are gestures lost in the city, lost on the platforms of railway stations, lost everywhere. . . . Pleasure, seduction: buckets and water and stones and the muscles of shoulder and arm. (109)

This is a profound shift in perception: from distant horizon—the thing you focus on when your goal is to get somewhere else—to immediate foreground, the thing you focus on when "here" is where you want to be. It is the difference between, to explore the distinction as Moss does, between the North as means and the North as end, between seeking a Northwest

Passage and Ultima Thule (135). It is the difference, to explore the distinction as Wiebe does, between desiring "True NORTH" and "PASSAGE to anywhere" (114).

Support for the process here—not just developing new modes of seeing in the North but a new mode of being in the North (Moss, 135)—comes from what may seem, at first, a strange quarter: from prairie writing. A handful of things recently written about the prairie provide deep insight into the North's importance and the importance of these three works.

It was not a northern writer, but an American writer, William Least Heat-Moon, who first offered me insight into and literary confirmation of a phenomenon I have experienced in just two environments: on the Prairies and in the North. In the first pages of *PrairyErth*, which he calls a "deep map," he suggests that he, like most Americans, saw the grasslands as "little more than miles to be got over" (27). He talks about the special effort needed to "search out [the prairie's] variation, its colours, its subtleties" (27) and the need to "think open and lean" (28). He then says, describing perfectly I believe, the Far North: " . . . most prairie life is *within* the place: under the stems, below the turf, beneath the stones. The prairie is not a topography that shows its all but rather a vastly exposed place of concealment" (28).

This idea is developed in another prairie book of great value to those who want to understand the power of the northern landscape: Kathleen Norris's spiritual geography, *Dakota*. In it, she describes her move to her ancestral home in the small Dakotan town of Lemmon and her rich, yet ascetic, life there, a life deepened by the spartan landscape about her. Over and over she mentions—like van Herk and Moss and Wiebe—the land's apparent silence and "emptiness." She also says that "where I am is a place that does not readily render its secrets or subtleties" (108). Early on, she quotes a Benedictine monk, Terence Kardong, who says that "we who are permanently camped here see things you don't see at 55 mph"; then Norris adds, making the connection with the North not just possible but complete, "the so-called emptiness of the Plains is full of such miraculous 'little things'" (10). Repeatedly, she returns to this important, essential point:

> Here, the eye learns to appreciate slight variations, the possibilities inherent in emptiness. It sees that the emptiness is full of small things, like grasshoppers in their samurai armour clicking and jumping as you pass. (156)
>
> A person is forced inward by the spareness of what is outward and visible in all this land and sky. The beauty of the Plains is like that of an icon; it does not give an inch to sentiment or romance. (157)
>
> Maybe seeing the Plains is like seeing an icon: what seems stern and almost empty is merely open, a door into some simple and holy state. (157)

It is no accident, I suggest, that two of the three writers we have been examining come from and have written about the Canadian Prairies. Indeed, it is Aritha van Herk who allows us, finally, to fix this link between prairie and Far North. In her "Prairie as Flat as . . ." she says that to see the prairie as flat "reveals a terribly myopic view of the secret and undulating world around us" (127). To see the prairie as simply flat or the North as empty is to not see either. "God," says Kathleen Norris, "is in the details" (188).

Norris's remark points us towards what we must, finally, recognize about these works: what I can only call their religious or spiritual intent. All three of our writers seek in the North, and to a greater or lesser extent, find, the ecstatic experience of the ascetic. "You must," says van Herk, "help yourself achieve geografictiones of the soul, moments of erasure only available in fiction and on desert islands" (87). Moss writes:

> Not every writer finds the Arctic barren. Some write the landscape into literature; but some, a few, risk the gape of gravity and soar—and write their language into Arctic landscape, and in their writing carry readers to the very edge of territories undreamed in the dreams of others. In their ecstatic, sometimes haunted records of encounters with the Arctic's awesome beauty or its subtle grace are implications, intimations, of a visionary world more real than actuality. (132)

"Look for me here," says Moss, "in the silencing of words; look here, I am tremulous with language, between wind and the land" (158). And in the final pages of *Playing Dead*, Wiebe quotes Rasmussen quoting an Inuit elder from Pelly Bay who talks about how song is found:

> A person is moved just like the ice floe sailing here and there out in the current. Your thoughts are driven by a flowing force when you feel joy, when you feel fear, when you feel sorrow. Thoughts can wash over you like a flood, making your breath come in gasps and your heart pound. Something like an abatement in the weather will keep you thawed up. And then it will happen that we, who always think we are small, will feel even smaller. And we will fear to use words. But it will happen that the words we need will come of themselves. When the words we want shoot up of themselves—then we get a new song. (119)

Wiebe says he wants to understand Orpingalik. He wants to "prepare" himself. He wants to walk into "the true north of [his] own head between the stones and the ocean" (119). He wants a new song (119). He says that if he finds it he will sing it for us (119).

And so, out of these writers' experience, out of their distrust of the traditions that they have inherited, in their careful observation and in their unrelenting efforts to use words that are faithful to, come from, the landscape, each work demonstrates at least in part what Moss calls, rightly I think, the "best in Arctic writing." That is, in each

> . . . our estrangement from the natural world yields to atavistic convolutions of the text that connect us, as outsiders, directly to the land—words evoke nostalgia for a world remembered by its absence. It is not, however, that wilderness has been made domestic, the feral subdued, but that art has breached the barriers between language and experience, imagination and the world imagined. The achievement, remarkable in letters, leaves the landscape untouched. (60)

But, I would add, the writer and the reader are not left untouched. They have been changed.

That the co-ordinates Wiebe is the first to plot are accurate is at least partly supported by van Herk's *Places* and Moss's *Dreams*. Support also comes, as we've seen, from American writers like William Least Heat-Moon and Kathleen Norris who have made similar explorations in a not dissimilar landscape. But the most compelling evidence that a new literary geography of the North—one that is truer to both the actuality and spirituality of the place—also comes, I suggest, from the publication of *A Discovery of Strangers* which is, surely, Wiebe singing the new song he says he is seeking in *Playing Dead*.

Recently, I was reminded of this book's importance. I am not referring to the book's receipt of the Governor-General's Award for Fiction. Rather, I am referring to an altogether simpler, but more telling event. Several weeks ago, one of Yukon College's English instructors gave me a copy of a paper that had been prepared for her English 220 class, a course that looks at representations of the North in Canadian literature. Its author, a woman of the Carmacks-Little Salmon First Nation, had written about three "northern" novels. About one of the three works Marybeth Westman said that "due to [her] romanticised beliefs about the Yukon, the author is unable to portray a sense of reality and a sense of place, leaving the reader bewildered and disappointed . . ." (3). About another Ms. Westman said that it "gives the reader a picture of only black and white . . . he ends up presenting the North as romantic" (10). From these two works Ms. Westman carefully distinguished the third, Wiebe's *A Discovery of Strangers*. She wrote:

> . . . Rudy Wiebe's *A Discovery of Strangers* is different. . . .
> Wiebe has consciously taken a new approach [to] writing about the

north. Wiebe . . . does not manipulate the landscape. Instead he works together with the landscape and allows it to find its own shape and patterns. (4)

I can think of no better endorsement for the risks that Wiebe and, by extension, Moss and van Herk have taken as they have begun the important work of rethinking the literary relationship between Canada and its North.

WORKS CITED

Eliot, T. S. "Tradition and the Individual Talent." *Selected Prose of T. S. Eliot.* Ed. Frank Kermode. New York: Harcourt, 1975. 37–44.

Least Heat-Moon, William. *PrairyErth (a Deep Map).* Boston: Houghton Mifflin, 1991.

Mitcham, Allison. *The Northern Imagination: A Study of Northern Canadian Literature.* Moonbeam: Penumbra, 1983.

Moss, John. *Enduring Dreams: An Exploration of Arctic Landscape.* Concord: Anansi, 1994.

Norris, Kathleen. *Dakota: A Spiritual Geography.* New York: Ticknor and Fields, 1993.

Purdy, Al. *North of Summer.* Toronto: McClelland and Stewart, 1967.

Ross, Shannon. "Icebergs and Archipelagoes: Form, Structure and Arctic Landscape in John Moss's *Enduring Dreams.*" *The Northern Review* 12/13: 167–174.

Senkpiel, Aron. "From the Wild West to the Far North: Literary Representations of North America's Last Frontier." *Desert, Garden, Margin, Range: Literature on the American Frontier.* Ed. Eric Heyne. New York: Twayne, 1992. 133–142.

———. "Of Kiwi Fruit and Moosemeat: Contradictory Perceptions of Canada's North." *The History and Social Science Teacher* 23.2 (Winter 1988): 77–81.

———. "Review of *Playing Dead.*" *The Northern Review* 3/4 (Summer/Winter 1989): 141–145.

van Herk, Aritha. "Prairie as Flat as . . ." *A Frozen Tongue.* Sydney: Dangaroo Press, 1992. 127–138.

———. *Places Far from Ellesmere.* Red Deer: Red Deer College Press, 1990.

Westman, Marybeth. *Three Stories of the North.* Unpublished essay, 1995.

Wiebe, Rudy. *A Discovery of Strangers.* Toronto: Alfred A. Knopf, 1994.

———. *Playing Dead: A Contemplation Concerning the Arctic.* Edmonton: NeWest, 1989.

Yates, J. Michael. "The Hunter Who Loses His Human Scent." *Man in the Glass Octopus.* Vancouver: Sono Nis, 1968. 52–61.

Questions of Being: An Exploration of *Enduring Dreams*

LORRIE GRAHAM AND TIM WILSON

We isolate ourselves
on the surface of a sphere;
locate ourselves with mathematical
exactitude, the metaphysics of geography.
But maps are not the same as memories;
the erotics of space
are now, at best, a dream.

JOHN MOSS, *Enduring Dreams*

At times *Enduring Dreams* seems more like a philosophical treatise than a narrative. What, then, is the nature of this philosophy? How does Moss define metaphysics when he uses a phrase like "the metaphysics of geography" (27)? "The struggle to define geography is a question of being" (2), he writes. Of course, the struggle to define metaphysics itself also becomes a question of being. Perhaps by exploring Martin Heidegger's definition of metaphysics in relation to Moss's definition of geography, the meaning of Moss's phrase "the metaphysics of geography" will be revealed and the implications of Moss's thought more fully understood. Heidegger, like Moss, wants to let beings or landscapes reveal themselves as they are, on their own terms. Metaphysics, on the other hand, has always gone beyond beings themselves in determining the truth of that which exists: "meta" meaning beyond and "physis" meaning nature or the physical.

The first few lines of *Enduring Dreams* reach toward definition:

> Trying to define geography: the imposition of knowledge on experience in a specified landscape. That's what I mean to say, but it's so terse it seems evasive. Geography is essentially propriocentric; it does not exist outside our awareness, but is entirely separable both from us and our presence within it. The mind opens like an eye on the landscape, and defines what it sees in terms of itself. The eye measures light; distance and direction—geography articulates our solipsistic vision of the world as knowable, as what we mean it to be. (1)

Moss's attempt here to define geography closely corresponds with Heidegger's efforts to delineate the modern metaphysical relation to beings. For

Heidegger, as for Moss, modern metaphysics is the metaphysics of the subject; things exist within this metaphysics as objects defined by terms set up by the subject; things exist as re-presented by the subject, as opposed to allowing "the things" to "present" themselves on their own terms. In other words, for Heidegger, in the modern epoch, the essence of truth or being "has been transformed into certitude, i.e., into the self-certitude of the human being in his self-positing, and that this latter is based on the subjectivity of consciousness" (*Parmenides*, 91).

This modern metaphysics of the subject and its self-positing culminates, for Heidegger, in the functional metaphysics of the will to power—for instance, in the metaphysics of Jacques Derrida where the essence of existence is the functional relation of interchangeable signifiers. With the culmination of modern metaphysics in the will to power, things exist as a function of relations, as an interpretation imposed by the ruling will to power, or perspective; things lose their autonomy, are absorbed into their relations. The self is posited by the willing self; hence, no distinction exists between subject and object: \both exist as a relation of interlocking forces, or perspectives of willing. For instance, Heidegger opposes willing to mere striving in as much as in the latter the self and the goal, what is striven for, are not absorbed into one another as functions of willing; that is, in mere striving the self is not *put before the self* as the goal of the willing. Heidegger notes that "striving can be indeterminate, both with respect to what is actually striven for and in relation to the very one who strives. In striving and in compulsion we are caught up in movement toward something without knowing what is at stake. In mere striving after something we are not properly *brought before ourselves*" [our emphasis] (*Nietzsche*, 41).

Just as, for Heidegger, in the culmination of modern metaphysics in the will to power, existence becomes defined as a function of forces or perspectives (for example, the definition of the willing self as a function of perspectives posited by that self), so, too, Moss argues the culmination of the geographical relation to existence means the revealing of being as a function of forces or "conditions." For instance, he writes, "Geography is a discipline, of course; and location—in a proscriptive sense, patterns determined by rule." Moss continues, "Geography is *conditions*, meant almost as metaphor. Arctic geography; conditions of climate, of *will*. To endure, be endured" [our emphasis] (2). In a like manner, Moss notes, "The Arctic, [is] reduced by geographic explication to ciphers, digits, points that occupy no space, lines with no dimension; words shatter, become facts" (9); finally, he states, "Perception and notation are *functions* of experience; not *being* itself" [our emphasis] (17).

For Heidegger, then, the metaphysical relation to beings means their functionalization and the loss of the things themselves; that is, the culmination of this metaphysical relation to beings means the withdrawal of Being itself. Simply put, things arise within modern metaphysics without limits; for Heidegger, beings only *are* within certain limits; in this way, in as much as modern metaphysics dissolves the things themselves into forces, the things themselves lack Being or the limits of what is proper to them. Similarly, Moss argues that geography forces the landscape to arise as a functional set of relations—that is, as a function of "ciphers," "digits," or "lines with no dimension." To the extent that geography abstracts the landscape into lines without dimension, geography loses the landscape by erasing the horizons of landscape as the limits of what is proper to it. In this way, then, just as Being has withdrawn for Heidegger, so too, for Moss, geography subsumes landscape. Moss refers to landscape as "the antithesis of geography" (5); in addition, he states that "[g]eography has displaced the landscape; misplaced it perhaps . . ." (17).

As an example of the way in which modern metaphysical geography displaces the landscape, Moss turns to certain metafictional writers. To make this relation of metaphysics and geography more clear, we shall refer to one of the texts Moss discusses in *Enduring Dreams,* Aritha van Herk's *Places Far from Ellesmere.* When referring to another of her works, *In Visible Ink,* Moss notes, "van Herk discovers herself on sinuous ocean ice between Resolute and Grise Fiord as invisibled by awe. The conceit is metaphysical, deconstructing on the page to make her point (the hypothetical intersection of consciousness and icescape, occupying no space)" (74). Why does Moss relate van Herk's work to modern metaphysical geography? In what way, in other words, does Moss see landscape arising for van Herk?

As we have noted, within the culmination of modern metaphysics in the will to power, the essence of existence is defined as a plurality of forces or perspectives in relation or a plurality of texts or signifiers in infinite referral. Thus, in as much as textuality is the essence of existence for van Herk, she is a metaphysical geographer. For example, one of the epigraphs in *Places Far from Ellesmere* quotes Foucault's definition of a discursive formation:

> A discursive formation is not, therefore, an ideal, continuous, smooth text that runs beneath the multiplicity of contradictions, and resolves them in the calm unity of coherent thought; nor is it the surface in which, in a thousand different aspects, a contradiction is reflected that is always in retreat, but everywhere dominant. It is rather a space of multiple dissensions; a set of different oppositions whose levels and roles must be described. (9)

Like Foucault, then, van Herk sees existence as the intersection of discursive formations: an interrelation of texts that are equally interchangeable; things exist as a function of signifiers in the ruling perspective of "power/ knowledge" or the will to power. According to van Herk, existence is a web of signifiers or texts to be read. She refers to Edmonton as "a reading, an act of text, an open book" (47). Earlier, van Herk also notes, "And will it hang black crepe over the same strings of Christmas lights before it dies: will it read past its own murder: un/read its eagerness to read the future: read its certain demise, its accidental blood and sweat" (35)?

In a more dramatic textualization of existence, she says:

> Edberg: this place, this village and its environs. A fiction of geography/geography of fiction: coming together in people and landscape and the harboured designations of fickle memory. Invented: textual: un/read: the hieroglyphic secrets of the past. Come home. (40)

Because van Herk sees existence as the interchangeability of signifiers, Anna Karenina, as character and text, can be de-contextualized—taken from one context, or relation of texts, and placed in another discursive formation. For instance, even though the narrator is in Edberg, van Herk, through the intertextuality of the reading, brings Anna Karenina on the scene,

> and Anna Karenina will get off to pace the platform for a few moments, just long enough to see Tolstoy's coachman and to remember that illegitimacy lurks everywhere, she has only to read the story differently, her own story waiting to be un/read by the light of these places: all places with acts of reading as their histories, and all of them your homes. (36)

van Herk also insists that we readers "must free [Anna] from the constraints of the novel she has been imprisoned in, shake her loose from the pages of her own story so that she can float over the landscape here in this landscape of a woman" (131).

Thus, Anna, like the narrator, is never rooted in a site, in a horizon where beings can reveal themselves—a horizon where beings are revealed but are also concealed. For example, van Herk states, "One old touring car: reading the wake of a passing people: a site effaced" (30); and similarly, she writes, "How, then, do you occupy a place: a site effacing itself, a town dis/appearing, dis/allowed" (29)? The nature of a horizon is that things fade in the distance, and that which is near shades off at the sides; all perspectives are not available simultaneously. However, just as modern metaphysics effaces the limits of beings, so too does the geographer efface the horizon of a landscape. van Herk as metaphysical geographer has access to Tolstoy's Russia as text beyond any limitations of a particular horizon. She notes that "Siberia is never far away: visible just over the horizon" (125). Anna, since she exists outside of a horizon, is available to the ruling will from all possible perspectives: Anna in Russia, in Tolstoy, in Edberg, Alberta, in the Arctic, as island.

This textualization of existence means a radical de-contextualization as well. In the section on "Allowances and Forbiddences," van Herk characterizes writing as that which proclaims the codes, what is allowed and what is forbidden. On the one hand, then, writing operates as a law or a limitation of being. For example, she claims that "Tolstoy insist[s] that sex is dangerous: sexual desire an unleashed demon that should be controlled and organized, *scripted* and domesticated" [our emphasis] (107). On the other hand, more strikingly, writing is that which transgresses all limits for van Herk. That is, reading or textuality allows Anna to transgress nineteenth-century social norms; in van Herk's reading, Anna is taken out of the context of nineteenth-century Russia and placed in Ellesmere. These two aspects of textuality, as law and as transgression, are characterized by van Herk as writing and re-writing, or the read and the "un/read."

Therefore, that which exists is that which is written and re-written. Existence arises as an inter-relation of signifiers and a plurality of perspectives. In van Herk's text the already written is the nature of existence as schematized by one perspective or will: "Everything on schedule, your packs arriving in Edmonton even before you do—perhaps you have already taken this trip and are only following your future. Perhaps your record of reading *Anna Karenin* on Ellesmere is already written, already un/read" (83). The re-written would then be the overcoming of that perspective and the imposition of a new one, a re-drawing of the lines.

This new perspective in no way moves beyond the modern metaphysical conception of existence as will to power. As Heidegger points out, in relation to Nietzsche's philosophy,

> as a mere countermovement it necessarily remains, as does everything "anti," held fast in the essence of that over against which it moves. Nietzsche's countermovement against metaphysics is, as the mere turning upside down of metaphysics, an inextricable entanglement in metaphysics. . . . ("Nietzsche's Word . . . ," 61).

In this way, van Herk's textual overcoming of the existing perspective is merely the essence of will to power as the will to overcome. Heidegger argues that the essence of will, for Nietzsche, is power (*Nietzsche*, 37), and the essence of power is over-coming or enhancement: "Power itself only *is* inasmuch as, and so long as, it remains a willing to be more power" (*Nietzsche*, 60). In other words, just as textuality is a law and a transgression, so too is will "in itself simultaneously creative and destructive" (*Nietzsche*, 63). Writing and re-writing are merely the supreme examples of putting the self on the scene, of projecting the self onto the landscape, of seeing "woman as island." It is a supreme example of seeing existence as merely the ruling interpretation, as merely a fictional configuration of the written, as a "geografictione."

If van Herk's narrative is an example of the metaphysical, geographical, or geografictional relation to beings or to landscape, Moss's book is the attempt to think of an alternative to this relation to beings. As Moss asserts,

> You cannot participate in history simply by reading, or by writing and rewriting the past. Any moment in your life is more complex than all the convolutions of historical narrative. But you can write yourself into the present; as an explorer you can document your passing. The danger, of course, is in believing your own account, confusing your own vision of the world with the world itself. (107)

We do not mean to suggest that Moss and van Herk exist as opposite poles to each other. For one thing, Moss himself praises the work of van Herk throughout *Enduring Dreams*. Also, Moss himself does not always avoid the modern metaphysical or geographical relation to beings.

While pointing to an alternative to the contemporary relation to the landscape as textual projection, Moss also dwells, at times, within that space:

> Images converge: lines connect; lines separate, divide. When you enter Arctic narrative, you enter every narrative of the Arctic ever written. When you enter the Arctic in person, you become part of the extended text. When you write the Arctic to affirm your presence in the world, you become in writing an imaginative creation. You could imagine anything and write it down and it would seem real forever. (105)

Although Moss exists at times within this space of textual projections, the core of *Enduring Dreams* is that which keeps the question of Being open. Alternative possibilities for Being and alternative relations to the landscape as landscape are explored. The alternative to the modern metaphysical relation to beings is profoundly "postmodern," that is, postmodern as postmetaphysical: an openness to beings that allows them to arise in themselves as themselves, on their own terms. Rather than the positing of the self-on-the-scene which accompanies the textualization or functionalization of existence as will to power, Moss argues that "[t]hrough memory caught in writing with humility, perhaps we can perceive meaning in landscape, instead of imposing it" (43). Moss calls us to a primordial openness to Being as landscape: "Until we journey through the landscape literally with books in hand, we are unable to escape the world as text, aware only of unease between remembered readings of the Arctic and our own experience there" (43).

One way in which Moss's primordial experience of openness to beings and landscape manifests itself is in the endurance run—the Marathon, that early Greek, pre-metaphysical event. Here the truth of existence is experienced as an unconcealing of beings within the openness of the runner's horizon.

> The horizon forms a line at the edge of your perception. Imagine running toward the horizon; a line of hills, or better, plane on plane of hills, like a Chinese painting. You will never reach the horizon, of course, but time will end just the same. Now, imagine yourself, with humility born from the depths of commitment, inseparable from the land—the horizon no longer a personal affront, the boundary of consciousness; it is a promise, the affirmation of an unseen but substantial world extending without limits, forever. (65)

This unconcealing which occurs within the runner's horizon also involves a concealing of landscape as it shades off in the distance of what is past; that is, Moss recognizes that that which is beyond the horizon is substantial and real; at the same time, he understands that this reality is beyond his perception. The runner cannot access this unknowable place beyond the horizon; it is not available through the inter-relation of textual referrals. In *Enduring Dreams,* then, Moss thinks of landscape in terms of its temporal revealing; he thinks Being as Time:

> With every foot fall the Arctic
> rises to embrace you;
> pellucid air displays the landscape
> like a Chinese painting—
> the primacy of perspective, vestigial,
> you, the runner, are
> inseparable from what you see. (25)

WORKS CITED

Heidegger, Martin. *Nietzsche: Vol. I, The Will to Power as Art,* trans. David Farrell Krell. New York: Harper Collins, 1979.

———. "Nietzsche's Word: God is Dead." *The Question Concerning Technology and Other Essays.* Trans. William Lovitt. New York: Harper and Row, 1977. 53–112.

———. *Parmenides,* trans. André Schuwer and Richard Rojewicz. Indianapolis: Indiana University Press, 1992.

Moss, John. *Enduring Dreams: An Exploration of Arctic Landscape.* Concord: Anansi, 1994.

van Herk, Aritha. *Places Far from Ellesmere: a geografictione.* Red Deer: Red Deer College Press, 1990.

The Spirit of the Arctic
or
Translating the Untranslatable
in Rudy Wiebe's
A Discovery of Strangers

KENNETH HOEPPNER

*I could be more accurate if I had a reliable interpreter who would make a
reliable interpretation.*
RUDY WIEBE, *"Where Is the Voice Coming From?"*

Since the death of the transcendental signified, how
does one read a new novel by a writer whose previous novels have posited
transcendent vision as the essence of political action? I cannot pretend to
be the reliable interpreter, but I can venture a reading. One temptation is
to read it as a more subtle enactment of earlier themes, and while I think
such a reading of Rudy Wiebe's *A Discovery of Strangers* is possible, it prede-
termines our reading of a complex, polyphonic novel. Seeing *A Discovery
of Stangers* as continuing the exploration of Wiebe's earlier themes would
be in accord with Penelope Van Toorn's demonstration that Rudy Wiebe's
fiction may be read as concerning itself with the relationship between religious belief in an absolute and postmodernism's relativization of knowledge. She has argued that Wiebe, even in the most recent novel she
considered, *My Lovely Enemy* (1983), cannot accept a truly dialogic position.
She cites the appearance of the mortician in *My Lovely Enemy* as evidence
of what she calls Wiebe's lingering nostalgia for absolute truth: "This last-
minute appearance of a *deus ex machina* in the otherwise highly dialogized
text suggests that, as in his other novels, Wiebe cannot entirely suppress
his own lingering nostalgia for the fundamentalist vision of a monologic
God" (288). She goes on to state that Wiebe believes that humans may yet
be able to articulate absolute truth (293).

I propose to suggest that in Wiebe's *A Discovery of Strangers* the
desire for that monologic God disappears as the novel accepts the postmodern challenge, not by celebrating carnivalesque free play, but by
engaging in the dialogical process of exploring the interplay between
community and "truth." The fact that community makes meaning invites
a celebration of community. The community becomes the sign of the

transcendent; the transcendental is signified by the here and now. Paradoxically, then, the transcendent "presence" is the community here and now.

I would suggest that Wiebe's earlier novels try to translate the "Word" into the language of particular communities, while knowing that the "Word" exists only in translation, and that a community talks back to the "Word". *A Discovery of Strangers,* more strongly than any of Wiebe's previous work, emphasizes the untranslatability of the "Word", but untranslatability is not equivalent to unknowability or indeterminacy, for such equivalence assumes that language is necessary for knowledge.[1] In *A Discovery of Strangers,* Wiebe situates the dialogue between Christian and native spirituality in the intertext of the meeting between the Tetsot'ine and the members of Franklin's first expedition. *A Discovery of Strangers* is not a discovery of the words that articulate the Word; it is a discovery that the communion of the flesh creates the Word. As do Wiebe's earlier novels, *A Discovery of Strangers* emphasizes the significance of the spiritual, but unlike the earlier novels, here the spiritual is not particularly Christian. It is rooted in people and place, untranslatable into language, but signifiable by making love, making strange.

In order to share in that revelation, readers must develop what Northrop Frye calls the "double vision." The process of reading the novel provides a simulacrum of the process of developing that vision. First I will try to establish that Wiebe suggests the possibility of a non-materialist view of history in which facts are the "accidents" of history; patterns are its essence, and the essential pattern of history is transcendence through " a discovery of strangers." The novel establishes a pattern in which the truly dialogic transcends whereas the monologic destroys. The novel suggests that pattern through the motif of the communion of flesh exemplified in the love between Greenstockings and Robert Hood. That love transcends language, for neither ever understands a word the other speaks (157, 159), but their flesh makes the "Word," makes love, creating a knowledge that is outside of language. Cannibalism is the monologic, profane inversion of the dialogic, sacralizing knowledge of and through the body.

Second, I will suggest that the novel is structured so that its reading results in revelation. As is the case with Wiebe's other novels, readers must try to understand unfamiliar voices, and the familiar is made strange. Readers must learn a new language.[2] As in his other historical fiction, Wiebe transforms the facts into story, giving voice to those who speak only in the gaps of published accounts. He translates those voices, in this case the voices of the Tetsot'ine, back to their "strangeness," simultaneously showing the "strangeness" of the white account of the Arctic and its people. But, as Keskarrah says, "stories are like ropes, they pull you to incomprehensible places" (126), and "discovery" is possible. Unlike "Thick English," the contemporary reader discovers that, in order to belong to the Arctic, one must know the place without being told [paraphrase of Keskarrah, 124]. People must become one with the spirit of the place in order to dream its meaning, in order to know the names of places. But that spirit has changed. As Keskarrah's translation of the whites' story of origins demonstrates its inadequacy, its essential maleness [126], so, too, the encounter between the Tetsot'ine and the whites changes the Tetsot'ine. Bigfoot remarks at the beginning of the novel: "Yesterday we had not seen any of it. And I would be as happy as you if we never had, but unfortunately, now we will never be able to say we haven't" (26), and Greenstocking's bearing the child Robert Hood fathered confirms it near the end. Readers must know the place in order to "know something a little."

Finally, I will suggest that knowledge of place constitutes Wiebe's translation of the "Word" into the spirit of the Arctic, simultaneously demonstrating its particularity and its untranslatability. In so doing, Wiebe follows Yoder's description of the way in which Anabaptist Christianity embraces postmodernism's challenge to the transcendental signified:

> Transcendence is kept alive not on the grounds of logical proof to the effect that there is a cosmos with a hereafter, but by the vitality of communities in which a different way of being keeps breaking in here and now. That we can really be led on a different way is the real proof of the transcendent power which offers hope of peace to the world as well. Nonconformity is the warrant for the promise of another world. (94)

Wiebe creates the vital community of the Tetsot'ine as an antidote to the sickness the Whites bring, the sickness of the "*spirit*, of *things*" (269), but the reader must translate what it means for the land to effect the cure: "Bigfoot finally asked, abruptly small again, 'But . . . what do you say? what can we do with these strangers?' . . . Keskarrah murmured, 'I think . . . it will have to be the land'" (267).

I
The Communion of the Flesh

Van Toorn's reading of *My Lovely Enemy* notes the significance of human sexuality in Wiebe's work: "In James's mind, and in Wiebe's text, passionate sexual love takes on figurative meanings: it serves primarily as a metaphor which permits imagination to grasp fully for the first time the too-familiar Christian abstraction of God's redemptive love for humanity" (275). That metaphorical reading may well apply to Wiebe's earlier fiction, but I do not read the relationship between Greenstockings and Robert Hood in those terms. The joy of the flesh transforms but does not necessarily redeem.

At the literal and figurative centre of the novel is the love scene involving Greenstockings and Hood. The imagery in this love scene confirms it as the thematic centre of the work. The novel's dominant image patterns of food, fire, song, and dream here unite with the idea that all that is alive is "already within everything else" (25). The fire draws them together. Hood, who has already fallen unfathomably into the freedom of wordlessness (82), now lets go of his desire for a word: ". . . he does not want to understand any word she ever speaks. None. The freedom of watching, of listening with incomprehension, fills him with staggering happiness: all the reports they are duty-bound to write, the daily journal, the data piled in columns upon page after page—but in this warm place thick with indescribable smells there is no listable fact, not a single word" (158). He loses his desire to make an image of Greenstockings: "he forgets his paper at last; his pencil falls . . ." (160), thus preparing him to fulfill Greenstockings' desire that he experience her directly: "why does he keep trying to make her outline on paper? If he wants it, why doesn't he feel it with her face between his hands?" (160). Now Hood learns to listen with his body (162), to know with his body. Greenstockings' food is sacramental, uniting herself and Hood with all living things. The song to the animal "Give me your stomach, /Sweet animal" (162) she also sings for Hood. Hood sings back "Drink to me only with thine eyes," the communion of bodies. For Greenstockings also, Hood's "incomprehension gives her freedom" (160). Then, almost simultaneous with their bodies joining, Hood gives her the stockings that become her name (177).

The communion of flesh renames Keskarrah's daughter and in this joining of flesh, Hood actualizes his name, "draw[ing] his name out of his bone" (31), as Angélique says. Hood also dies to the origins of his name, the folk-tale fairy-tale English pastoral world. In this union of flesh, Greenstockings and Hood discover each other and they discover the strangeness of the "other." That their knowledge is genuine is signified by its contrast with the quest for false knowledge. The scene of their love-making is intercut with Birdseye's dream of the failure of the expedition's quest for knowledge. Ironically, the survivors of that quest survive by profaning the life-engendering communion of flesh through cannibalism.

Significantly, Greenstockings's and Hood's discovery and transformation occur outside of language, thus calling into question the poststructuralist idea that, as Catherine Belsey puts it, "we can only *know* in language, which is culturally relative" (*Desire,* 14). The play on names and naming in this central love story also invites our reconsideration of another dominant poststructuralist tenet, namely, the arbitrariness of the name.

II
The Untranslatable Language

From the beginning, the novel draws attention to the significance of names. One way of reading explores the idea that names are determined rather than arbitrary. Another way of reading suggests that names, words, never constitute "presence." In the first section of the novel, Wiebe invites us to question the naming of the cow: "If the three-tined cow with her calf alive beside her had had a name, it would have been? Elyáske" (4). What does this name signify? The name is one already known but not thought about. It expresses the essence of the "three-tined cow," but how, in what language? The idea that names have power is developed in the paragraph immediately following: "he [the wolf] would have defied any animal, and that included the seven members of his pack, to know his name" (4). The suggestion that names have power, that they contain the essence of that which is named, becomes an explicit statement in the section "Into a Northern Blindness of Names." The name equals place: "Of course, every place already was its true and exact name. Birdseye and Keskarrah between them knew the land, each name a story complete in their heads" (24). That verb form "was" in the statement makes the equation. Name equals place equals story.

In contrast, "These English . . . tried to name every lake and river with whatever sound slips from their mouths . . . it is truly difficult for a few men who glance at it once to name an entire country" (22). Clearly, names may be determined; the relation of signifier and signified need not be arbitrary; "presence" is possible, but not in a language that is translatable. Just as the language of the body expressed through the communion of flesh admits no substitutes, so the proper name cannot be learned except through direct experience. The novel tells us that "Keskarrah . . . is powerful and old enough to draw the picture of the world in the sand and name a few places what they are" (20). No picture drawn on the sand is permanent; no naming constucts a totality. But as pictures and names come out of people's places and experiences, they combine to form stories that "pull us to incomprehensible places" (126). Beginnings, origins, are incomprehensible, but stories can provide a comprehensible translation. The novel contains Keskarrah's telling of two stories of beginnings, the People's story and the Whitemud story. Keskarrah's assessment that "the Whitemud story . . . is not happy" (126) . . . "[it] tells them that everything is always wrong" with the result that "wherever they go, they can only see how wrong the world is" (132) contrasts with his assessment of his own people's story of "the man and the ptarmigan-woman and how they made snowshoes together" (126). Keskarrah goes on to recognize the similarity of the two culture's stories of origins, but recognizes the danger of their difference (126). The people's story confirms the necessity of men's and women's coming together; the Whitemud's "stories seem to be only about men, they say their Soul Everywhere is a man also" (126). We are invited to infer that the Judaeo-Christian story of origins does not fit this place.

Conventional Christian piety results in the telling of stories that misrepresent, or in the ignoring of stories that might reveal. Franklin refuses to consider possibilities that he considers un-Christian: "he does not know (and if such knowledge of his future were offered him, he would refuse to consider it, as being un-Christian) that . . . Robert Hood . . . has, in fact, left him. . ." (142). As Richardson and Hepburn are starving, Richardson refuses to believe that Christian Englishmen would kill other humans in order to eat them, "One would expect the strong, as good Christians, to aid the weak" (241), but Hepburn's subsequent account of survival through cannibalism illustrates the folly of Richardson's belief. Similarly, Richardson's account of Hood's death, emphasizing Hood's religious devotion to the end, misrepresents Hood's thoughts as the novel presents them: "Robert Hood's mind is sodden with texts, touch him and he floods, his doors wrenched open and the rivers of sacred English words dammed up in his memory stream out, all of them into this Arctic dawn, visible and blaring aloud" (244). The blaring words, like the texts Richardson reads, reveal to Hood that "he was such a silly, gullible child, a child who thought he knew everything because he knew only the confident, simple world of English games, and endlessly elaborated, confident duty, words" (251). Hood's experience of "eating starvation" unlearns those texts. Greenstockings replaces Jesus in the fragments of gospel songs that he recalls. The apple taste of Greenstockings's nipples becomes linked with the sweetness of the name of Jesus "in a believer's ear" (229); her arms become the "everlasting arms" (230); and her body becomes his haven as in the song "safe into that [thy] haven guide" [O receive my soul at last] (231).

Other instances of parodic allusion reinforce the idea that the language system the English use to construct knowledge must be replaced. Birdseye dreams the expedition's future in which ignorance speaks to its members, parodying Knowledge's speech to Everyman: "I am your most faithful ignorance. I will go with you and be your guide, in your most need to go by your side" (155). Further parody links Knowledge's speech to Everyman with Jesus's statement to his disciples: "But determined ignorance will ride on each shoulder, will whisper so softly and tenderly: 'Lo, I am with you alway, even unto the end of the world.'"3 The body's knowledge, individual and communal, is the antidote to this ignorance.

III
The Spirit of the North: "It will have to be the land"

Keskarrah is the teacher-figure, a figure, as Van Toorn observes, common to all Wiebe's novels (287). Unlike other teacher-figures who monologically speak the Word, Keskarrah provides an outline of how to live in the place he knows. One can only know the "Soul Everywhere" by knowing the place in which one lives. Keskarrah remarks on the inability of the English to know a place or to know the "Soul Everywhere":

> They always have to hold something in their hands, something to make marks on, or to look at things or through unknowable instruments that the sun distorts first, and then draw something of it onto paper, with names that mostly mean nothing. As if a lake or a river is ever the same twice! When you travel and live with a river or lake, or hill, it can remain mostly like it seems, but when you look at it with your dreaming eye, you know it is never what it seemed to be when you were first awake to it. Again and again Thick English talks about the Soul Everywhere, but he himself never looks for the sun. He and his men always stare at it through something else, and I think the sun uses their instruments to blind them. To make them think living things are always the same. (75)

The universalism of the idea of a Soul Everywhere is at odds with the particularity of place.

Wiebe chooses the Tetsot'ine community in the north during the time of that community's encounter with members of Franklin's second expedition as the site of discovery. Why does he choose the north? I could outline the features of Tetsot'ine life that illustrate their living as a community in oneness with the land: their sense of oneness with all animals; their devaluation of material goods that interrogates the foundations of consumer-based economies as illustrated by Richardson's idea that natives must learn about money. "'If they understood money, they would work harder to get more of it, in order to buy what they want." Franklin shook his head. "But it seems they want so little." "Exactly," Richardson murmured, closing his notebook. 'They must want more than they need. That is civilization'" (59). I could cite their elders' ability to know the essence of the place, to name it and to dream it; I could also cite their developing gender equality as illustrated in Greenstockings's development (302). However, to regard these qualities as the essence of utopia here and now would be to mistake the accidents for the essence.

Instead, the spirit of the North is an "impenetrable, life-giving cold" (*Discovery*, 317). The North requires "a different way of being"; it requires silence instead of "blaring aloud". That silence is a precondition for transcendence, a point Wiebe has made in his meditation on silence in his essay "The Words of Silence: Past and Present." He quotes from the *Ancrene Riwle*: "in silence and in hope shall be our strength," and "she may also hope that she shall sing through her silence sweetly in heaven" (17). For those who listen, the silence speaks; it says "be still and know that I am

God" as the Psalmist writes (Psalm 46:10). Who is this "I" who claims to be God? *A Discovery of Strangers* does not say, but its stories suggest that it is not I or we, nor entirely the Other. It is a place of incomprehension where we recognize ourselves as strangers who can begin to discover "a different way of being."

Let me conclude by rereading John Howard Yoder's comments on the significance of that discovery:

> Transcendence is kept alive not on the grounds of logical proof to the effect that there is a cosmos with a hereafter, but by the vitality of communities in which a different way of being keeps breaking in here and now. That we can really be led on a different way is the real proof of the transcendent power which offers hope of peace to the world as well. Nonconformity is the warrant for the promise of another world. (94)

NOTES

1.   A pattern that may be emerging in my reading of Wiebe's fiction could be called "Rudy Wiebe's Northward Journey: Away from the Prairie Mennonite spiritual world to the Northern spiritual world." In *Peace Shall Destroy Many* and *The Blue Mountains of China*, Wiebe explores the interpenetration of the Christian word and the Mennonite community, simultaneously considering the question of evangelizing. In *First and Vital Candle*, he focusses attention on how to present Christianity to the aboriginal community, but does not fully attend to the dialogic process; he doesn't help readers hear what aboriginal spirituality is saying back. *The Temptations of Big Bear* and *The Scorched-Wood People* give aboriginal and Métis spirituality a voice in the dialogue, while *My Lovely Enemy* completes the circle by returning to question the nature of Mennonite Christianity from a postmodern perspective. That questioning finds its answer in native spirituality represented by Keskarrah's pantheism when he says: "'It is for us to look. Perhaps we will recognize how everything alive is already within everything else'" (25).

2.   The Anabaptist scholar, John Howard Yoder, one whose influence Wiebe acknowledges, comments on the significance of language: "It is a significant anthropological insight to say that language can steer the community with power disproportionate to other kinds of leadership. The demagogue, the poet, also the journalist, the novelist, the grammarian, all are engaged in steering society with the rudder of language. This applies both to rhetoric as a skill and also to the place of any set of concepts in predisposing what kinds of thoughts the members of a given community are capable of having" (32).

WORKS CITED

Belsey, Catherine. *Desire: Love Stories in Western Culture.* Oxford: Blackwell, 1994.

Van Toorn, Penelope. *Rudy Wiebe and the Historicity of the Word.* Ph.D. Thesis, University of British Columbia, 1991.

Wiebe, Rudy. "The Words of Silence: Past and Present." In E.D. Blodgett and H.G. Coward, *Silence, The Word and The Sacred.* Waterloo: Wilfrid Laurier University Press, 1989.

————. *A Discovery of Strangers.* Toronto: Knopf, 1994.

Yoder, John Howard. *The Priestly Kingdom: Social Ethics as Gospel.* Notre Dame, Indiana: University of Notre Dame Press, 1984.

Go North Young Woman: Representations of the Arctic in the Writings of Aritha van Herk

MARLENE GOLDMAN

Currently the north is hot—especially within the fictions of Aritha van Herk. Her writing may well convince Canadian authors, particularly women, to adjust their bearings and set their compasses due north. In her experimental fiction *Places Far from Ellesmere* (1990), the narrator stages a daring rescue of Tolstoy's tragic heroine Anna Karenina from the clutches of her author's fatal plot. Part of the rescue operation involves a subversive rereading of the novel which takes place in the Arctic: "Go north, Anna, go north," the narrator says. "If there are westerns, why can there not be northerns? Northerns of the heart. Anna has been punished too long. Take her with you to Ellesmere" (85). In giving this advice, is the narrator simply putting a playful spin on an old genre, namely, the "western," or do her fictions open a potential narrative space for a new feminist genre, referred to here as "northerns"?

As one might expect, the "northern" did not suddenly spring up, fully formed, on the Canadian fictional horizon. Critics such as Sherrill Grace and Robert Kroetsch have traced its development for quite some time.[1] Typically, critics define the Canadian "northern" by contrasting it with the American "western." Yet, if the western's portrayal of the antisocial, violent hero[2] sets it apart from the northern, which supposedly features a "community of peoples,"[3] then, as we will see, van Herk's fictions fall under the category of the western. By the same token, however, if, as Robert Kroetsch asserts, in Canadian fictions characters typically face a wilderness that they do not want to conquer, but hope will conquer them, then some of van Herk's writing can also be classified as "northerns" (Kroetsch, 54).

Ultimately, her novels do not conform to the tidy labels. Readers familiar with her writing know that she revels in taking up liminal positions that explode totalizing categories.[4] She has created her own parodic brand of "northern," whose arrival was preceded by a careful exploration of the feminist possibilities afforded by the north in earlier fictions, including *The Tent Peg* (1981) and *No Fixed Address* (1987). However, due to their parodic nature, van Herk's northern fell under the shadows cast by previous fictional treatments of the west and the north, which raises important questions: namely, to what extent do van Herk's fictions constitute a meaningful departure from the traditional narratives which inform her work? More precisely, do her fictions, which portray the Arctic as a no-man's land, signal a comic rejection of genres which invoke this image, or do they simply replicate the imperialist projections which gave rise to the western, and account for its pervasive description of an empty, feminine landscape waiting to be conquered?[5]

Writings which depict the north typically bear witness to a Eurocentric perspective. As John Moss states, "Everything written on the Canadian Arctic is, in effect, a northwest passage, the expression not only of the traditions but the geography and history of another world" (40). Of course, this does not mean that all writing about the north is complicit with imperialist practices dating back to the search for the Northwest Passage. But it does highlight the fact that writings on the north inscribe the landscape in terms that reflect the language and desires of the outsider. Even a feminist author such as van Herk, bent on unreading classical texts, conveys the ideological perspectives of the south.

In his book *Culture and Imperialism,* Edward Said underscores the role of narrative, and novels in particular, in the spread and entrenchment of imperialism. He affirms that, while the "main battle in imperialism is over land ... when it came to who owned the land, who had the right to settle and work on it, who kept it going, who won it back, and who now plans its future—these issues were reflected, contested, and even for a time decided in narrative" (xii-xiii). While Said's work treats European writings on Africa, India, the Far East, Australia, and the Caribbean, the concerns of his study provide a direction for this analysis, which examines the way in which van Herk's fictions, beginning with *The Tent Peg,* represent the north and play a part in delineating who has possession over it.

Generally speaking, van Herk does not directly signal the political ramifications of narrating the north in her writing. Nevertheless, in the process of creating the feminist space of her "northern," her texts implicitly and explicitly foreground the problems surrounding attempts at narrating the north that contribute to (or leave unchallenged) the claims of imperialism.[6] Simply put, her works both install and subvert traditional features of this discourse.

This ambivalent response is evident in *The Tent Peg,* where the heroine, Ja-el, disguises herself as a boy in order to escape the city and join an all-male geological team sent to the Yukon's Werneke mountains to map potential mining sites. Pulling a hat low over her brow, she flees north.

Under the cover of a set of initials, J. L., she is able to fool the expedition leader, Mackenzie, into believing she is a man and hiring her on as a cook. In the episode where she first learns from Mackenzie how to handle a gun, J. L. identifies her new-found confidence with the northern landscape. As she says:

> It made me realize my own power, that I could turn a gun on them and pull the trigger, that up here there are no rules, no set responses, everything is new and undefined, we are beyond, outside of the rest of the world. There are no controls here.
>
> It frightens me and yet I know now that I don't have to be afraid of them, no not afraid at all. Out here my anger is as real as theirs, can have as great an effect. (86)[7]

On the one hand, the story celebrates J. L.'s escape from her gender role, and locates this subversive feminist practice in the northern landscape. On the other hand, J. L.'s transformation into one of the boys, an angry gunslinger who exults in her freedom from the restraints imposed by civilization, highlights the story's debt to the traditional western (see Slotkin 403–404). In this case, the western takes a decidedly feminist turn because, rather than battle hostile Indians, J. L. engages in a shootout with sexist members of her own culture.[8]

As the summer draws to a close, however, J. L. compromises the freedom associated with the northern landscape when she assists in the staking of a newly discovered gold mine. By participating in this venture, J. L. becomes complicit with imperialist practices which historically depend on acts of naming and claiming.[9]

In van Herk's subsequent novel, *No Fixed Address*, the heroine does not compromise her freedom. Instead of staking out a territory or selecting a "fixed address," the itinerant and irreverent heroine, Arachne Manteia, drives her 1959 Mercedes through all "the towns and villages and hamlets" of the west, plying her trade as an undergarment salesperson. Like J. L., Arachne longs to escape traditional female roles and she, too, eventually heads north. As she sees it, by heading in this direction, "she will be going nowhere, into a lost and limitless world she might not emerge from" (301).[10]

For the most part, Arachne portrays the north in the familiar terms of the "frontier." The text's subversive casting of a female picaresque character destabilizes certain narrative stereotypes, although this reversal does not prevent the text from maintaining significant links with traditional discourses. For example, when she enters the north, Arachne behaves like any other westerner. Searching for a frontier that can be colonized, she is both fearful and hopeful. As the narrator explains:

> She is steeling herself to enter the blank, the dislocated world of
> the North. Afraid, she is, afraid. After this there is nothing. What
> happens when the road comes to an end? After this there is no
> turning back. . . . Perhaps she will be able to find a place to settle
> in, colonize. (302)[11]

As in *The Tent Peg,* where the north is portrayed as a space "beyond, outside of the rest of the world" (86), in *No Fixed Address,* the narrator
describes the Arctic as "the ultimate frontier, a place where the civilized
melt away and the meaning of mutiny is unknown, where manners never
existed and family backgrounds are erased" (316). Despite their playful
tone, both of these texts raise serious questions about the relationship
between the desire to alter representations of female subjectivity and the
repercussions of imposing this desire on the northern landscape.

At least since the Renaissance, explorers, missionaries, scientists,
and sportsmen have been captivated by the Arctic. For the most part, they,
too, have envisioned it as "empty," waiting to be conquered.[12] Likewise,
the settlers who came to America, and gave rise to the "western" desired
above all "a tabula rasa on which they could inscribe their dream" (Slotkin, 38).

To some extent, van Herk's depictions of the northern, with their
tentative depiction of a feminist space, re-inscribe elements of the traditional genres they supposedly attempt to subvert. "Northerns" and "westerns" alike share the tendency to represent a coveted territory as an empty
space, "the ultimate frontier," which serves as a testing ground for antisocial and occasionally violent individuals.[13] Viewed in this light, the transformation of the northern landscape into a literary genre does not seem
to differ radically from the earlier transformation of the west into the western. Furthermore, van Herk's early treatments of the north prompt one to
ask: from whose vantage point does the north appear as an absence? Certainly not the Inuit's. Historically, the representation of the Arctic as no-
man's land has had tangible political consequences.

During the Cold War period, the government felt the need to
respond to the tendency of other nations to regard the north as a no-
man's land, specifically, the assumption that "in the Arctic the laws and
rules of Canada, or indeed of any country, do not apply."[14] According to
historian Shelagh Grant, in 1953, the government's response took the
form of an effort to "re-Canadianize" the Arctic and prompted what she
describes as a bungled attempt to relocate seventeen Inuit families from
the Port Harrison area in northern Quebec to Grise Ford, near the Craig
Harbour police post on Ellesmere. The details of this "experiment" and
the Inuit's experience are hotly contested and have come under close
scrutiny.[15] The fate of the Inuit who were transplanted to the far north
captured public attention when, in 1982, sixteen families requested finan-

cial assistance to cover the cost of returning to Port Harrison. A Parliamentary standing committee recommended that the government recognize the role played by the Inuit in protecting Canadian sovereignty, extend a formal apology, and, finally, compensate the Inuit for the "wrongdoing inflicted upon them" (Grant, 4). Instead of following these recommendations, however, the Government maintained that the situation did not warrant compensation because the relocation project was motivated by a concern for the Inuit, who were starving in northern Quebec, and not by a desire to solidify Canadian sovereignty in the Arctic. My goal here is not to solve this dispute.[16] The details of the case are relevant to my analysis of van Herk's writing only insofar as they highlight the political implications of viewing the Arctic as absence. The case is particularly important because the drama unfolded on Ellesmere Island, the setting for van Herk's most unconventional exploration of the Arctic.

In *Places Far from Ellesmere*, the links between the Arctic desert of Ellesmere Island and feminist attempts to subvert traditional representations of femininity become even more apparent. In this work, the narrator mediates on four "exploration sites," including the author's hometown of Edberg; the city of Edmonton, where she went to university; Calgary, where she currently resides; and, finally, Ellesmere Island. It is on this floating polar desert that the narrator enacts the rereading of Tolstoy's *Anna Karenin* mentioned earlier.

As in the previous novels, in this text, the Arctic once again promises to fulfil the dream of empty space: the "tabula rasa" (77).[17] Furthermore, the island, portrayed as "absence," satisfies the desire for "a hesitation where you can pretend there are no telephones in the world, no newspapers, no banks, no books" (77). This portrayal confirms geographer Rob Shield's view that fictional treatments of the north sustain an "oppositional spatialization whereby Southerners construe the North as a counter-balance to the civilized worth of the Southern cities, yet the core of their own, personal, Canadian identity" (163). Shields argues further that the fictional treatments of the north often disguise the "realities of the exploitation of the north for southern profit" (193).

On the topic of southern exploitation or "internal colonization," as the core/periphery relations are also known,[18] van Herk's novel remains silent; no mention is made of "experiment" involving the Inuit. To be fair, van Herk's trip took her to Lake Hazen and not to Grise Ford. (She does, however, describe her travels to Grise Ford in her subsequent collection of essays, *In Visible Ink*.) On the whole, *Places Far from Ellesmere* does not address the political and imperial agendas that continue to determine the fate of the Arctic. Instead, the north becomes what Moss describes as "a sprawling metaphor, a mirror of southern realities and dreams" (49). In keeping with the tendency to view the landscape as a metaphor, the text identifies features of the Arctic, such as the puzzle-ice, the contours of a mountain, and the prolonged daylight with the characters in Tolstoy's novel and the process of unreading.[19]

Eventually, the entire landscape is transformed into an image of Anna's body—a transformation signalled by the title of this exploration site: "Ellesmere, woman as island" (77). In a passage that meditates on Tolstoy's heroine, the narrator draws an explicit connection between Anna and Ellesmere:

> One thing about Anna: she is not the expected feminine principle, not a slim, streamlined adolescent, but a woman on the verge of flesh, with a full figure, solid. . . . And Ellesmere is a fat island, the tenth largest in the world, fat with the flesh of heated snow, of dazzling cold Fat with distance, with unreachability, with mystery. (96–97)

Throughout this section, the Arctic is portrayed as a site of seduction for the southern explorer.[20] The narrator refers to the northern landscape as "this mystery of polar desert" (89), and, later, as "this book of the north, un/read because mysterious, this female desert island and its secret reasons and desires" (130). The repeated emphasis on the north's "mystery" recalls descriptions of the "mysterious East" in the works of European authors who, as Edward Said states, knowingly or unknowingly supported the efforts of imperialism (Said, xi). In van Herk's text, both the "desires" of the "clean-swept northern desert" and the pleasures "of oblivion" that it supposedly teaches are utopian attributes drawn from traditional European narratives. Along these same lines, the repeated deployment of the extended metaphor of the landscape-as-woman underscores the fact that the imposition of Tolstoy's classic nineteenth-century novel onto the Arctic signals not so much a radical departure from traditional, masculine narratives as a modification of these narratives. Although van Herk's narrator would like to begin anew, and claims that she has freed Anna from the "shadows" that follow her—including the shadow of her lover, her husband, her brother, her son, and even the shadows cast by her "damnable literary history," and her "author" (108)—whether she recognizes it or not, *Places Far from Ellesmere* remains in the shadow of previous canonical texts, which represent the landscape as an alluring, elusive female.

An important difference between van Herk's text and prior fictional treatments of the north lies in the narrator's understanding of the connections between traditional narratives and imperialist practices. At one point, the narrator lists a host of European surnames which have been imposed on the bays and mountains of the Arctic landscape: "These names, every mapped configuration male/lineated . . . Name, name, leave names on everything, on every physical abutment, leave behind one's father's name, the names of other men, the names of absent and abstract/ ideal women (88). She goes on to note that, long before the explorers ever existed, some forty-two hundred years ago, "hunting bands roamed beside the inlets and fjords of Hazen Plateau. They had a name for Elles- mere. You are sure of that" (98). Ironically, the narrator's awareness of the existence of this eclipsed name does not prevent her from describing the island as if these bands had never existed; for her, as it was for the explor- ers, the Arctic is imagined as a "tabula rasa."

While readers may be entranced by van Herk's imaginative fictions, myself included, some may wonder, and feminists, in particular, whether it is sound political strategy to champion invisibility and escape, and inscribe these subversive activities on the supposedly "blank great white page of the north." If feminists are going to claim a territory, why appropriate a site on the margins? Why not reinvent an urban space?

I am certainly not alone in raising these concerns; perhaps what I most admire about van Herk is that she wrestles with the problems raised by her own work. In her most recent collection of essays, *In Visible Ink: Crypto Frictions* (1991), a concerted effort has been made to rethink and resolve some of the more troubling issues which constellate around her previous representations of the north. In the first essay, discussing a trip which she took to the Arctic, the narrator once again champions the plea- sures associated with its supposed promise of escape and invisibility (8).[21] In this case, the notion of invisibility so prominent in her writing is subtly adjusted because, at the same time that the narrator becomes invisible, she acknowledges that she has, in fact, entered into an alternative lan- guage. In the journey referred to above, an Inuit guide leads her and addresses her in his language, Inuktitut. As the narrator explains, "He gives me *his* words, and thus names me, writes my invisible and unlan- guaged self into his archaeology. I am written, finally with that nomadic language" (10). This passage reveals an important change in van Herk's conception of the "northern." The text no longer drapes the Arctic in metaphors shaped solely by the desires of a Western feminist. Instead, the narrator modifies the familiar goal of becoming invisible and links it with the process of becoming *visible* in terms of another marginalized dis- course, here represented by Pijamini's "nomadic language."

On the whole, van Herk's fictions have been moving in a northerly direction and have tentatively begun to set themselves apart from tradi- tional, imperialist discourses—a direction which allows room for the per- ceptions of both self and other. With any luck, her works will prompt "explorers" from the south both to readjust their compasses and to recog- nize that some of the most exciting possibilities associated with the narra- tion of the north are bound up with the perceptions of people like Pijamini—people who read the "northern" as home.

NOTES AND WORKS CITED

1.   For a discussion of the northern, see Sherrill E. Grace's "Comparing Mythologies: Ideas of West and North" in *Borderlands: Essays in Canadian American Relations* (Toronto: ECW, 1991), 243–262; as well as her article "Western Myth and Northern History: The Plains Indians of Berger and Wiebe," *Great Plains Quarterly* 3.3 (1983):146–156. See also Robert Kroetsch's essay "The Canadian Writer and the American Literary Tradition," in *The Lovely Treachery of Words* (Toronto: Oxford University Press, 1989), 53–57. Francis W. Kaye's study, "The 49th Parallel and the 98th Meridian: Some Lines for Thought," *Mosaic* 14.2 (1981): 165–75 also outlines the perceived differences between Canadian and American fiction. Many thanks to Dr. Sherrill Grace for helping me to clarify van Herk's unusual treatment of the northern.

2.   In his book *Regeneration Through Violence* (Middletown, Conn.: Wesleyan UP 1973), 403–413, Richard Slotkin suggests that the hero of a western is typically a violent male, "whose courage, prowess, and intelligence are proven in a struggle for survival against the wilderness and the savages" (410). Leslie Fiedler makes a similar argument in *The Return of the Vanishing American* (New York: Stein and Day, 1968), 24. See also Wallace Stegner's view of the western hero in *The American West as Living Space* (Ann Arbor: University of Michigan Press, 1987), 74–81.

3.   This phrase is taken from Grace's essay "Western Myth and Northern History," 150.

4.   In her essay "Stranded Bestride in Canada," *World Literature Written in English* 24.1 (1984), 13, van Herk celebrates the liminal position of the Canadian writer. As she says, "We have been blessed with the quixotic need to assume such a range of identities and characters that we can never be fixed . . . we are nowhere and we are no one. It is true that sometimes we writers feel that we are caught in the unfortunate and ball breaking position of a person who has a foot in each territory. We *could* split up the middle and disintegrate. Still, the edge is a fine place to write from."

5.   As Annette Kolodny explains in her book *The Lay of the Land* (Chapel Hill, N.C.: University of North Carolina Press, 1975), since the pioneer period, the western landscape has been perceived in terms of a myth that identified the land as Woman—an empty, virginal space waiting to be colonized.

6.   My use of the word "imperialism" refers to Edward Said's definition in *Culture and Imperialism* (New York: Random House, 1994), as "the practice, the theory, and the attitudes of a dominating metropolitan centre ruling a distant territory" (9).

7.   van Herk, Aritha. *The Tent Peg.* Toronto: McClelland and Stewart-Bantam, 1981. Reprint, New Canadian Library N196, 1987.

8.   More specifically, J. L. battles the misogynist assistant party-chief, Jerome, who attempts to rape her. As Ian MacLaren points out in his essay, "A Charting of the van Herk Papers," in *The Aritha van Herk Papers: First Accession* (Calgary UP, 1987): xi-xlv, Jerome is faithful to "his saintly namesake, the Church Father whose legendary sarcasm and invective van Herk retells superbly . . ." (xxviii). Seen in this light, J. L.'s battle with Jerome supports Leslie Fiedler's view that, in the western, the hero's essential enemy may well be repressive forms of Christianity (141).

9.   Richard Slotkin also traces the way in which the hero in American fiction similarly betrays "the woods and its creatures . . . destroying what they had come to save . . ." (412–413). In his introduction to van Herk's papers, Ian MacLaren suggests that by participating in the staking, J. L. claims "a stake in the northern map of a hitherto unitary male discourse" (xxxi).

10.   van Herk, Aritha. *No Fixed Address: An Amorous Journey.* Toronto: McClelland and Stewart-Bantam, 1987.

11.   In this passage, the narrator combines a romantic perspective of the north with a view that portrays it as a land of opportunity. As Shelagh Grant notes in her essay

"Myths of the North in the Canadian Ethos," *The Northern Review* 3+4 (1989): 15–41, this seeming contradiction, which links "the lure of the wilderness and the vision of a settled north," was prominent in Canada in the 1940s (34–35).

12. Knud Rasmussen's claim that Greenland Eskimos had a right to hunt on Ellesmere Island because it was a "No-Man's Land" fuelled the government's concerns over Canada's sovereignty in the Arctic. Rasmussen's comment is cited on p. 6 in Shelagh Grant's study, "A Case of Compounded Error: The Inuit Resettlement Project, 1953, and the Government Response, 1990," *Northern Perspectives* 19.1 (1991): 3–29. Political scientist Oran Young suggests that the perception that the Arctic is an "empty stage" constitutes one of the dominant factors that has produced "an attitude of benign neglect toward the Arctic" (6). See his study *Arctic Politics: Conflict and Cooperation in the Circumpolar North* (Hanover, NH: University Press of New England, 1993), 6.

13. In his book *Places on the Margin: Alternative Geographies of Modernity* (London and New York: Routledge, 1991), Rob Shields also notes that the north is portrayed as a "masculine-gendered liminal zone of *rites de passage* and re-creative freedom and escape" (163) where "'civilised' social norms are suspended . . ." (194). Shield's view of fictional treatments of the north sheds light on van Herk's textual strategies and, in conjunction with this study, dismantles the standard critical opposition between the northern and the western.

14. This quotation, cited in Grant's essay, "A Case of Compounded Error," 10, is taken from a letter the secretary to the Cabinet wrote in January 1953 to the Minister of Citizenship and Immigration, requesting some form of customs and immigration control in the Arctic. For a thorough analysis of these concerns and the relocation project, see Grant's study. Note that Gerard Kenney's *Arctic Smoke and Mirrors* (Prescott, Ont.: Voyageur Publishing, 1994) presents a view of the relocation project which challenges Grant's perspective. My thanks to Dr. Graham Rowley (who was secretary of the advisory committee on Northern Development at the time of the relocations), for outlining the government's position and for recommending Kenney's book.

15. As Kenney explains, the case has involved "the Canadian Human Rights Commission, the Parliamentary Standing Committee on Aboriginal Affairs, the Royal Commission on Aboriginal Peoples, the Department of Indian Affairs and Northern Development and a number of Inuit organizations." Kenney goes on to lament that, in addition, a "half a dozen or more major reports have been written and the two sides are as polarized as ever" (139).

16. I must admit, I find it perplexing that Kenney, who seems to be arguing that sovereignty issues took a backseat to concerns about the welfare of the starving Inuit, asserts that, as a result of the relocation, there "would now be Canadian Inuit in the high Arctic to help with the police work of patrolling the North. No longer would [Henrey Larsen's] men be in the ridiculous position of using Greenland Inuit to protect Canadian game animals against unauthorized hunting including hunting by Greenland hunters" (35–36). The stress placed on the national identities of the participants—these are not Inuit, but *Canadian* Inuit—implies that sovereignty issues were very much at stake in the decision to move the Inuit to the far north.

17. van Herk, Aritha. *Places Far from Ellesmere: a geografictione.* Red Deer, Alta.: Red Deer College,

18. For information concerning the notion of "internal colonization" see Oran Young's *Arctic Politics*, 18–19.

19. In an article published in *Arctic Review* 10 (1993): 198–200, Patricia Robertson argues that this constant metaphorical treatment detracts from the text: "Too often . . . she uses images of landscape as reminders of Anna's 'imprisonment' in the novel, so that what is actually in front of her becomes merely a series of symbols" (200).

20. It is interesting to note that, although the narrator views her fellow travellers as outsiders: "The Yellowknife/Resolute plane full of Arctic adventurers and outfitters, strange southerners seeking something stranger. Tour groups, hiking and kayaking groups," she never puts herself in this category (84). She is even more contemptuous of the American missionaries who have come to the Arctic: "here to teach Sunday school—Christian Bible school?—to the Inuit children. You are unforgivably profane in light of what you read as pure stupidity. . . . The Inuit of Resolute need American Christian fundamentalist missionaries?" (85–86). Her anger is ironic because, while she is no missionary, she is certainly on a mission to save Tolstoy's heroine.
21. van Herk, Aritha. *In Visible Ink: Crypto-frictions.* The Writer as Critic Series: III. Edmonton: NeWest, 1991.

Gendering Northern Narrative

SHERRILL E. GRACE

> *The greatest deeds have always been accomplished in high latitudes, because the highest latitudes produce the greatest men.*
>
> CHARLES TUTTLE, *Our North Land, 1885.*

> *Out on the open ice, the Arctic temperature prods every nerve, every bone. A reminder of where I am, and that who I am does not matter a writ in this cryptically enduring world.*
>
> ARITHA VAN HERK, *In Visible Ink, 1991.*

I

When Zoom the cat knocks on the door of his friend Maria's Victorian mansion in the children's book *Zoom Away,* he is about to embark on an Arctic adventure.[1] As Maria tells him, Zoom's uncle, Captain Roy, has gone missing on a voyage to the North Pole, and Maria wants Zoom to help search for Uncle Roy and his Catship. Maria leads Zoom through her strange mansion where the air is very cold, snow drifts fill the corners, icicles hang "like teeth" from all the archways, and the halls are "carpeted with snow." As they go down the corridors, from room to room, the snow becomes deeper, howling wolves can be heard, and Maria must check her astrolabe before stopping for lunch in a room festooned in snow and icicles.

Finally, the two come to a "little" room where Zoom finds himself before a "little" door with the words "Northwest Passage" carved above it. When Maria opens the door, Zoom can hear the wind howling "louder and more ferocious than a pack of wolves." Nothing daunted, he dons his snow goggles, lights his lantern, and prepares to pass through the door to begin his expedition. There is only one problem: he will have to go alone because the "doorway [is] very small. Too small for Maria. 'I'll have to find a different way,' she said. 'I'll meet you on the other side'."

As one might expect in a delightful story for children, Zoom successfully negotiates the Northwest Passage to find himself at the North Pole. Throwing off his goggles in an excess of joy, he skates off across the Arctic Sea applauded by appreciative seals and birds—until he spies Uncle

Roy's three-masted Catship "stuck in the ice." The ship (like so many similar sailing vessels we've heard of) is beset and abandoned, but the good Captain has left a note, "To whom it may concern," explaining that he and the crew are heading south on an iceberg "in a merry mood" and will be back for the ship "when the ice melts."

But *where* is Maria? Zoom is now cold, tired, and lonely. His uncle has gone and Maria said she would meet him "on the other side" of that little door. Then suddenly, inexplicably, Maria appears with a sled made "out of two oars and some sailcloth." She tucks Zoom onto the sled, and four short lines later he wakes up before the fireplace in Maria's Victorian sitting room.

II

I have chosen to begin my exploration of gender in/of the North with Tim Wynne-Jones's *Zoom Away* for several reasons. It is a beautifully crafted narrative with wonderful illustrations by Eric Beddows, but it is also an historically resonant and explicitly gendered story about the North and about Arctic adventure. The issues I am particularly interested in here are right on the surface: Maria's house, through which we travel to reach that special "little" door, is exuberantly northern; its icicles, snow drifts, and wolves identify it as Canada, while Maria's map and Victorian furnishings signify a more symbolic, imaginative northern space. And although the adventure is Maria's idea and must begin on her home ground, so to speak, she cannot take the Northwest Passage to the Beaufort Sea. The Arctic adventure is only for Zoom—or for Captain Roy and his men. So while northern space itself is gendered feminine, as represented by Maria and her house, the acts of exploration, adventure, free movement in that space are exclusively masculine. Maria's role is to provide the space travelled through, to be the mediator between Zoom and his uncle/adventure, and to provide a safe, warm haven at the end.

The paradigm I have sketched here is in many ways familiar, and *Zoom Away* is another inscription of socially constructed/narrated gender identities that posit masculine as essentially active, feminine as essentially passive, masculine as distinct from and independent of nature, feminine as synonymous with nature. But further than that there is no need to go. Feminized nature in *Zoom Away* is as mysteriously benign as Maria herself, and Zoom is after all just a little cat. The story is useful, however, because it clearly demonstrates some important ways in which white, southern Canadians have constructed and gendered their representations of North. In the discussion that follows, I will pursue this representation by examining examples of plays, fiction, and visual art that resist the gendered categories we see in *Zoom Away*. In order to do that, however, I must begin by clarifying, first, what I am not looking at and, second, how I read the social semiotics of what I am calling the dominant masculinist tradition of Canadian northern narrative.

There are many things I cannot consider here because they are beyond the scope of this study or my expertise. I am not, for example, going to examine at length where or what "north" and "Arctic" are, nor am I going to explore in detail the gendering of the dominant discourse of North.[2] To do so would be to devote all my time and space to a discussion of the dominant, thereby leaving little room for the emerging counter-discourse. Most importantly, I am not examining *northern* artistic self-representation, and there is a wealth of such material: the music of Susan Aglukark, the Great Northern Arts Festival; Sedna myths and sculpture or the 1994 exhibition *Inuit Women Artists: Voices from Cape Dorset*; the stories of Markoosie and Ipellie or those of Michael Kusugak; métissage life writing or the poetry, prose and drama collected in *Writing North*.[3] What I will do is trace an emerging counter-discourse of southern representations of North and show how these re-negotiate and re-articulate the semiotics of gender and the conventions of northern narrative.

To say, as many have, that the north is a state of mind, is to speak as a southern Canadian who has never lived north of North Vancouver or North York, let alone, north of sixty, or as a southerner who has vacationed in, worked briefly in, and passed through the vast hinterland of taiga, tundra, and ice that stretches north of the industrial, urban, agricultural Canadian base line.[4] I speak as such a Canadian. To describe the North as a state of mind is to speak in metaphors, sometimes dismissive, sometimes romantic and mystic, sometimes terrifying and apocalyptic, and these metaphors have always done a lot of serious cultural work in Canada. As Carl Berger points out in his important essay "The True North Strong and Free," the images and rhetoric of "the north" constitute one of those central "myths and symbols [that] nourish and sustain the emotional taproot of nationalism, and impart to it an intellectual content which itself has an attractive power" (4).

For at least the last two hundred years, that northern taproot has nourished a complex, wide-spread "narrative of the nation" (Bhabha, 294) that sends up shoots "sudden as summer" (Scott, 58), that celebrates our landscape, that fills our airport gift shops with northern curios, that *explains* our oil and gas exploration, our military ventures (such as "Project Franklin" in 1967), our "tammarniit," and that has constructed the image of a distinctly Canadian identity comprising hardy, virile masculinity, intellectual, spiritual, and racial superiority (of white, northern European stock), and imperialist authority.[5] However, this northern narrative of nation, I would argue, is not a master-narrative in Lyotard's sense (although it is often wielded as if it were), so much as a discursive formation, and as such it is always open to change and always capable of resisting origins and subverting essentialist agendas.[6]

One of these sites of change and resistence is gender. As should already be apparent, I view gender (and other categories of identity such as class and ethnicity) as a social effect produced by and maintained in political and cultural intersections. In *Gender Trouble*, Judith Butler analyses the ways in which gender identity works/is used to instate an hegemony of normative, hierarchical, asymmetric binaries that validate and enforce a phallogocentric heterosexuality. However, she also demonstrates the underlying epistemological fallacy of such gendered "expressive" notions of "stable identity" and argues that "gender is an identity tenuously constituted in time, instituted in an exterior space through a *stylized repetition of acts*" (140). For Butler, in short, gender is "performative" (141), not pre-existent, fixed, or essential, and if we agree with her that gender is performative then we can see ourselves as always able, as "culturally enmired" subjects, to negotiate our gender relations (Butler, 143). One of the places to look for these negotiations—or re-negotiations—of gender is in that aspect of the discursive formation of North (and Canada) that emerges in northern narratives. By the term "narrative" I mean all those texts—visual art, films, plays, music, fiction, poetry, biography and autobiography, history, geography, ethnography, and so on—that produce culture and participate in (by constituting and re-constituting) discursive formations.

The gendering of the familiar, dominant northern narrative that I see replicated so clearly in *Zoom Away* has been with *us* for a long time. Carolyn Merchant traces the gendering of mother earth back to the Greeks, and she locates the modern politics of that gendering (as does Lisa Bloom) within a capitalist, mechanistic, scientific framework. The masculinist, imperialist ideology that emerged in the seventeenth century allowed western man to objectify the natural world and its resources as raw material without agency or purpose, except insofar as it could be controlled and exploited by civilization. When the natural world in Canada appeared to co-operate with this project, it was deemed to be benign—"Our Lady of the Snows" (Kipling, 148–149)—but when it appeared to resist it became the dangerous virago so dramatically evoked in the metaphors of Robert Service or Earle Birney, or the sexual challenge imaged by Don Gutteridge and J. Michael Yates, or the abstract female force described more conventionally by many explorers.[7]

Human agency (and with it power, freedom, individuality) has been constructed in northern narratives, and elsewhere, as exclusively male, aggressively heterosexual, and masculinist. From the nineteenth-century fur-trapping stories of Robert Ballantyne to Robert Kroetsch's *But We Are Exiles* (1965) and *Gone Indian* (1973) and Mordecai Richler's postmodern epic narrative of nation *Solomon Gursky Was Here* (1989), the north is figured as the place of male adventure, the space for testing and proving masculine identities, where sissies and wimps will be turned into real men or be destroyed, or be sent home/south to the women or the bottle.[8]

This masculinist paradigm is duplicated in the other arts: theatre, film, painting, and music. The northern symbolism of Herman Voaden's plays inscribes and naturalizes a familiar asymmetric binary: an essential masculinity is the transcendent force at one with the spiritual, mystic power of "the North"; women (as female characters or as a feminized nature) are essentialized as the passive element against which the masculine principle must assert and define itself.[9] A similar southern masculinist ideology is imposed on the Inuit in Hardin's *Esker Mike and His Wife Agiluk* (1973) and Peterson's *The Great Hunger* (1958), and it appears to be unironically reproduced by Gwendolyn MacEwen in her verse drama *Terror and Erebus*.[10]

Southern films about the north narrow and intensify, if anything, this already over-determined, gendered and hierarchized semiotic. Robert Flaherty's *Nanook of the North* (1922) is the classic, original example, made by the "father of documentary"; in it Flaherty imbricates race with gender to construct an image of the "ethnographic other" for the white, southern, masculinist gaze.[11] The very popular film *Never Cry Wolf* (1983) reinforces the same stereotypes of gender and race (although racial stereotyping is more complex here), thereby constructing the North as the idealized space for a solitary, boyish, white hero to become a man and conflating the uncorrupted Inuit "Other" with nature.[12] The film's concluding message, that to look is to destroy, comes too late—too late for the wolves, the Inuit, the environment—because we have already looked. Thanks to the supreme power of technology (here planes and film cameras), the innermost secrets of nature (most dramatically figured in our hero's entry into the wolf den) have been penetrated, indeed violated, and exposed fully to view. A similar apocalyptic, masculinist celebration of science and technology informs *Frozen in Time* (1987), both the book and the CBC "Nature of Things" documentary.[13]

But if there is any accuracy in the masculinist paradigm of northern narrative that I am sketching here, it should also be discernable in other, less representational, artistic forms. What about painting and music? Admittedly the ice is a little thinner here, the adventure a little more hazardous, but let me suggest a few avenues for exploration. Lawren Harris, of all the Group of Seven painters except Jackson, is the most closely identified with northern, even Arctic, adventure. He went farther north, more often, than the others, and his snow-capped peaks, abstracted northshore landscapes, and remote, pristine icebergs have become symbols of Canadian identity, keys to the Canadian spirit and imagination, icons of the idea of North. Moreover, Harris theorized the north; it was, for him, the "mystic North," the source of pure, transcendent, transfiguring power, subject only to the painter's dominating gaze and expressive palette.[14] It is also, I would argue, a phallogocentric power, represented in and by Harris's *natural* forms and spaces, which are always devoid of people, but full of phallic presence/logos. Compare, for example, *North Shore, Lake Superior* (1926) with *Winter Comes from the Arctic to the Temperate Zone* (1935–1937). As we know, this vision of the north has been enormously influential: Voaden adapted Harris canvasses (their forms and colour) in his lighting and sets; other painters (for example, W.P. Weston) have imitated the Harris landscape, and Toni Onley went so far as to follow literally in his footsteps (and those of Jackson), and to paint and write about his Arctic adventures. In *Onley's Arctic*, the artist self-consciously installs himself within the masculine genealogy of explorer-painters, including Harris and Jackson, that stretches back into the last century.[15]

Music, that most anti-representational of the sister arts, has also fallen under the spell of the North. For example, in the first part ("Blue Mountain") of his 1957–1958 three-part composition for Chamber Ensemble called *Images*, Harry Freedman has translated the "line, colour, and mood" of Harris's *Lake and Mountains* (1927) into the lines, registers, and tempi of music;[16] Glenn Gould invokes Harris and the Group in *The Idea of North* (a pivotal work for the gendering of North); and in *Music in the Cold* (1977), R. Murray Schafer advocates an aggressively masculinist, racist, colonialist project that replicates the arguments made by R.G. Haliburton in his 1869 lecture *The Men of the North and their Place in History*.[17] Haliburton assures his audiences and readers:

> A glance at the map of this continent, as well as the history of the past, will satisfy us that the peculiar characteristics of the New Dominion must ever be that it is a Northern country inhabited by the descendants of Northern races. (2)

Schafer tells us:

> The art of the North is the art of restraint.
> The art of the South is the art of excess.
> It is the soft art of dancing girls and of the slobber.
> Of necessity, conservation of energy begins in the North.
> It begins with lean stomach and the strong bow.
> Prodigality is centred in the South,
> and the waste of energy begins at the mouth.
> Some of this waste energy is called art.
> It is thought that warm climates are the best incubators of it. (65)

Haliburton's "Northern races" are, of course, northern European, and the heroes who will kindle nationalism and make it blaze forth "in the icy bosom of the frozen north" (2) are virile, heterosexual males. Schafer's northerners are similarly masculine and white, and the northern artist is male, "pure," solitary, "impassive"; "his" mind mirrors an empty wilderness and "his" "imagination howls with the wolves" (66).

III

The dominant discourse of the Canadian northern narrative, which has been primarily constructed by men for men, is at once masculinist and racist, and it has simultaneously served to reinforce by naturalizing, and to facilitate by empowering and rationalizing, the hegemony of the Canadian state. Inscribed within this narrative is a comprehensive set of binaries that are hierarchically gendered and, furthermore, code what Eve Kosofsky Sedgwick describes as the "homosocial desire" (4–5) that negotiates land, resources, territory, and local/hereditary inhabitants in an economy of exchange between men. But the apparently normative, univocal hegemonic power of this discourse is just that—*apparent.* As theorists like Edward Said, Homi K. Bhabha, Judith Butler, and V. Spike Peterson have demonstrated, gender, narrative, nations—like history itself—are "historically contingent way[s] of organizing human interaction" (Peterson, 241), and once we recognize them as such we are better able to hear the muted counter-discourses that are always there.

I believe that over the past decade, or so, a growing number of voices has emerged, each speaking in its own way, but all speaking against, in order to interpellate themselves and disrupt, the masculinist narrative of North that I have just outlined. Many examples come to mind, from the fiction of Paulette Jiles to the music of Alexina Louie.[18] Margaret Atwood has always targeted, with deadly precision, the "tension between subject and object" that constitutes and destroys *us* as pioneers, and in "The Age of Lead" she marks our refusal, until it is too late, to apply the lessons of the north (here Beechey Island) in downtown Toronto.[19] In the rich trajectory of his career, from *First and Vital Candle* (1966), through "The Naming of Albert Johnson" (1982) and *Playing Dead* (1989) to *A Discovery of Strangers* (1994), Rudy Wiebe has participated in both the replication of the dominant discourse and the disruption of its hegemony. But I would like to take my examples from other sites of resistance: plays by Wendy Lill and Geoff Kavanagh, fictions by Elizabeth Hay and Aritha van Herk, and visual art by Judith Currelly and Marlene Creates.

The subject of Lill's play *The Occupation of Heather Rose* is southern *representation* of the north and southern *construction* of a Canadian identity predicated upon the colonization of the north. Heather Rose is a young middle-class nurse, fresh out of nursing school and thoroughly conditioned by the "Florence Nightingale" ideal of service and the white man's burden. She arrives in a northern native community full of girlish enthusiasm, romantic dreams of adventure, and zealous paternalism: "Heh, look at me," she gloats upon her arrival in the float plane. "I've really done it! I'm *here*! In the middle of an adventure" (70).

Structurally, however, the play is a memory/monologue being re-told and re-lived from the shattered, angry perspective of a *dis*illusioned present. Nurse Rose's nursing station has been occupied by an old Indian woman who is waiting for a prosthesis (which the government is taking months to send); she has succumbed to the very evils and weaknesses she attributed to the natives and the "white trash" around her, and she has recognized herself, and what she stands for, as the problem. Played out face to face with an audience (presumably southern, urban, and largely white), Heather Rose's revelations become "our" self-representations; Heather anatomizes not only the sufferings caused by southern paternalism but the historically contingent processes by which the system is constructed and maintained. By parodying the familiar story and re-telling it in a female voice, this play about northern adventure looks south at the creators/perpetrators of the myth, undermines the binaries of gender, race, and narrative that we have been taught to see as essentially normative, and shows us a southern construction used to rationalize a complex oppression.[20]

Kavanagh's unpublished play *Ditch* (1994) takes the Franklin story and turns it inside out. The two characters in this play are sailors who are dying and have been abandoned at "the Boat Place" on King William Island when their companions returned to the ships. Kavanagh may have tinkered with the facts (and the flora and fauna), as we know them, but his chief transgression is to gender his dying men as gay. In the course of the play, the openly homosexual man gradually convinces his determinedly heterosexual companion to acknowledge his homosexual desires and to confirm them in words and gestures of human tenderness and love. Placed side by side with examples from the dominant discourse on Franklin, whether from Dickens's *The Frozen Deep* (1857) or *Solomon Gursky Was Here*, *Ditch* works to reveal the underlying homosocial desire repressed and channeled by obligatory heterosexuality, the blurred non-essentialist processes of gender formation, and the violent imperative to conquer and exploit that informs the disciplined, masculinist, military-style activity of Arctic exploration.[21]

As Harold Innis has told us, the Canada we know was founded on and developed by the fur trade *as a northern* nation under the paternal aegis of the Hudson's Bay Company. The beaver, as material base to an economic superstructure, as cultural metaphor, national icon, and sexist joke, informs the idea of Canada as a northern nation at every turn. In her remarkable hybrid narrative, *The Only Snow in Havana* (1992), Elizabeth Hay meditates upon the connection between snow and fur and the power vested in their conjunction to script and control our inner lives, our language, our stories (and history), and our national identity.

Through the process of her travels, she re-maps what we thought of as familiar territory (our geography and history) and deliberately, carefully opens up spaces for re-interpretation and re-articulation of the Canadian trade in fur. What she releases is a "body of words, a captive soul, a small bound tongue" (69) that can speak "the sound of snow" (69) and "the language of fur" (70) by *em/bodying* them. "Once I taped the sound of snow," she tells us:

> I held a microphone between my teeth and taped myself skiing across a lake. The sound was gravelled over by the rubbing of my parka and the clicking of my teeth.
>
> Now I keep writing feel for fell. Feel, fell, felt—a new conjunction in the language of fur. I touched fur, and the memory is as compressed and worn as felt, the texture of emotion, of felt things. (69–70)

Hay's new "language [of snow and] of fur" is hybrid; it enables her to feel/say/do many things. With it she can construct an identity and a place in history for Tookoolito (Hannah Ebierbing), Charles Hall's "Esquimaux" translator and, together with her husband and children, his loyal, ethnographic victim. "Hannah," Hay tells us, "was real snow," the page on which white, southern, masculine history wrote its glorification of Hall and erased the woman herself—silencing her voice, erasing her name, and refusing Hannah's request for her identity by labelling her "Esquimaux" instead of Inuit (65). With her new language, Hay can re-contextualize the great explorers and fur traders like Alexander Mackenzie, who exchanged a pair of scissors for a fur robe ("Europeans snipped the lives of everything they encountered," 51), or David Thompson, who erased his half-Cree wife from his *Travels* (116), but lamented at length the over-harvesting of beaver. "Such a female fate," Hay muses, "to be trapped by desire and worn as a fur coat" (170). With this language, Hay reminds us that in Canada, "Fur is what we negate. The animal" (120), but that really "to begin a northern story" is to begin with "something warm. Glenn Gould's hands in gloves even in summer" (27).

On her fourth and final geografictional site exploration in *Places Far from Ellesmere*, Aritha van Herk takes us to the place itself: North— "Ellesmere, woman as island" (77). Unlike Franklin, however, she carries only one book with her to this Arctic desert: Tolstoy's *Anna Karenina*. Why? Well, to release her—Anna—from the narrative clutches of her deadly masculinist construction. But why North, why take her *north*? The answer can be found, I think, in the dominant gendered discourse of North, in R. Murray Schafer's insistence that the north is only for men, that the south is good enough for dancing girls, effeminacy, shallow entertainment, and "the slobber." In going north with Anna, Aritha is invading the last frontier known to man, a frontier equated with Woman, but denied to women: "Terror of women=terror of the north. Lost in one frozen waste or another, lost to women or the wiles of Ellesmere" (123).

Ellesmere becomes for van Herk a site of reclamation, a feminine, natural space, and a name wrested from the nineteenth-century explorer/ colonizer, be *he* the Earl of Ellesmere, the "male/lineated" (88) cartographers, Earle Birney's "men who 'guard the floes that reach to the pole'" (89), or *Canada*. She stakes her claim to the island's happy, remote inaccessiblity in order to access the female desire and energy that are rightfully hers, that enable her to "*unread* Anna" (133) and to *re*write the northern of masculine desire for adventure, domination, and death as the northerne of feminine desire for experience, co-existence, and rebirth.

In *Places Far from Ellesmere* van Herk turns the tables on the male adventurer/author/narrator by re-place-ing him, but that replacing is not so much an erasure—she does not simply excise him from history or murder him by story in a manoeuvre of reverse sexism—as an opening up of fiction and geography to another discourse, a double-voiced discourse that is personal, angry, witty, subversive, and celebratory. What it celebrates is its own ability to *imagine* and *construct* woman as Ellesmere and on Ellesmere, free to move about Ellesmere and, thus, able to free Anna—all women—from the essentialist heterosexuality (which invites, but punishes female adulterers) of patriarchal binaries. Anna (and Aritha) go north to reclaim themselves.

My last two examples of resistance and rescription of the northern narrative are from the visual arts. Judith Currelly is a painter and a bush pilot working in the western Arctic; Marlene Creates is a photographer and installation artist from Newfoundland whose work, whether based in Labrador, Great Britain, Vancouver Island, or the shores of Lake Nipissing, is about the land. Both women have actually gone north, and both are working within/against a Canadian tradition of landscape art.[22] Despite profound and crucial differences in their choice of media and presentation, both artists, like Hay and van Herk, are teaching us a new language with which to unlearn the masculinist narrative so forcefully contructed by Harris and the Group.

It is no accident, I suspect, that these artists are women: where Toni Onley (or more recently, Vincent Sheridan) goes North to follow in the footsteps of Franklin, Stan Rogers, and Harris, and Allen Smutylo goes North to seek balance and structure in an empty, pristine, essentially "other" Arctic world, Currelly and Creates go north to *re*present humans and animals living within, fully integrated with, the natural landscape.[23] The fundamental masculinist binaries of nature/culture, female/male simply do not apply in their work. Currelly describes her painting as coming "from my involvement with 'wild places' ... about experiencing the interaction and interdependance between human beings and their environment ... about knowing through touch, smell, feel, and through the energy generated by physical presence" (Artist's Statement). Creates explains that her work is inspired by "the relationship between human experience and the landscape" (*Distance*, 15); it is "about places and paths: absence and presence, leaving and arriving, identification and dislocation" (*Landworks*, 18).

Most of Currelly's northern works are large, individual oil paintings on wood; a few are triptychs or multiple, connected constructions of near mural size. All have a strong narrative quality in that they animate and people the landscape, filling it with presence and story. What at first glance may appear to be a barren, empty terrain of stone and tundra is, on closer inspection, marked with the signs of its inhabitants. Both *Caribou Tracks* (1993) and *Phantom Herd* (1993), which are typical of her most recent work, present a land suffused with warmth and filled with present and remembered life. *Earth's Secrets* (1995), reproduced on the cover of this volume, rejects the superficial visual and narrative clichés of empty barrenness to represent the wealth of human and animal story contained within the north. In this large work (37 x 84 3/4 inches), the flat landscape, painted in rich, glowing orange tones, cracks open to reveal layers of animal and human life inscribed (literally—on the surface of the wood) within its depths. This charcoal grey opening moves into the picture plane, twisting and narrowing as it welcomes us into the waiting, distant hills.

Whether consciously or not, in this painting Currelly is responding to the masculine, empty iciness of a work like *Lake and Mountains* by reversing, contra-dicting it: this is neither Harris's blue-grey "mystic north," an idealized refuge for the injured, urban spirit or the male ego, nor a romaticized, ahistorical virgin territory with the occasional primitive "Other." It is a "home," and Currelly insists that we see it as such. To do otherwise is to indulge in what she describes as the "dangerous and ultimately destructive" essentializing binaries of "patriarchal culture" that oblige us to ignore the personal and global interdependency necessary for our survival. Currelly rejects the notion that the North is a state of mind:

> When people live in 'sparsely settled areas', the living land is not just an idea or a primal memory—nor is it 'Wilderness'. It is familiar and real, a functioning ecosystem of which we ... are a part. ...
> I want my work to communicate this [osmotic awareness and connection] and to challenge the patriarchal concepts of 'man's' nature and 'man's' universe. (Artist's statement)

In *The Distance between Two Points is Measured in Memories, Labrador 1988*, Marlene Creates has created a series of assemblages with five elements: in a row on the wall there is a black-and-white photograph of a person sitting inside his or her home, then a hand-drawn "memory map," then a printed transcription from an oral story by the subject, and then a black and white photograph of the geographical site described in the person's map and text. On the floor, beneath thirteen of the eighteen assemblages, sit actual physical objects—a piece of wood, a stone, a square of blackberry sod—from the remembered places described in the texts.

Moving from one assemblage to another, the gallery visitor is invited to participate in and share the eighteen human stories and the artist's exploration of human relationship to the land. Each assemblage is subtle, complex, contradictory, and thoroughly dialogised; each suggests a mutual interaction and marking of the land by people, but also of the people by the land, and the assemblages map those marks or traces. As a series the assemblages re-duplicate, replicate, and reiterate each other while preserving differences; they interrogate and interact with each other and the viewer to construct a highly nuanced, often ironic, experiential and interpretive process. Just the activity of moving close to see detail or to read and moving back to see the larger contiguities involves us and challenges our expectations and assumptions about art and life. And shifting from portrait to landscape photograph, from verbal text to cartography, dislodges our essentialist categories, our urge to classify and control, to keep things like moss, stones, tundra, or drift wood (not to say words, maps, and pictures) in their proper places.

Art historians would call this type of work "Land Art" or "Art in the Land," but the best theoretical term I can imagine for *The Distance between Two Points Is Measured in Memories* (the title says it all) is Bakhtin's concept of the "chronotope."[24] Creates, it seems to me, has reconstituted the co-ordinates of time and place, history and geography, so that we must register them together, as inseparable forces that inform each other, rather than as separate disciplines or categories for the control and domination of culture and nature. Her refusal of binaries recurs in all aspects of the work: sophisticated technology (the camera) sits side by side with simple hand-drawing; private interiors are juxtaposed with the open spaces of taiga, tundra, and water; constructed artefacts hover above (but are, in a paradoxical sense, rooted in/by) natural artefacts.

Perhaps most significantly, these heterogeneous, dialogic images give voice to men and women of Inuit, Naskapi Innu, and Euro-Canadian settler origins, thereby reminding us that, like the land itself, the people are heterogeneous, not homogeneous. The "unity" of the work exists in its meticulously iterated and sustained narrative differences and its insistence upon our connection, through memory, with the world. Like Currelly, Creates believes that,

the ideological distinctions we (western industrial society) have made between nature and culture have separated us from the non-human part of the world, reinforcing the idea that nature exists

separate from us ... [and] that there needs to be a re-connection
between what is experienced as culture and ... nature. (15)

IV

If it is appropriate to describe the dominant narrative of north as masculinist, then *is* it equally appropriate to call the alternative narrative (or
counter-discourse) that I have just traced feminist? These labels do not, of
course, identify or delimit all that could be said about either, but they are,
I suggest, useful starting points. There are problems, however, with this
terminology. To oppose "masculinist" and "feminist"—as ecofeminism
often does, and as Bloom implicitly does in *Gender on Ice*—is to run the
risk of merely replicating the old binaries, of lapsing back into an essen-
tialism that classifies masculinist as essentially bad and feminist as essentially good.[25] Moreover, to label the counter-narrative of North "feminist"
is to insist upon a position of extreme vulnerability because, as we know,
that narrative, which must co-exist with, live alongside, to some degree
articulate itself in and by re-articulating the dominant narrative, is always
open to reinscription within the masculinist story. Such reinscription
reads the feminist northern as a superficial, emasculating, feminization of
the North, a turning—to adapt Schafer's rhetoric—of North into South,
of virility into "the Slobber." Are women inevitably trapped by this binary,
excluded, like Maria, from ever taking the Northwest Passage? Must we
either accept our exclusion or disguise ourselves as little cats in order to
slip through the door and infiltrate that world of masculine adventure? Or
can we, following Butler, perform our own escape from such asymmetric,
gendered categories? Are there other terms that better describe the Canadian counter-discourse of North?

To date, the dominant narrative has been (and continues to be)
constructed by southern, Euro-Canadian men (exceptions like MacEwen
and K. M. Graham prove the rule), while the narratives of counter-discourse are being articulated, to the best of my knowledge, *primarily* by
women. But my analysis of the gender of northern narratives far exceeds
the biology or sexual orientation of the artist. Moreover, the newly emergent northern discourse refuses the monologic hegemony of the masculinist story: by its very nature, which means its very construction, it is
heterogeneous, inclusive, dialogic; it gives voice to a range of genders, ethnic identities, classes, and landscapes; it speaks from the margins of the
nation, and employs a variety of strategies to interpolate its message into
—and thereby, to decentre and dis-place—our idea of *the* true north
strong and free. It is "liminalist" and "carnivalesque."[26]

The works I have examined critique and undermine binaries,
especially that central one of nature/culture. They foreground their own

construction and their own processes of representation; they interrogate official history, forcing it to make room for previously silenced and excluded stories; they re-map our geography by embodying it, moving it from a totalizing, abstract cartography to a lived, relational topography. They rewrite traditional masculinist genealogy (what van Herk calls the "male/lineated" image of the world), by opening up the incomplete stories of Mackenzie, Thompson, and Franklin, by rescripting Tolstoy, by reimagining the interrelationship of nature and culture, men and women. In the place of a monologic male/lineated/narrated world, they offer us a complex variety of gendered possibilities, multiple voices and perspectives, re-accentuated texts whose power derives from hybridity—even in a seemingly single-voiced, tightly unified memory/monologue play like *The Occupation of Heather Rose*.

Above all, this emerging discourse de-romanticizes the very concept of northern adventure as a physical, spiritual, and artistic challenge available only to real men. Indeed, northern adventure, at least as it has been constructed by the dominant discourse, is viewed in this counter-discourse as a dangerous paradigm that rationalizes racist and sexist behaviour, validates the central authority of the nation state, and facilitates the destruction of the ecosystem of which we are all a part. In none of the texts that I have considered does the artist advocate that we all become Grey Owls or Anahareos converted to a naive, individualistic version of conservation, but throughout this discourse we are reminded that northern narrative, like northern adventure, insists upon our participation in the story and our responsibility for its next chapters.

NOTES

I would like to thank Peter Dickinson, Stefan Haag, and Gabriele Helms, and the graduate students in my "Representing North" seminars for their practical help and intellectual debate.

1. *Zoom Away* is a short unpaginated children's book with alternate full-page illustrations and verbal text.

2. I take up the question of where or what North is, or has been represented as, in my book-in-progress *Canada and the Idea of North*. For discussions of the question see Grant and Hamelin. For the purposes of this article, the Arctic is defined as a discursive space within the larger discursive formation of North.

3. In addition to the work of Markoosie, Ipellie, Kusugak, and the volume *Writing North*, see Petrone, Pitseolak, and the interdisciplinary journal *Northern Review*.

4. Perhaps the best known expression of the idea that the north is a state of mind is Glenn Gould's *The Idea of North*, but many other Canadians have referred to the northerly regions of the country, as well as to the Arctic, in this, or similar, metaphoric ways.

5. For a discussion of "Project Franklin," see Wonders, and for a discussion of the "tammarniit" of Inuit relocation, see Tester and Kulchyski.

6.   In developing my theoretical understanding of narratives of north and my methodological approach to the many different texts considered in this study, I have drawn upon Said's concepts of staging and specularizing the "other," Lyotard's discussion of narrative, Bhabha's discussion of narrations of nation, and Butler's formulation of "performative" gender. However, central to my thinking on these issues are Foucault's model of discursive formation and Bakhtin's concepts of dialogism, chronotope (which helps to explain how the counter-discourse I outline in part III actually works), and the carnivalesque.

7.   A consideration of gender at the level of imagery, rhetoric, or specific locutions in poetry and prose cannot be undertaken here, and one must be cautious about generalizations. In *Strange Things*, Atwood traces a female northern landscape through the work of many male writers, but she notes that when the writer is a woman things get more complex: with female characters the landscape is neuter but with male characters it is female (108), sometimes "with a vengeance" (114). However, for some specific examples of gendered northern landscapes and adventures see: Robert Service's "The Law of the Yukon" where the Yukon is personified as a potentially fruitful woman who waits for strong men to "win" and "bless" her; Earle Birney's "madcap virgin/mother of ice" or, still farther north, the Arctic "Hoarding her cold passion" in "The Mammoth Corridors" (32–33), or his men—remembered by van Herk—who "guard the floes that reach to the Pole" (21); J. Michael Yates's escape from women to the woman of the North with whom he unites towards the end of his meditations. Exploration narratives (including Mowat's top of the world trilogy) frequently speak of the Arctic as a space to be penetrated and as Mother Earth, who is barren or fertile, depending on the latitude. In his journal, Robert Hood describes his relationship to the Pasquia Hills, north-east of Lake Winnipeg, in gender specific terms: "The gifts of nature are disregarded and undervalued till they are withdrawn, and in the hideous regions of the Arctic zone, she would make a convert of him for whom the gardens of Europe had no charms" (64).

8.   For a discussion of Ballantyne's boys' stories see Phillips. In Jeffrey's play *Who Look in Stove*, a reenacting of the John Hornby story, the men die, and in *Solomon Gursky Was Here*, Moses Berger is a confirmed alcoholic, though it is Solomon, as much as the north, that drives him to drink. I have examined Kroetsch's gendered construction of North and his intertextual use of Grey Owl as a northern trope in "Robert Kroetsch and the Semiotics of North."

9.   This is particularly true in Voaden's symphonic expressionist play *Northern Song*, but it is true more generally of his work. See my discussion of Voaden in *Regression and Apocalypse*, 119–129.

10.   MacEwen's play is a complex retelling of the Franklin disaster, and while her all male cast describes the Arctic as a destructive female whose explicitly sexual embrace will crush any man who attempts to penetrate her—and explorers' narratives often speak of "penetration"—one *might* argue that the play constructs the Europeans as victims of their own narrative desire and narrators of their own fate.

11.   I discuss Flaherty's film in "Exploration as Construction: Robert Flaherty and *Nanook of the North.*" It is worth noting here that, in *Kabloonak*, the 1994 Canada-France co-production about Flaherty and his film, gender and race are essentialized in more overt, sensational ways than in *Nanook*.

12.   The semiotics of *Never Cry Wolf* are more ambiguous and complex than this brief summary suggests. In a remarkable scene, Tyler runs naked with a herd of caribou as if to illustrate his awareness of his place within nature, and the young Inuk betrays the wolves, literally selling them out to Rosie the pilot, in order to earn enough money for a set of false teeth. The Inuk elder, however, is portrayed stereotypically as silent, wise, cheerful, and even childlike, and as able to appear or disappear at will within the landscape.

13. The narrative and epistemological climax towards which *Frozen in Time* moves is apocalyptic revelation: a revelation of the faces of the frozen corpses, made especially significant for one member of the research team who is related to one of the dead men, but also profoundly staged for reader and viewer; and a revelation, through technology and science, of the Truth about the fate of the Franklin expedition. Nothing, not even permafrost and time, is impenetrable, undiscoverable; no natural mystery can elude the power of science and technology to identify origins and control matter.

14. See Roald Nasgaard's *The Mystic North.* Harris describes the significance of the North, as he saw it, in notebooks and poems; see *Lawren Harris,* 7, 11, 39, 45, 61.

15. I have discussed the influence of Harris, the Group of Seven, and Frederick B. Housser on Voaden in *Regression and Apocalypse,* 122–23. As Ian Thom has noted (*Weston,* 7), Lawren Harris and Fred Varley should be seen as part of the landscape influences (together with Carr) on the B.C. painter, his claims to the contrary notwithstanding. The influence of Harris seems obvious in Weston's *The Far Place* (1936) and *Mt Whitecap* (1954). But it is Onley who makes the masculine genealogy of northern adventure and painting unequivocal in his reiteration of the names of all the explorers and artists who preceded him. For Onley, the Arctic is made sacred by the daring of these men, and nothing less than Canadian identity is created by their presence.

16. I would like to thank the University of Victoria musicologist Joan Backus for her help with Freedman's *Images* and for sharing with me her thoughts on music and painting. She also brought to my attention David Parsons's MA thesis "Landscape Imagery in Canadian Music" (1987) in which Parsons discusses a wide range of compositions inspired by the North.

17. Haliburton is, so to speak, the tip of the iceberg and Canada's answer to Frederick Jackson Turner. His basic premise, usually gender inflected if not overtly racist, is repeated by generations of eminent Canadian historians from W. L. Morton to Harold Innis. See the essays in Wonders's *Canada's Changing North* and Berger's critical assessment of this nationalist historiography. To give Haliburton his due, he argues that, unlike the southern man who demonstrates a general lack of chivalry, a northern man respects his northern woman who will live and die at his side!

18. In *North Spirit,* Jiles re-writes the story of the southerner who goes north for adventure to demonstrate the dependence of the white person on the native and to explore the rich culture of the northern world, and Alexina Louie captures her sense of north in *Winter Music.*

19. I have discussed Atwood's story and her use of *Frozen in Time* in "'Franklin Lives': Atwood's Northern Ghosts," *Various Atwoods,* 146–166.

20. For a discussion of the play and its representation of Woman-Nurse-North, see Grace and Helms.

21. *Ditch* premiered at the 1993 SummerWorks Festival and was remounted at Tarragon's Extra Space Theatre in January 1994. Both productions were directed by Colleen Williams, and I would like to thank Williams and Kavanagh for sending me a typescript of this hitherto unpublished play. I have discussed *Ditch* in "Reinventing Franklin."

22. As I have suggested above, I see this tradition of Canadian landscape art as predominantly male and masculinist (Emily Carr being an interesting exception). Its masculinist qualities, most dramatically imaged by Harris, include its emptiness, its formal abstraction, and its appeal to mystic transcendent meaning, or Logos.

23. In his most recent Arctic work from 1994, Smutylo has included images of whales and people, thereby suggesting his growing interest in the interaction of humans with their environment.

24. Bakhtin discusses chronotopes, with a glance at Lessing's *Laocoön* (where the sister arts were defined as primarily temporal or spatial), in his third essay in *The Dialogic*

Imagination. By "chronotope" he means "the intrinsic connectedness of temporal and spatial relationships" (84), and he identifies two chronotopes—the road and the threshold—as especially significant in narrative (250), although both "art and literature are shot through with *chronotopic values*" (243). Creates's narrative deploys both of these key chronotopes: the five images constitute stops along the road of time/life, and the entry into domestic interiors, and the reproduction of "memory maps" are all instances of their conjunction. In her essay on Creates in *The Distance Between Two Points* (53), Jacqueline Fry discusses the concept of "Land Art." Currelly's *Earth's Secrets* is also arguably, chronotopic, although it is less obviously narrative than some of her other work. The central image of the crevice/crevass invokes a road and a threshold. I would like to thank both Creates and Currelly for their assistance and the Diane Farris Gallery for images of Currelly's work. Very special thanks to Currelly for permission to reproduce *Earth's Secret* (see cover).

25. For a discussion of this essentialist game and the debates surrounding "feminization" see Bowlby.

26. In coining the term "liminalist" here, I am thinking of Bhabha's discussion of the function of "*internal* liminality that provides a place from which to speak both of, and as, the minority, the exilic, the marginal, and the emergent" (300) as these voices seek to articulate "counter-narratives of the nation that continually evoke and erase its totalizing boundaries" (300). Carnivalesque is, of course, Bakhtin's term for textual *and social* strategies for abolishing hierarchies and celebrating marginality and otherness.

WORKS CITED AND CONSULTED

Atwood, Margaret. *Strange Things: The Malevolent North in Canadian Literature.* Oxford: Clarendon Press, 1995.

Bakhtin, M. M. *The Dialogic Imagination: Four Essays,* ed. Michael Holquist, trans. Holquist and Caryl Emerson. Austin: University of Texas Press, 1981.

Beattie, Owen and John Geiger. *Frozen in Time: Unlocking the Secrets of the Doomed 1845 Arctic Expedition.* New York: Plume, 1987.

Berger, Carl. "The True North Strong and Free." *Nationalism in Canada,* ed. Peter Russell. Toronto: McGraw-Hill, 1966. 3–26.

Bhabha, Homi K., ed. *Nation and Narration.* London: Routledge, 1990.

Birney, Earle. *The Mammoth Corridors.* Okemos, Michigan: Stone Press, 1980.

Bloom, Lisa. *Gender On Ice: American Ideologies of Polar Expeditions.* Minneapolis: University of Minnesota Press, 1993.

Bowlby, Rachel. "Breakfast in America—Uncle Tom's cultural his-tories." *Nation and Narration.* 197–212.

Brannan, Robert Louis, ed. *Under the Management of Mr Charles Dickens: His Production of 'The Frozen Deep'.* New York: Cornell University Press, 1966.

Butler, Judith. *Gender Trouble: Feminism and the Subversion of Identity.* New York: Routledge, 1990.

Creates, Marlene. *The Distance between Two Points Is Measured in Memories, Labrador 1988.* North Vancouver: Presentation House Gallery, 1990.

———. *Marlene Creates: Landworks 1979–1991.* Cat., Art Gallery, Memorial University of Newfoundland. St. John's Newfoundland, 1993.

Currelly, Judith. "Artist's Statement." 1990.

Foucault, Michel. *The Archeology of Knowledge,* trans. A. M. Sheridan Smith. London: Routledge, 1972.

Freedman, Harry. *Images.* 1958. Toronto: BMI Canada Ltd., 1960.

Fry, Jacqueline. "Essay," in Creates, *The Distance between Two Points Is Measured in Memories.*

Gould, Glenn. *The Idea of North.* 1967. *Glenn Gould's Solitude Trilogy: Three Sound Documentaries.* CBC Records, 1992.

Grace, Sherrill E. "Exploration as Construction: Robert Flaherty and *Nanook of the North." Essays on Canadian Writing.* Forthcoming.

———. "'Franklin Lives': Atwood's Northern Ghosts." *Various Atwoods: Essays on the Later Poems, Short Fictions, and Novels,* ed. Lorraine York. Toronto: Anansi, 1995.

———. *Regression and Apocalypse: Studies in North American Literary Expressionism.* Toronto: University of Toronto Press, 1989.

———. "Re-inventing Franklin." *Canadian Review of Comparative Literature* 22. 3–4 (1995): 707–725.

———. "Robert Kroetsch and the Semiotics of North." *Open Letter* 5/6 (1996): 13–24.

Grace, Sherrill and Gabriele Helms. "Dismantling Southern Repre-sentation: *The Occupation of Heather Rose.*" Paper presented at "Northern Parallels," 4th Circumpolar Universities Cooperative Conference, February 1995.

Grant, S. D. "Myths of the North in the Canadian Ethos." *Northern Review* (Summer/ Winter 1989): 15–41.

Gutteridge, Don. *The Quest for North: Coppermine.* Ottawa: Oberon, 1973.

Haliburton, R. G. *The Men of the North and their Place in History. A Lecture.* Montreal: John Lovell, 1869.

Hamelin, Louis-Edmond. *The Canadian North and its Conceptual Referents.* Ottawa: Ministry of Supply and Services Canada, 1988.

Hardin, Herschel. *Esker Mike and his Wife Agiluk.* Vancouver: Talonbooks, 1973.

Hay, Elizabeth. *The Only Snow in Havana.* Dunvegan, Ontario: Cormorant Books, 1992.

Houston, C. Stuart, ed. *To the Arctic by Canoe, 1819–1821: The Journal and Paintings of Robert Hood.* Kingston: McGill-Queen's University Press, 1974.

Innis, Harold. *The Fur Trade in Canada: An Introduction to Canadian Economic History.* Toronto: University of Toronto Press, 1970.

Ipellie, Alootook. *Arctic Dreams and Nightmares.* Penticton, B.C.: Theytus Books, 1993.

Jackson, Christopher. *Lawren Harris. North By West: The Arctic and Rocky Mountain Paintings of Lawren Harris, 1924–1931.* Calgary: Glenbow Museum, 1991.

Jeffery, Lawrence. *Who Look in Stove.* Toronto: Exile Editions, 1993.

Jiles, Paulette. *North Spirit: Travels Among the Cree and Ojibway Nations and their Star Maps.* Toronto: Doubleday, 1995.

Kabloonak. 1994. Director: Charles Massot.

Kavanagh, Geoff. *Ditch.* 1993. Unpublished script.

Kipling, Rudyard. "Our Lady of the Snows" (1897), in *The Complete Verse.* London: Kyle Cethie, 1990.

Kusugak, Michael Arvaarluk and Vladyana Krykorka. *Hide and Sneak.* Toronto: Annick Press, 1992.

Lawren Harris, ed. Bess Harris and R. G. P. Colgrove. Toronto: Macmillan, 1969.

Lill, Wendy. *The Occupation of Heather Rose,* in *NeWest Plays by Women.* Eds. Diane Bessai and Don Kerr. Edmonton: NeWest Press, 1987.

Louie, Alexina. *Winter Music.* Chamber Music for Eleven Instruments, 1989.

Lyotard, Jean-Francois. *The Postmodern Condition: A Report on Knowledge,* trans. Geoff Bennington and Brian Massumi. Minneapolis: University of Minneapolis Press, 1984.

MacEwen, Gwendolyn. *Terror and Erebus. Tamarack Review* (October 1974): 5–22.

Markoosie. *Harpoon of the Hunter.* Kingston: McGill-Queen's University Press, 1970.

Merchant, Carolyn. *The Death of Nature: Women, Ecology, and the Scientific Revolution.* New York: Harper, 1980.

————. *Ecological Revolutions: Nature, Gender, and Science in New England.* Chapel Hill: University of North Carolina Press, 1989.

Morton, W.L. "The North in Canadian History." *North* VII.i (1960): 26–29.

Mowat, Farley. *Canada's North.* Toronto: McLelland and Stewart, 1969.

————. *The Snow Walker.* Toronto: McLelland and Stewart, 1975.

Never Cry Wolf. 1983. Director: Carroll Ballard.

Northern Review: A Multidisciplinary Journal of the Arts and Social Sciences of the North. Whitehorse: Yukon College.

Onley, Toni. *Onley's Arctic: Diaries and Paintings of the High Arctic.* Vancouver: Douglas and McIntyre, 1989.

Parsons, David. "Landscape Imagery in Canadian Music," MA Thesis, Carlton University, 1987.

Peter Pitseolak (1902–1973): Inuit Historian of Seekooseelak, ed. David Bellman. Montreal: McCord Museum, 1980.

Peterson, Leonard. *The Great Hunger.* Agincourt: Book Society of Canada, 1967.

Peterson, V. Spike. "Disciplining Practiced/Practices: Gendered States and Politics." *Knowledges: Historical and Critical Studies in Disciplinarity,* ed. Ellen Messer-Davidow, David R. Shumway, and David J. Sylvan. Charlottsville: University Press of Virginia, 1993. 243–267.

Petrone, Penny, ed. *Northern Voices: Inuit Writing in English.* Toronto: University of Toronto Press, 1988.

Phillips, Richard. "A Space of Boyish Men and Manly Boys: The Canadian North West in Robert Ballantyne's Adventure Stories." *Essays in Canadian Writing.* Forthcoming.

Pickthall, Marjorie. "Canada's Century." *The Complete Poems of Marjorie Pickthall.* Toronto: McClelland and Stewart, 1936.

Purdy, Al. *North of Summer: Poems from Baffin Island.* Toronto: McLelland and Stewart, 1967.

Richler, Mordecai. *Solomon Gursky Was Here.* London: Penguin, 1989.

Said, Edward. *Orientalism.* New York: Random House, 1978.

Schafer, R. Murray. *Music in the Cold* (1977). Indian River, Ont.: Arcana Editions, 1984.

Scott, F. R. "Laurentian Shield," in *The Collected Poems of F.R. Scott.* Toronto: McLelland and Stewart, 1981.

Sedgwick, Eve Kosofsky. *Between Men: English Literature and Male Homosocial Desire.* New York: Columbia University Press, 1985.

Tester, Frank and Peter Kulchyski. *Tammarniit (Mistakes): Inuit Relocation in the Eastern Arctic, 1939–63.* Vancouver: University of British Columbia Press, 1994.

Thom, Ian. *W.P. Weston.* Vancouver: Heffel Gallery Ltd., 1991.

van Herk, Aritha. *In Visible Ink (crypto-frictions).* Edmonton: NeWest Press, 1991.

————. *Places Far from Ellesmere.* Red Deer: Red Deer College Press, 1990.

Voaden, Herman. *A Vision of Canada: Herman Voaden's Dramatic Works, 1928–1945,* ed. Anton Wagner. Toronto: Simon and Pierre, 1993.

Wiebe, Rudy. "The Naming of Albert Johnson," in *The Angel of the Tar Sands and Other Stories.* Toronto: McLelland and Stewart, 1982. 88–99.

————. *Playing Dead: A Contemplation Concerning the Arctic.* Edmonton: NeWest, 1989.

Wonders, William C., ed. *Canada's Changing North.* Toronto: McLelland and Stewart, 1971.

————. "Search for Franklin." *Canadian Geographical Journal* 76.4 (1968): 116–127.

Writing North: An Anthology of Contemporary Yukon Writers, eds. Erling Friis-Baastad and Patricia Robertson. Whitehorse: Beluga Books, 1992.

Wynne-Jones, Tim and Eric Beddows. *Zoom Away.* Vancouver: Douglas and McIntyre, 1991.

"A Brave Boy's Story for Brave Boys": Adventure Narrative Engendering

RENÉE HULAN

Arctic adventure narratives contribute to a representation of the north which is, in the words of Hugh Brody, "the saga of a
few heroic individuals" (Brody, 17). Whether faced with the challenges of
endless possibility or intractable circumstance, the white, solitary, adventurous male hero thrives in this setting. In early exploration literature, this
figure enjoys an erotic embrace with the landscape as he follows rivers
ever deeper into his sublime, mother nature; later, he lives the masculine
fantasy of the American frontiersman, that solitary wood dweller Annette
Kolodny's research caught happily penetrating the virgin landscape (5).
While adult adventurers become these rugged individuals by defining
themselves outside social relations, adventure tales written for and about
boys construct rugged individuals through complex relations with men. In
order to peel away the layers of gender, social, and racial characteristics
informing these relations, this paper situates an adventure story based on
the life of an Inuit boy named Pomiuk within the paternalistic tradition of
"muscular Christianity" advocated by the Victorian Social Reform movement. Within this tradition, the discourses of medicine, gender, class, and
religion converge to convert, cure, or otherwise overcome difference, an
erasure necessary to colonial expansion.

In *Empire Boys: Adventures in a Man's World,* Joseph Bristow links the
popularity of heroic adventure at the end of the Victorian period to "a
number of shifts in attitude towards juvenile publishing and curriculum
design" (20–21), which emphasized the importance of turning boys into
good citizens of the British Empire (19).[1] Boys' literature of the late Victorian period was a prolific genre with a substantial audience, especially
for magazines like the influential *The Boy's Own Paper* , which had a circulation ranging from two-hundred thousand to one million copies (Dunae,

"Empire," 107; Drotner, 115). While its counterpart, *The Girl's Own Paper,* advised readers in matters of etiquette, health, work, and education, emphasizing "activities that were seen as necessary bulwarks against feminine dissipation and inactivity" (Drotner, 150), *The Boy's Own Paper* was filled with exploration and adventure in far-away lands. As literary representation engaged in "wider discussions of the moral and physical well-being of boys" (Bristow, 2), boys' magazines and novels engendered good citizens by promoting "wholesome adventure, cold baths and Christianity" (Moyles, 47). Education and Social Reform movements endorsed adventure narrative as a moral teacher: the education system added the *Empire Readers* series to the curriculum, and the Church formed organizations like the Religious Tract Society, which published the *Boy's Own Paper* (Bristow, 20–21). Adventure narratives set in Canada, in magazines like *The Boy's Own* or in novels like R. M. Ballantyne's *Ungava; or, A Tale of Esquimeaux-land* "fixed the Canadian north as a great stage for boy's adventures" (Waterston, 132) with the people inhabiting the territory, the Inuit, enhancing the scenery as guides or "Huskies," as "queer little men" or savages, and later as friends.[2]

Adventures from every corner of the British Empire represented masculine action and virtue and reflected the concerns British Social Reformers had about the education of boys. In Britain, Social Reform addressed the concerns about the education of boys by targeting the working-class boys who, like the working class generally, were "regarded as more primitive and in greater need of socialization into the dominant culture" (Slemon and Wallace, 12). The "rough lad," as the working-class boy was known, paradoxically embodied the romantic and primitive nature of boys admired by reformers as well as the potential danger of letting that nature run wild as "hooligans" (Koven, 374). Upper-class men tried to prevent hooliganism by founding boyss social and athletic clubs in working-class areas aimed at improving boys by establishing "vertical bonds of comradeship across class lines" (Koven, 365). Boys were malleable subjects who could transcend their social positions by becoming like their gentleman friends.

Social Reform was a movement based on cross-class companionship (Koven, 370), but its goals could be translated into cross-cultural and cross-racial contexts, too. Just as generational difference masked class difference between the British Social Reformers and their "rough lads" (Koven, 368), so missionaries could mask racial difference by establishing a paternal relationship with the colonized.

Pomiuk: A Waif of Labrador (1903), the book whose epigraph provides the title of this paper, tells the story of one such relationship between Doctor Wilfred Grenfell and a young patient who was one of the Inuit Labrador displayed at the Chicago World's Fair in 1893. The book's author, William Byron Forbush, had already published *The Boy Problem* (1901), a study that advocated athletics and friendship as key to boys' social development, when he turned his attention to Pomiuk's story in 1903. In *Pomiuk,* Forbush presents a story based on the exploits of real-life adventurers, a type of adventure made popular by boys' magazines: the hero is the doctor and missionary, Grenfell, who struggles against all odds in a harsh, exotic environment to rescue Pomiuk from physical and spiritual ill health.

The story of Grenfell's involvement with Pomiuk demonstrates how the goals and principles of "muscular Christianity" straddled Britain and North America at the turn of the century. At the time when Social Reform settlements were being established in London, Wilfred Grenfell was a medical student who emulated the Reformers he admired, including Charles Kingsley, by working as a Sunday school teacher and sporting club leader in the city's East End.[3] In Labrador, Grenfell continued the work of the Social Reform Movement by starting a social club, a foot-ball club, and a Scripture Union Society for the fishermen (Forbush, 69), and earning a reputation as "a heroic figure whose practical missionary work served as an example of how much difference an individual Christian could make to the world" (Rompkey, 193).

In America, as in Britain, adventure was "the energizing myth of empire" (*Great* , 4), and, as Martin Green argues, American adventure stories combined ideals of patriotism and manliness to prepare young men for the frontier (2). Such stories took their bearings from British adventures like *Waverley* and *Crusoe,* the stories of "the dream that made young Britons want to go out and spread the empire" (3). Although the stage for the adventure described in *Pomiuk* is the Canadian north, Forbush, an American, addresses American children with his book and dedicates it to Grenfell, a Briton. The dedication includes a photograph of Grenfell bearing the caption "A Christian Viking," a title which gives Grenfell's career the shape of the Viking adventures his pen traced in stories of Labrador such as his book *Vikings of To-Day.*[4]

According to Martin Green, adventures patterned on the sagas flourished at the turn of the century, illustrating the belief of one author that "English boys were too straightforward to like the Greek gods, while the Norse ones would appeal directly to their natural 'Teutonic' impulses" ("Adventurers," 83).[5] Arguing for the racial origin of the tradition, another Victorian author wrote: "The sagas reveal the characteristics of our branch of the Aryan race, especially the personal courage which is so superior to that of the Greek and Latin races, and which makes the Teutonic epics (whether the *Niebelungen Lied,* the *Morte d'Arthur,* or the *Njala*) much more inspiring than the *Iliad,* the *Odyssey,* or the *Aeneid"* ("Adventurers," 83). As imprecise in geographical terms as adventures tend to be, those inspired by the sagas evoke an Arctic environment as an appropriate setting for new sagas in which British characters display their Viking spirit and heritage. The Inuit, who act as representatives of racial difference, are caught up in Viking conquest.[6] In the story of *Pomiuk,* Grenfell's medical, religious, and social missions converge in this imperial project of imaginatively claiming the inhabitants of the land.

Cases like Pomiuk's offered men like Grenfell an opportunity to flex Christian muscle. In *Off the Rocks,* Grenfell describes coming upon the boy, whom he treated for a broken and diseased hip, in his tent in Labrador: "on the stones of the beach that served for a floor lay a naked boy of about eleven years, his long, jet black hair cut in a straight frieze across his forehead, his face drawn with pain and neglect, his large, deep, hazel eyes fixed wonderingly on us strangers" (Grenfell, *Off the Rocks,* 42). In this passage, Pomiuk is the object of pity and desire inspiring Grenfell's Christian charity.

Forbush's book, written as it was to educate boys in their Christian duties and gender roles, picks up this erotic content but focusses on the transformation from "lively young sportsman" to invalid, thus differentiating him from the vigorous doctor who rescues him (54). According to Forbush, the Inuit abandoned Pomiuk who was orphaned but healthy when he arrived at the Esquimaux Village at the Chicago World's Fair.[7] Forbush lays the blame for Pomiuk's injury on his guardian Kupah, calling it "probable that it was the roughness of Kupah which had broken the little boy's hip" (56–57). Implicating Kupah disperses any blame that might befall those who put Pomiuk and the others on display in Chicago;[8] moreover, Forbush considers Kupah to represent the yet unredeemed state of his race: "All these people are heathen, because they came from a part of Labrador which was farther north than any to which missionaries had ever gone" (56). The cruelty of the heathen contrasts with "the kind care of missionaries" (58), especially that of Dr. Grenfell, whom Forbush refers to as a friend "guided by God" to Pomiuk in his tent (60).

The medical dimension of Pomiuk's difference forms the basis of his relationship with Grenfell. To highlight it, Forbush's narrative contrasts the once healthy, active boy who delighted in those activities appropriate to boys—hunting, fishing, and sports (28–29) with the "Waif of Labrador" evoked in the title: crippled, bed-ridden, abandoned by his own people, awaiting the intervention of missionaries. As an invalid, he represents the "physical helplessness and moral courage" exemplified in suffering and Christian selflessness (Nelson, 98–99). The narrative aligns this physical infirmity with the supposed spiritual degeneracy of the Inuit, as Pomiuk's body and soul submit to medical intervention and religious conversion. The bond of friendship between the boy and Grenfell erases differences in age, race, and culture, replacing them gradually with similarities of gender and religion. Becoming like the "Christian Viking" who saved him effaces Pomiuk's Inuit identity, his racial difference. The boys reading Forbush's account are to identify with both examples, the missionary-doctor and the native convert and patient.

While receiving medical care, Pomiuk also received an education in masculine and Christian qualities, the first step being his christening with the name "Gabriel," which according to Grenfell means "God's man." Throughout Pomiuk's hospital stay, Grenfell trained him in acceptable masculine behaviour; for example, he prohibited Pomiuk from crying, warning that the doctor "did not like little boys who cried" (113). Grenfell kept a list of the days of the week posted on which he would write "G" or "B" depending on whether or not Pomiuk had cried that day (92, 113), and "[w]hen he got so many G's, some little present would be given him" (92).[9] While Forbush makes Grenfell and the others who helped Pomiuk into Christian teachers by example, he represents Pomiuk as a model student of Christian goodness, gratitude, and patience,[10] a lad who was "as happy as can be, laughing merrily over almost any happy thing, as a Christian ought to do" (98).

Pomiuk's religious and social education as represented in Forbush's book encodes masculinity mediated by Christian values and provides an occasion for contact between readers. Readers learned of male bonding between Pomiuk's benefactors as they read about his rehabilitation in medical, religious, and gender terms. The main reference to such bonding occurs when Grenfell reads the letter sent by an American known only as Mr. Martin: "It was an impressive moment when Doctor Grenfell opened the letter which was to connect the two friends of Pomiuk as helpers of him and of each other for life (Forbush, 82). The sick body of Pomiuk unites the two men in friendship, bringing together Grenfell, the Christian Viking, and Martin, the former missionary and editor for the children's section of a Christian weekly. Grenfell's own account of this triangle of friends in *Off the Rocks* refers to Pomiuk's naked body and to the love the boy bears for both his benefactors:[11]

> Only one treasured possession he had—besides his naked body—a letter we had received from the Hudson's Bay agent. It was addressed to Pomiuk and told of an old man in Andover, who loved and was praying for this lost sheep away in the mountains. It contained a photograph, and when I showed it to Pomiuk he said: "Me even love him." (43)[12]

The opportunity for male contact and friendship offered by Pomiuk's situation extended beyond Martin and Grenfell to the Sunday School children across North America who learned of Pomiuk's story. One boy's club, called the "Captains of Ten," a name which referred to the goal of "mastering" their ten fingers by doing whittling and woodcarving, began raising money for Pomiuk's care by selling their crafts (Forbush, 96). As boys in various countries were bonded in the act of helping him (Forbush, 121), Pomiuk's suffering taught "the comfortable American children" to "be glad to feel that through their gifts these little ones who would have died of starvation and sickness were warm and cozy and receiving Christian care" (Forbush, 119).

At the end of September 1897, just as another Inuit boy and his father were arriving in New York to be put on display and to raise money for the expeditions of Robert Peary, Pomiuk died. Forbush eulogizes Pomiuk in the book by calling him "an example and comfort to all" (127) and admiring how "he endured bravely and patiently the limitations of a crippled life . . ." (127). At his death, the northern lights appear as a sign of "joy in the City of God" (128).[13] Pomiuk's life, at its end, becomes an example of gender expectations for Christian boys to emulate; however, his death also differentiates him from the boys in the audience and resituates his life within the context of what Grenfell considered to be the dying Inuit race. The sacrifice of Pomiuk, despite efforts to save his body and soul, makes him an even more perfect example of the values expressed in the adventure of Grenfell—built as it is around the heroic self-sacrifice of missionary service. *Pomiuk: A Waif of Labrador* signifies how brave white Christian boys should be and what burden their brave shoulders should carry.

NOTES

1. For Christian Social Reformers, like Kingsley and his admirer Grenfell, the Church would educate boys in these matters and help eliminate social disparities.
2. For example, these terms are repeated in various stories in the *Boy's Own Annual* for 1907–1908 (73–74; 85–86; 106–108; 586–588). For a study of conventions in depicting racial difference, see Patrick A. Dunae's "Boy's Literature and the Idea of Race, 1870–1900."
3. In his letters, Grenfell describes reading and enjoying Charles Kingsley's novels (Rompkey 24) and admits his religious views are "much those of Kingsley" (Rompkey, 192). But, while Kingsley is known to have visited the Grenfell home at Parkgate (Rompkey, 199), the anecdote Forbush relates in which Kingsley took the young Grenfell on his knee and proclaimed him "a real Saxon" (65) is unsubstantiated; in fact, Grenfell asks his mother in one of his letters for details of this very meeting (Rompkey, 199).
4. In *Vikings of To-Day*, Grenfell draws on the sagas and establishes Viking heritage as common ground uniting the histories of England and Labrador: "while Northmen and Saxon were struggling for pre-eminence in the England of ours, bold Vikings from Iceland visited Labrador" (3).
5. In boarding school stories, references to the Viking spirit rationalize the sometimes brutal behaviour of male adolescents ("Adventurers," 84), and in other texts, imperial success was often attributed to the Viking heritage of both British and American cultures ("Adventurers," 80).
6. In *Children's Periodicals of the Nineteenth Century*, Sheila A. Egoff describes the use of Vikings in *The Boy's Own Paper* (15).
7. This is one of many inaccuracies in Forbush's story. According to Grenfell's account, the murder of his father and the second marriage of his mother occurred while Pomiuk was at the Fair (*Off the Rocks*, 42).

8. Forbush's remarks on the Exhibition are tinged with fatalism: "There is something sad, however, about the exhibiting of human beings as objects of curiosity and it was especially pathetic to think that had not Pomiuk come to America he would perhaps never have been injured" (56–57).

9. Forbush's account also tells how reports of a mere girl's superior stoicism was used to "shame" Pomiuk into suffering bravely (90–92).

10. In *Off the Rocks*, Grenfell singles Pomiuk out from the other Inuit even before his sickness develops, calling him "the soul of them all" and articulating Mr. Martin's hope that Pomiuk would "share his own priceless treasure, the consciousness of a heavenly Father's love" (37).

11. Forbush's book repeats the homoerotic scene, adding Martin's delighted response to a kayak Pomiuk had carved: ". . . how much of love as well as of skill the little cripple's hands put into this token of his affection!" (116).

12. As R. G. Moyles notes in "A 'Boy's Own' View of Canada," this kind of dialect or unpolished English was a conventional sign differentiating the natives from the English (and heroes from scoundrels) in stories for boys (52).

13. This sentence refers to the story of Minik which is told in Kenn Harper's *Give Me My Father's Body: The Life of Minik, the New York Eskimo.*

WORKS CITED AND CONSULTED

Ballantyne, R. M. *Ungava; or, A Tale of Esquimeaux-land.* Illustrated by the author. London: Ward, Locke, 1857.

Bratton, J. S. *The Impact of Victorian Children's Fiction.* London: Croom Helm, 1981.

Bristow, Joseph. *Empire Boys: Adventures in a Man's World.* London: HarperCollins Academic, 1991.

Brody, Hugh. *The People's Land: Eskimos and Whites in the Eastern Arctic.* Harmondsworth, Eng: Penguin, 1975.

Dunae, Patrick A. "Boy's Literature and the Idea of Empire, 1870–1914." *Victorian Studies* 24.1 (1980): 105–121.

———. "Boy's Literature and the Idea of Race, 1870–1900." *Wascana Review* (1977): 84–107.

Drotner, Kirsten. *English Children and Their Magazines, 1751–1945.* New Haven: Yale University Press, 1988.

Egoff, Sheila A. *Children's Periodicals of the Nineteenth Century.* Pamphlet No. 8. London: Library Association, 1951.

Forbush, William Byron. *Pomiuk: A Waif of Labrador.* Boston: The Pilgrim Press, 1903.

Green, Martin. "Adventurers Stake Their Claim: The Adventure Tale's Bid for Status, 1876–1914." *Decolonizing Tradition: New Views of Twentieth-Century "British" Literary Canons,* ed. Karen R. Lawrence. Chicago: University of Illinois Press, 1992. 70–87.

———. *The Great American Adventure.* Boston: Beacon P., 1984.

Grenfell, Wilfred. *Off the Rocks: Stories of the Deep-Sea Fisherfolk of Labrador.* 1906. Freeport: Books for Libraries Press, 1970.

———. *Vikings of To-Day: Or Life and Medical Work Among the Fishermen of Labrador.* London: Marshall Brothers, 1905.

Harper, Kenn. *Give Me My Father's Body: The Life of Minik, the New York Eskimo.* Frobisher Bay, NWT: Blacklead, 1986.

Kolodny, Annette. *The Land Before Her: Fantasy and Experience of the American Frontiers, 1620–1860.* Chapel Hill: University of North Carolina Press, 1984.

Koven, Seth. "From Rough Lads to Hooligans: Boy Life, National Culture and Social Reform." *Nationalisms and Sexualities,* ed. Andrew Parker, Mary Russo, Doris Sommer, and Patricia Yaeger. New York: Routledge, 1992. 365–391.

Moyles, R. G. "A 'Boy's Own' View of Canada." *Canadian Children's Literature* 34 (1984): 41–56.

Nelson, Claudia. *Boys Will be Girls: The Feminine Ethic and British Children's Fiction, 1857–1917.* New Brunswick: Rutgers University Press, 1991.

Slemon, Stephen, and Jo-Ann Wallace. "Into the Heart of Darkness?: Teaching Children's Literature as a Problem in Theory." *Canadian Children's Literature* 63 (1991): 6–23.

Waterston, Elizabeth. *Children's Literature in Canada.* Twayne's World Authors Series 823, ed. Ruth K. MacDonald. New York: Twayne, 1992.

Imagination and Spirituality: Written Narratives and the Oral Tradition

SHELAGH D. GRANT

$\mathbf{F}$or over a millennium, Inuit history and culture were carefully nurtured and preserved by the oral tradition. With the arrival of the Qallunaat, a second, quite different history and identity began to take form in the written narratives of the Arctic explorers. For a while, each evolved in isolation, as if the other did not exist, with both cultures believing in their own superiority. One was written, the child of western civilization; the other was oral, passed down from generation to generation by the indigenous peoples. One was based on the observations of a transient newcomer; the other on the experience of a long-time inhabitant. The former was driven by imagination; the latter by spirituality. Although moulded and reshaped by the twentieth century, similar distinctions exist even today.

Based on long-standing cultural traditions, these disparate views of Arctic history represent quite contradictory views on the capability of humans to survive in the Arctic environment. The nineteenth century exploration narratives expounded the tenets of Social Darwinism and Judaeo-Christianity, extolling the superior ability of man, not woman, to conquer the natural world. Beau Riffenburgh in his definitive study, *The Myth of the Explorer*, related how, in an era of imperialistic nationalism, "men who achieved remarkable feats were more than just popular heroes; they were symbols of real and imagined nationalist or imperialist cultural greatness" (Riffenburgh, 2). In nineteenth century Europe and America, the Arctic represented the ultimate challenge to both man and nation—the Ultima Thule. And so began Western civilization's fascination with the Arctic landscape and exploration history, replete with nineteenth-century ego-centrism, chauvinism and nationalism, and a vista distorted by vivid imagination.

The Inuit, as well, had incorporated a set of moral values in the representation of their history. Initially expressed in their ancient legends and reinforced by later stories, a distinctive code of ethics was established to govern Inuit social behaviour. Guided by a unique form of spirituality, the objective was to maintain an egalitarian society in peaceful harmony with the environment. To do so demanded respect for the land, the animals, the birds, and creatures of the sea. As Ivaluardjuk, a Netsilik Inuk, explained to Knud Rasmussen in 1922:

> ... the greatest peril of life lies in the fact that human food consists entirely of souls. All the creatures that we have to kill and eat, all those that we have to strike down and destroy to make clothes for ourselves, have souls, like we have, souls that do not perish with the body, and which must therefore be propitiated lest they should revenge themselves on us for taking away their bodies." (quoted in Rasing, 72)

Their philosophy implied a co-dependence between the "hunter and the hunted" (Brody, 73)— a contract, as it were, between equal partners. As described more recently by an Inuk from Baker Lake, the relationship was "so close that it seemed like the animals understood Inuktitut" (Tulurialik, "The Fish Story"). Co-operation and sharing were key to survival; conflict and dishonesty would be avenged by the spirits. Such a thing as "luck," as we know it, did not exist in nineteenth century Inuit culture (Rasing, 72).

The most powerful member of a pre-Christian Inuit community was the Shaman or Angakok, who possessed the multiple role of "priest, physician and prophet" with special powers to contact the spirits (Petrone, 4).

> The angakut were acknowledged or authorized teachers and judges on all questions concerning religious beliefs; and this belief in many ways acting upon the customs and social life of the people, the angakut necessarily became a kind of civil magistrate; and lastly, they had not only to teach their fellow-men how to obtain supernatural help, but also to give such assistance directly themselves. (Rink, 59–60)

Once someone violated a strict taboo, the only means of release from the consequences was a public confession, usually with the assistance of the shaman. Even then, the transgression would be considered a "sin" rather than a "crime" (Rasing, 116). Honesty was key to survival for the small hunting communities. Unacceptable behaviour, such as displaying arrogance, taking others' property, committing adultery without consent, or failing to share food or shelter, was controlled by diverse methods of social ostracism ranging from rude remarks and gossip to a fate worse than death—banishment. Aggressive behaviour was unacceptable among family and friends, and, if possible, to be avoided when in contact with strangers. Murder was tolerated only if everyone agreed that the individual posed a serious threat to the community (Rasing, 117–132; Rink, 32–35).

In many respects, the ancient legends and teachings of the oral tradition might be compared to those of the Judaeo-Christian Bible. Both explained origins and provided the tenets for a strict code of social behaviour. In the Inuit culture, however, there was no worship of one "God," or even several gods, but there was a profound fear of supernatural powers capable of rewarding or punishing behaviour. These spirits were "concealed in nature" and something "to which human life [was] subordinated" (Rink, 36–7). To show disrespect or cause a creature to suffer would likely incur some form of revenge, whether by disease, starvation, or accident. To the Europeans, belief in spirits and immortal souls of animals was considered pagan and evil. Thus to civilize the primitive natives, they must first be introduced to Christianity. As explained by one missionary, "to watch the Eskimo pass from a sinful and degraded paganism into the faith and practice of Jesus Christ is the true romance of the Arctic missionary, beside which all else is as nothing" (Fleming, 1917, 112). Two cultures—two perceptions. One believed in the right to conquer evil and Nature; the other hoped to avoid evil and live in harmony with Nature.

Both the written narrative and the oral tradition were considered a means of entertainment, as well as education. For the Inuit, storytelling was frequently accompanied by songs and dances. Here, the messages conveyed in the lyrical poetry were simple, but profound.

> And yet, there is only
> One great thing,
> The only thing;
> To see in huts and on journeys
> The great day that dawns,
> And the light that fills the world.
> (Recorded by Knud Rasmussen, in Bruemmer, 1985, 144)

Traditionally, happiness was derived from the Inuit's love and respect for their environment. Their surroundings were called Nunassiaq meaning simply the beautiful land (Bruemmer, 1974, 61). No other description was necessary.

By contrast, the language used by the Qallunaat to describe the Arctic landscape could hardly be described as simple or succinct. Beginning in 530 A.D., when the Irish monk St. Brendan wrote of "floating crystal castles" and on through to the early nineteenth century, the Arctic landscape was portrayed as vast, cold, barren, yet mystical (Bruemmer, 1974, 29–42). Although most accounts written in the early nineteenth century, such as those by Captains Wm. E. Parry and G. F. Lyon, seemed understated and "full of mundane details" (Loomis, 101), this did not prevent Europeans from creating their own images of a frozen, lifeless horizon of icebergs and glaciers, surrounded by stormy seas and misty snows, as depicted in Coleridge's *Rime of the Ancient Mariner* and Shelley's *Frankenstein* (Riffenburgh, 14). While John Moss has suggested that "no rendering of the landscape can ever quite describe what is actually there" (1991, 37), in this case, the British Admiralty's more rational descriptions were largely ignored. As a result, fantasy and illusion would dominate in the profusion of Arctic literature that followed in the latter half of the century.

In the Victorian era, authors of narratives, poetry, and fiction needed little encouragement to vent their imagination, and they employed all manner of literary expression to convey the splendour and mystery of the Arctic landscape. Literary analysts have divided the descriptive techniques employed into two categories: the "picturesque" and the "sublime." The picturesque interpretation was employed to depict the Arctic landscape in terms familiar to the readers (Maclaren, 89–90), as did Charles Ede in 1878, when he wrote of "huge icebergs . . . moving southward, in a solemn state, mimicking in their varied forms the towers, spires, and steeples of some far city" (12). The Arctic sublime, on the other hand, was the antithesis of familiar landscape and employed superlative imagery to create an awe-inspiring vista of unearthly grandeur: of sheer cliffs, contorted icebergs, and radiant northern lights, interspersed with scenes of ferocious white bears and gargoyle-like walruses. Riffenburgh argues that the "knowledge the public thus gained of the Arctic was a compound of fact and fantasy, and was dominated by the power of the sublime" (17).

To reinforce the imaginative literary prose, publishers embellished their books with fanciful etchings of majestical spires and sheer cliffs, while framing dwarfed sailing ships with grotesquely contorted icebergs. These romanticized images of the Arctic landscape (McClintock, 1859; Kane, 1894) were in sharp contrast to early Inuit drawings that illustrated the most significant factors in their lives: people, their clothing and homes, hunting techniques, and the creatures they depended upon for their survival. The former was based on a foreigner's imagination, fuelled by nationalism and chauvinism; the latter from a lifetime of experience and cultural pride.

According to Barry Lopez, the aim of Euro-American dramatization of the Arctic landscape was to establish an ilira—an unconscious "fear that accompanies awe" (7). Initially, the scene was dream-like, but in 1854 the Arctic took on a nightmarish quality when it was reported that the Franklin expedition had died of scurvy and starvation—with evidence of cannibalism (Loomis, 98–105). As the horror of the expedition's fate began to register in the literary world, some authors resorted to melodramatic exaggerations to turn fear into terror. One of the more spectacular examples appeared in the Preface to an American novel, *The Polar Hunters,* published in 1917:

> It is a world of evil magic, that world of the Frozen North, where the terrible conditions of life bring about an unparalleled conflict between Man and the Demons of Hunger and of Cold. It is a war against Titans, and Titans have been defeated. Every incident in that grim struggle thrills with danger and excitement, every detail of life is weird and strange. (Rolt-Wheeler)

While admitting that much of his knowledge of the Arctic came from the American Museum of Natural History, the author went on to describe the feat of planting the Stars and Stripes at the North Pole as "the most stupendous geographical triumph in the world . . . achieved by an American for Americans," with reference to the "scores of unburied skeletons . . . on the unknown shores or beneath the eternal ice." He also emphasized that "the secret of the Arctic lies hid in the life of the Eskimo, in the understanding of whom, American scientists and American explorers stand foremost." Embodied here are the key elements that fired the imagination of the Victorian Age: sublime imagery, mystery, conquest, heroism, and national pride.

Although most British authors tended to be more restrained, Charles Dickens was less so, employing rhetorical vernacular to its extreme in his essays on the Arctic appearing in the magazine *Household Words* (Riffenburgh, 27). Other poets, novelists, journalists, and artists added their own interpretations, until the public became "instant authorities" on the mysterious Arctic they had never seen, nor expected to see. Chauncey Loomis suggests that "their imagined Arctic was a place of terror, but even in its terror it was beautiful in the sublime way that immense mountains or the vast reaches of space are beautiful" (110). Not surprisingly, Arctic fiction found a ready market with adventures more exciting and bizarre than those of the explorers, as in Percy St. John's *The Arctic Crusoe* and Jules Verne's epic tale of Arctic adventure that climaxed with Captain Hatteras planting the Union Jack on an erupting volcano at the North Pole (Verne, 1874).

Questions about accuracy were raised, particularly with regard to the sensational journalism appearing in the New York dailies after the United States joined in the search for the Franklin expedition. The American public thrived on excitement and Arctic stories sold papers. Understandably, editors began inserting misleading headlines to appease the public's insatiable appetite. Only rarely was there an attempt to correct false impressions. As a case in point, Lieutenant Doane, the United States commander of an unsuccessful attempt to colonize Ellesmere Island, wrote a rather cynical report that mysteriously found its way into *The Chicago Times* on 6 April 1881:

> We did but little, but left a great many things undone requiring some more courage to refrain from doing. We did not change the names of all the localities visited, as is customary, nor give them new latitudes. . . . We did not erect cenotaphs. . . . We received no flags, converted no natives, killed no one. . . . (Riffenburgh, 135)

In a few cases, the explorers themselves were to blame for exaggerated accounts, such as the Fifth Earl of Lonsdale, who became known as an unscrupulous storyteller. Ultimately, the bitter feud between Peary and Cook over who had reached the North Pole in 1909 would cast further doubts about the veracity of explorers' claims and exploits (Riffenburgh, 136–137.) Even then, it was difficult to wean the public from their long held images of the Arctic and its heroes.

Inaccurate impressions of the Arctic and its indigenous peoples persisted well into the twentieth century, with Vilhjalmur Stefansson arguing that the Arctic landscape was still viewed by most as "a lifeless waste of eternal silence" inhabited only by a few "Eskimos, the filthiest and most benighted people on earth, pushed there by more powerful nations farther south, and eking out a miserable existence amidst hardship" (Stefansson, 7). Yet his own attempts to alter these misconceptions in *The Friendly Arctic* were generally unsuccessful, since he too had resorted to "narrative manipulation" and fabrication to please his publishers, a fact that did not go unnoticed by his peers (Moss, 1991, 40).

The depiction of the Esquimaux of Northern Greenland as "wild and uncouth" (Kane, 119), and living in "filthy squalor" (Jones, 34) seemed more a legacy from Martin Frobisher's accounts of beast-like cannibals (Kenyon, 62) than from the descriptions by British Admiralty explorers such as Ross, Parry, Lyon, and McClintock, or those of earlier missionaries and traders settling in Greenland and Labrador. Similarly, there is little mention of the eighteenth-century Hudson's Bay supply ships to York Factory, or the extensive whaling activities in Davis Strait, reaching Lancaster Sound by the early 1820s. Images of peaceful Inuit, living alongside Europeans and at times bearing their children (Rink, 76–79) were not compatible with the concept of a heroic Arctic explorer. As one might expect, most fictional accounts would adopt the negative image.

Nor is there mention in the nineteenth-century narratives of those Inuit taken to Britain a century earlier, in some cases for schooling (Petrone, 57–59). In one instance, Mikak, a young Inuk woman who created a sensation in London in 1768, returned to Labrador and invited a visiting group of Moravian missionaries to stay. "You will see . . . how well we will behave, if you will only come. We will love you as our countrymen, and trade with you justly, and treat you kindly" (60). For the most part, Inuit visiting Britain in the late eighteenth century were treated well. Some received invitations to meet with royalty and were dressed suitably for the occasion. Others taken later for "exhibition" purposes were not so fortunate. The few who survived—most did not—invariably requested to return home as soon as possible (57–65).

By comparison, Inuit stories included many references to the first arrivals of the Qallunaat, literally translated to mean "the men of heavy eyebrows" (57). Initially, the Inuit thought the strangers and their ships were supernatural, and sought protection from their shamans. When the whaling ships reached Lancaster Sound in the 1820s, for example, the Inuit at Pond Inlet believed the men "had come to murder them," perhaps inspired by tales of the massacre by Frobisher's men centuries earlier. The shamans were called upon to intervene and "cast a spell on the qallunaat, and they could then do nothing" (Eber, 5). Once "protected," the Inuit welcomed the whalers and explorers because of their willingness to trade guns and goods in return for fresh food, skin clothing, information and other assistance. Eventually, the Inuit would become active participants in the whaling industry, with the men acting as "whaling mates" or manning the whale boats and the women providing "friendship" and warm clothing for the captains and their crew (28). The shamans' role changed too. By the mid-1800s, when the whaling ships appeared on the horizon, their chants summoned the whales to ensure there would be plenty to harvest (16). The Inuit benefitted greatly from the trade for guns and ammunition. The whalers profited commercially, and those who wintered over would depend entirely upon the Inuit for clothing and food. What existed was a state of "co-dependence."

Most British explorers tended to ignore or minimize the impact of European whalers on the lives of the Inuit. Captain Leopold McClintock, for example, made only passing reference to the whaling ships in his published chronicle (19, 101, and 126), but gave detailed descriptions of the various natives he encountered and their living conditions. He commended the Danes for their colonial policy in Greenland, noting particularly their generous assistance to the "Esquimaux" in times of distress and their apparent success in teaching them to read and write. His criticism of British policy was clear:

> Have we English done as much for the aborigines in any of our numerous colonies, even in far more favoured climes? We have thousands of Esquimaux within our own territories of Labrador and of the Hudson's Bay Company, have we ever attempted to do anything for their welfare?—and thousands more of them inhabit the north shore of Hudson's Strait and the west shore of Davis'

Strait, within three weeks' sail of us, and in annual communication
with our whaling ships. (13)

McClintock seemed convinced that colonial government was beneficial to
the native peoples. As an example, when he described the unhealthy living
conditions at a Moravian mission settlement near Godhaab, he noted that
this community was "not subject to Danish authority." Similarly, he reported
being repulsed by the "filth and wretchedness" of the Esquimaux dwellings
at Etah in North Greenland, but was quick to suggest that the "degraded"
condition of these people was a result of their being completely isolated
from the more civilized settlements in southern Greenland (114).

In spite of his charge of British neglect, McClintock found the
Inuit of North Baffin to be "better-looking, cleaner, and more robust"
than he had expected (136). More importantly, they possessed an unusual
memory for detail as illustrated in their descriptions of distant shipwrecks
that occurred decades earlier and of Sir Edward Perry's winter at Igloolik
in 1822–23. Perhaps even more surprising was their knowledge of Dr. John
Rae's stay two years earlier at Repulse Bay, some five-hundred miles away
(130–41).

Alas, not everyone was willing to accept the inherent accuracy of the
Inuit oral tradition. When Dr. John Rae recounted Inuit reports of cannibalism among the last survivors of the Franklin Expedition, he was ostra-
cized by British officials and the London press for daring to suggest that
members of the Admiralty were capable of such dishonourable conduct.
The Inuit were declared unreliable: in the words of Charles Dickens, they
were no more than a "handful of uncivilized people, with a domesticity of
blood and blubber" (Loomis, 108).

Americans as well were quick to discredit Inuit testimony. In 1873,
for instance, the United States Secretary of the Navy turned a blind eye to
statements by a trusted Inuk guide who claimed that the veteran explorer
Charles Francis Hall had died of arsenic poisoning at the hands of his
crew. In the national interest, a far more honourable explanation was
"death by natural causes" (Petrone, 69–71). As a consequence, the significance of accuracy in the Inuit oral tradition would be ignored for many
decades to come. Yet accurate and precise detail was of critical importance
to preserve the ancient legends that formed the foundation of Inuit culture and identity. As Petrone explained in *Northern Voices,*

> In ancient times the *word* was sacrosanct. It embodied the very
> essence of being. And it carried the power to make things happen.
> Through this sacred power, the Inuit sought to shape and control
> the cosmic forces that govern human life. (4)

There were a number of serious attempts in the nineteenth century to record the ancient legends, notably by Dr. Henry Rink, Charles

Francis Hall, and Franz Boas. Dr. Rink, a Danish scientist/explorer and later Governor of South Greenland, collected over five hundred legends and stories, filling over two thousand sheets of manuscript. Some were recorded as early as 1823 by Greenland Esquimaux, a testimony to the advanced educational opportunities provided under Danish rule. Noting only minor regional differences, Rink found distinct similarities in the legends told in the isolated Inuit communities of Greenland compared to those recorded in northern Labrador (Rink, 84–92). Almost a century later, Knud Rasmussen would find similar themes in legends elsewhere in the Canadian Arctic during his travels from east to west with the Fifth Thule Expedition (Petrone, 3).

Stories of more recent times dating back several hundreds of years were also preserved through the Inuit oral tradition of storytelling. Even today, they provide rich historical detail not found in the writings of western civilization. In the 1970s, for example, elders in Arctic Bay told stories about the Tuniit, recognized by anthropologists as belonging to the Dorset culture who were thought to have disappeared around 1300 A.D. By their description, the Tuniit were larger and stronger than the Inuit; they lived in small stone houses, wore parkas almost to the ground, carried their fire around their waists when hunting, and had very few material possessions. One elder also described how some Tuniit lived alongside Inuit families on Bylot Island until driven away to the north, possibly to Greenland (Cowan, 15).

Attempts by Qallunaat to record the ancient legends were not always successful. To gain Inuit trust required living among them for extended periods of time and learning their language. Even then, translating an Inuit story into English was difficult since Inuktitut is a language of phrases and ideas, rather than of words and structural sentences.

Also complicating early translations was a tendacy for Inuit to defer to the Qallunaat and tell them only what they wanted to hear. Usually described as simply not wishing to "offend," recent studies point to a long-standing Inuit tradition of dealing with any uneasiness about people or situations. In Inuktitut, such fears were called *ilira*, and the ancient legends taught the Inuit to respond by either withdrawing from the situation or showing "love" in order to appease the one who had instilled the fear. This latter response was known as *nagli*, but perceived by many Qallunaat as a "willingness to comply" (Rasing, 110–116). Although this form of response provided the Inuit with unusual self-control over mind and body when faced with perceived danger, present-day scholars and Inuit themselves are wondering if this response may have worked against them in dealing with the Qallunaat. (Rasing, 271, NBOHP Arnakallak).

A number of factors in the Inuit oral tradition encouraged consistency and accuracy. Storytelling and songs were considered a means of educating the young, and as Alootook Ipellie argues, the raconteur was required to have a phenomenal memory to ensure strict accuracy and attention to detail (1992, 16). Over a century earlier, Dr. Henry Rink had made a similar observation:

> The art requires the ancient tales to be related as nearly as possible in the words of the original version, with only a few arbitrary reiterations, and otherwise only varied according to the individual talents of the narrator, as to the mode of recitation, gesture, &c. . . . Generally, even the smallest deviation from the original version will be taken notice of and corrected, if any intelligent person happens to be present. (85)

Thus, while not everyone was considered a qualified storyteller, all were taught as children to value the importance of accuracy.

Although there is no evidence of ego-centrism in their legends and stories, the Inuit certainly believed in the superiority of their own race. Generally they thought the white men were "restless, time-obsessed, overweening, moody, totally lacking in manners, and boorish" (Bruemmer, 1974, 200). The problem, as explained to Knud Rasmussen, was that the white man and the Indian were offspring of an Inuit woman mated with a dog. The young were placed in a leaky boat which required constant bailing, and it was thought this might explain the "peculiarity of white men who are always in a hurry and have much to do." Moreover, it was thought that

> . . . white men have quite the same minds as small children. Therefore one should always give way to them. They are easily angered, and when they cannot get their way they are moody and, like children, have the strangest ideas and fancies. (200)

Another Inuk was more generous in his views, explaining to Rasmussen that "we have our customs, which are not the same as those of the white men, the white men who live in another land and have need of other ways" (cited in Petrone, 102).

The Arctic exploration narratives generally confirmed this attitude of superiority, although each interpretation varies. Dr. Elisha Kane in *Arctic Explorations,* for instance, related his first meeting with Greenland Esquimaux by describing them as "fearless," showing "no apprehension of violence from us," and in fact were "laughing heartily at our ignorance in not understanding them" (120–121). Lest they would think the explorers inferior, Dr. Kane declared it was critical to impose fear among the natives in order to gain their respect (260–264). As a result of his actions, the natives deserted the ice-bound crew who nearly starved to death as a consequence. Six years later, Captain McClintock observed a similar attitude among the Inuit of King Williams Island, claiming there was "not a trace of fear" even among the children (McClintock, 227).

Evidence that the feeling of superiority persisted well into the twentieth century is found in the notebook of an RCMP officer who was stationed in the Eastern Arctic from 1922–1935.

> At the back of the Eskimo mind, although seldom expressed, is a feeling of his superiority over the white man, and a belief we can show them nothing in connection with their country and animals which they do not know. There is a latent fear of us, deadened by contact, reduced by fair treatment, and almost turned into contempt by over familiarity, but always in existence. They have a strong opinion that we should not interfere too much in their affairs, and we should not unless necessary. (McInnes, Papers C/3/1)

Corporal McInnes also wrote that he believed the Inuit to be "the most ethical, the most moral, and the most communal people," he had ever met, and "better developed mentally than other people," with a "higher system of philosophy" than that of western civilization. (*Ibid.*) Alootook Ipellie, writing in 1992, confirms the high moral principles and caring among his people:

> Even though Inuit lived in one of the world's most inhospitable climates, they remained people warm of heart and always ready to help anyone struggling with life. If the art of human relations were to be measured among all peoples on the planet earth, Inuit would score high on a list of those expert at caring for their fellow beings. This is not surprising, given the fact they have always relied on one another to survive the forces of nature. (16)

Yet many Arctic explorers, Elisha Kane in particular, believed that Inuit assistance could only be acquired through manipulation, cunning, and the promise of material goods.

So entranced with the achievements of their polar heroes, the public accepted as fact the many misconceptions written about the Inuit. This was particularly true for the younger generation for whom the exploration narratives held a special appeal. In Britain, special editions were published as prizes for boys' grammar and public schools, with the school emblem etched in gold on the leather cover: as in an 1894 edition of Kane's *Arctic Explorations* (Wolverley Grammar School) or the abridged 1876 version by M. Jones, *Dr. Kane: the Arctic Hero* (Park School, Glasgow). In the United States, a number of children's editions were published by religious organizations, such as Captain William Scoresby's *The Arctic Regions*. Only a few books were written solely to inform about geographical and scientific facts, as was the case of Ascott Hope's *Wonders of the Ice World*. Stories about conquering nature, of courageous heroes with strong moral character, and of death-defying adventures in a fairy-tale land of icebergs, polar bears and primitive "Esquimaux" were all part of a young boy's education.

Some publishers sought to attract youthful readers by fictionalizing history. In the case of *Uncle Richard's Voyages for the Discovery of a Northwest Passage,* published in 1826, the anonymous author relates his stories as if he had accompanied such explorers as Parry, Lyons, Franklin in his overland expedition, and even Captain Cochrane in his travels to Siberia. He makes no pretence of his purpose, stating in the Preface that he hoped his young readers would be impressed by his conviction, "that courage, resolution and perseverance, will support men through toils and dangers, and enable them to act an honourable and useful part in the service of their country" (A2). Fiction and non-fiction alike were accompanied by imaginative etchings of grotesque icebergs, eerie illuminated skies, fierce bears and walruses, and all sorts of mysterious land forms.

By far the most injurious consequences of a vivid imagination were the misconceptions created in the young mind concerning the indigenous people of the Arctic. None were more misleading or vicious than the descriptions of the "Esquimaux" found in *Uncle Richard's Voyages*. Described repeatedly as "savages," the women in particular were characterized as "disgusting" (201), "poor wretches" (222), covered with a "coating of blood, grease and dirt." (195) To show the ultimate in degradation, the author repeats a story about how one woman had offered to give him her child in exchange for a knife. (169) He also claimed that the Esquimaux "shewed utter selfishness and insensibility to each other's sufferings" (239), and declared that "the old women are so truly hideous, with inflamed eyes, wrinkled skin, and black teeth, that I am not at all surprised at former voyagers reporting they had seen witches on this shore" (167). With such images, the youth of nineteenth-century Britain and America could not help but be convinced of the superiority of the Anglo-Saxon race and its Arctic heroes.

Although none were quite comparable to *Uncle Richard's Voyages,* many Arctic adventure novels appeared in the mid to late 1800s, each providing inaccurate images of both the land and its peoples. Several were written by R. M. Ballantyne, the son of a wealthy Scot, but who had spent a few years in Canada with the Hudson's Bay Company. Apparently he had never been north of York Factory, yet this prolific writer of boys' stories set a number of his tales in the Arctic, notably *Fast in the Ice, Ungava: A Tale of the Esquimaux* and *World of Ice*. Numerous editions appeared in both Britain and the United States, reaching many generations of young readers on both sides of the Atlantic. Although slightly milder in tone, Ballantyne would reinforce Uncle Richard's image of the Inuit as primitive savages, describing them as "fat, dirty and oily" (*Fast in the Ice*, 138) and, in one instance, "creeping on their hands and knees" out of their igloos "like dark hairy monsters" (*World of Ice*, 172). These and other books would leave behind a trail of misconceptions to be absorbed by the fertile minds of impressionable youth.

By the turn of the century, the original exploration narratives were often abridged and/or combined into anthologies. They still retained much of the distorted imagery, but were often written in a more simplistic style, as in William B. Wharton's *Tales of the Frozen North* or Irving Crump's *The Boys, Book of Arctic Exploration*. These adventure stories continued to extol the virtues of courage and manliness, as did W.H.G. Kingston's *Arctic Adventures* or Kirk Munroe's *Under the Great Bear*. By the twentieth century, much younger children became armchair participants in imaginary Arctic adventures, in works such as Harvey Ralphson's *Boy Scouts Beyond the Arctic Circle* and Milton Richard's *Dick Kent with the Eskimos*. For older boys, Oxley's *North Overland with Franklin* and Munn's *Tales of the Eskimos* would add further imaginative distortions of historical fact.

Once the North Pole had been "conquered" in 1908–1909, most adult literature seemed to take on a somewhat more subdued tone. Although fascination with the Arctic continued unabated throughout the first half of the twentieth century, it was now shared by more Canadians— both readers and writers. Following the Great War, British and American Arctic expeditions, once a source of intense national pride, were replaced by annual Canadian patrols with RCMP aboard to maintain sovereignty. For the same reason, new laws were introduced requiring explorers to obtain permission from the Canadian government. The major explorations of this period were Stefansson's Canadian Arctic Expedition (1913–1918), followed by Rasmussen's Danish Fifth Thule Expedition, and attempts by Admiral Byrd to fly over the North Pole. The whaling industry was finished and replaced by the fur trade which was soon dominated by the Hudson's Bay Company. As a sign of the times, Qallunaat women now appeared in the Arctic, either as nurses or wives of missionaries.

Subtle changes were also taking place in the written narratives. Not surprisingly, autobiographical narratives of "lesser" men and women began to dominate Arctic literature, written by RCMP officers, missionaries, fur traders, geologists, bush pilots, and nurses. There were still numerous stories about the more exalted: the Arctic aviators, sailing captains, and scientists, but when accompanied by black-and-white photographs, these books seemed to make the Arctic less mysterious and terrifying. Canadian artists also began to take an interest in the Arctic landscape but, with the exception of Lawren Harris's icebergs, the paintings of the Group of Seven and Maurice Haycock tended to portray a more gentle scene. Even the black-and-white, silent movies taken during the annual Eastern Arctic patrol seemed to reduce the polar bears, musk-oxen, and walruses to a reasonable size. The Arctic seemed less threatening, but the romantic image still predominated.

For the first half of the twentieth century, the Inuit were still viewed as curiosities—a quaint and happy people, who seemed to thrive in an environment most southerners found too rigorous and formidable. In this context, Robert Flaherty's *Nanook of the North* was filmed to fit the existing stereotype, rather than reality. Written narratives tended to support this image, with Peter Freuchen and Vilhjalmur Stefansson being the most prolific authors of adult literature. New children's fiction such as *Etu, Our Little Eskimo Cousin* (Wade) and *Brother Eskimo* (Sullivan) tended to be less racist but still patronizing, as were stories by the missionaries, such as *Dwellers of the Arctic Night* (Fleming) and *By Eskimo Dogsled and Kayak* (Hutton). As long as the Churches were willing to educate and the Hudson's Bay Company provided an economic base, there was little reason for public concern. In fact, the "noble savage" image seemed quite appropriate to the romanticized image of a pristine Arctic environment. Few anticipated that the image might someday turn into one of "the noble victim" (Tippett, 14).

Although anthropological studies pointed to the existence of a unique and distinct culture spread across the Arctic, most scholars and scientists did not think it could survive the dominant influence of western civilization. Most assumed that absorption and assimilation were inevitable, that after learning to read and write, the "primitive" natives would share in the future prosperity of the Canadian nation and likely move south by choice. Few, if any, saw Christianity as a threat to the Inuit oral tradition, to their culture, their history, and their identity. Yet, when the Inuit cast aside their beliefs in shamans and spirits, they inadvertently diminished the significance of the ancient legends and the moral principles that had guided their social behaviour for over a millennium. Syllabics began to replace the oral tradition, but the Inuit elders were slow to recognize the effect this would have on storytelling. The younger Inuit, however, were being educated under the direction of the missionaries who encouraged them to forget their language and all practices associated with their pagan past. Thus the *ilira*, which still unconsciously guided Inuit behaviour, would deter serious thoughts of transferring the ancient legends and stories to paper lest it offend their teachers (Petrone, 58).

Unexpectedly, the legends and teachings of the oral tradition did not disappear, partly as a result of Inuit paintings and carvings which allowed expression of the spirituality that had once dominated their lives. Other changes that took place following the Second World War caused severe social dislocation in family life, particularly the residential school system and the transference of TB patients to southern sanatoriums. Newcomers arrived to participate in military defence and mining activities, but they also brought alcohol, then drugs, to the once remote Inuit commu-

nities. Some Inuit adjusted—some did not. To the surprise of many Qallunaat, however, Inuit culture and identity survived.

Meanwhile, the Canadian public was still entranced with a
romantic image of its Arctic, thus quite content to believe government
reports of great progress in bringing education and health services to the
indigenous peoples. Photographic essay books and more autobiographies
flooded the book shelves. A few writers, like Richard Finnie and Farley
Mowat, attempted to defy the romantic myth and suggested there might
be problems hidden in the isolated north. Most Canadians were reluctant
to listen. Although James Houston and Harold Horwood successfully
placed the Inuit at the centre of their novels, it was not until scheduled air
flights and television documentaries brought the Arctic more directly in
contact with southerners that the romantic illusions slowly gave way to
concerns about the fragile Arctic environment and the indigenous people
who lived there.

By the 1980s, it was apparent that Inuit culture and identity had
not only survived, but was enjoying a rebirth as Inuit leaders sought to
rebuild self-confidence and pride among their people. Through local ini-
tiatives such as the COPE and the North Baffin oral history projects, there
was a concerted effort to seek out the wisdom of the elders and record
their stories on tape. Some have appeared in anthologies, like *We Don't
Live in Snow Houses Now.* Others have provided important resource material for new histories, as in the case of Dorothy Eber's *When the Whalers
Were Up Here.* New publications, by Inuit for Inuit, such as *Inuktitut, Inuit
Today,* and *Inuit Fiction Magazine,* were initiated as a means to encourage
young Inuit to write their own stories and poetry, in Inuktitut, English
and, in some cases, French. A few began to write full-length books. Some
were autobiographical like *I, Nuligak* or Armand Tagoona's *Shadows;* others were fictional, such as Markoosie's *Harpoon of the Hunter.*

Ancient legends and more recent stories also began to appear in
print; some were edited by southerners, as in the case of Robin Gedalof's
Paper Stays Put, or Penny Petrone's *Northern Voices;* others were collaborative
efforts such as Pitseolak and Eber's *The People from Our Side* or Nungak and
Arima's *Inuit Stories: Povungnituk.* Sometimes new stories and interpretations
were added, as in the case of Alootook Ipellie's *Arctic Dreams and Nightmares.* In school texts, Qallunaat stories were replaced with stories written
and illustrated by Inuit. Even adult story-telling experienced a revival.

The spirituality that was so central to the old stories is taking on
new significance and meaning. A new pride in Inuit culture is emerging
and with it, self-confidence and self-respect. In the words of Penny
Petrone, author of *Northern Voices,*

> Much of this ancient folklore has been lost over the years and
> much of what has survived is fragmented. Although oral narrative

was literature in performance that to a large extent defined its form and content, the extant corpus, even on the printed page, is testimony to a rich, precious birthright that is still a great source of spiritual energy and physical strength. (3)

From the beginning of time, spirituality had placed respect for the environment at the cornerstone of Inuit culture. Rebirth of that spirituality, in whatever form is acceptable to the Inuit people, may succeed in reinforcing the very foundations of their culture and ensure survival of their fragile environment.

Only a century ago, the exploration narratives were considered by Euro-Americans to be the core of Arctic history. Today, there is still a fascination with the Arctic, but the character of the narratives is changing. National pride is now shared by Canadians, Danes or Alaskan-Americans, and often challenged in a new genre of socio-political critiques. Many popular historians have included the Arctic in their repertoire, whereas professional historians are still rewriting traditional tales of discovery: Clive Holland's *Farthest North* and John Geiger and Owen Beattie's *Dead Silence: The Greatest Mystery in Arctic Discovery* as examples. Others, like David C. Woodman in *Unravelling the Franklin Mystery: Inuit Testimony,* are attempting to include Inuit voices in exploration history.

New autobiographies of Arctic experiences such as Donald Marsh's *Echoes from a Frozen Land* and Dewey Soper's *Canadian Arctic Recollections* suggest readers are still fascinated by real life experiences, but there appears to be even greater interest in Arctic fiction and poetry. Here the imagination seems to reside more in the creative talents of the writer, as in Aritha van Herk's *Places Far from Ellesmere,* rather than in a deliberate distortion of the landscape. In the field of historical fiction, Rudy Wiebe was singularly successful in placing the indigenous peoples at the centre of Franklin's overland expedition in *A Discovery of Strangers* and Peter Høeg's *Smilla's Sense of Snow* focusses on the present by exploring Greenland's cross-cultural disorientation in a mystery novel of suspense and science fiction intrigue. Meanwhile, countless coffee-table books still appear every Christmas, full of magnificent colour photographs of the Arctic landscape that reflect an ongoing Canadian fascination with the Arctic sublime and "ultima thule," although many now focus more on the Inuit, their communities, and their history. More thoughtful writers, notably Barry Lopez in *Arctic Dreams* and John Moss in *Enduring Dreams: An Exploration of Arctic Landscape,* are forcing us to look inward, outward and backward, to find new meaning in the Arctic imagery that was once rooted in western culture.

Like the ancient folklore of the Inuit, Qallunaat history of the Arctic has also been fragmented, with the once dominant exploration history now sharing honours with whaling, fur trade, missionary, military, economic, social, and political history. Yet many scholars now recognize that an all-inclusive Arctic history is impossible as long as the indigenous peoples remain on the periphery rather than at the core. Someday, and hopefully in the not too distant future, a truly comprehensive Arctic history will emerge with the indigenous peoples at the centre, written by an Inuk, and incorporating only those Qallunaat histories considered meaningful to the Inuit. Until then, there will continue to be two Arctic histories, two forms of Arctic narrative, and two distinct cultural perceptions—one still influenced by imagination, the other by spirituality.

WORKS CITED AND SELECTED REFERENCES

Primary Sources

Finley McInnes Papers. Private collection of diaries, reports, Inuit sketches, photographs, and correspondence of a former RCMP officer posted to Pond Inlet and other northern police posts, 1922–1935.

North Baffin Oral History Project (NBOHP) 1994—Parks Canada and GNWT, a collection of oral histories from Pond Inlet (unpublished).

Non-Fiction

Boas, Franz. *The Central Eskimo*. Washington: Smithsonian Institute, 1888.

Bernier, Captain J. E. *Master Mariner and Arctic Explorer*. Ottawa: LeDroite, 1939.

Brody, Hugh. *Living Arctic: Hunters of the Canadian North*. Vancouver: Douglas and McIntyre, 1987.

Bruemmer, Fred. *The Arctic*. New York: Quadrangle, 1974.

———. *The Arctic World*. Toronto: Key Porter, 1985.

Crump, Irving. *The Boys' Book of Arctic Exploration*. New York: Dodd Mead and Company, 1925.

Eber, Dorothy Harley. *When the Whalers Were Up Here: Inuit Memories from the Eastern Arctic*. Kingston: McGill-Queen's University Press, 1989.

Finnie, Richard. *Canada Moves North*. Toronto: Macmillan, 1948.

Fleming, Archibald Lang. *Archibald of the Arctic: the Flying Bishop*. New York: Appleton-Century-Crofts, 1956.

———. *Dwellers in the Arctic Night*. London: SPGFP, 1928

Freuchen, Peter. *Arctic Adventure, My Life in the Frozen North*. New York: Farrar and Rinehart, 1935.

Geiger John, and Owen Beattie. *Dead Silence: The Greatest Mystery in the Arctic*. Toronto: Viking, 1993.

Jenness, Diamond. *The Life of the Copper Eskimos: Report of the Canadian Arctic Expedition, 1913–18*. Vol. 12. Ottawa: F. A. Ackland, 1922.

Jones, M. *Dr. Kane, the Arctic Hero: A Narrative of His Adventures and Explorations in the Polar Regions*. London: T. Nelson and Sons, 1876.

Kane, Elisha Kent. *Arctic Explorations in Search of Sir John Franklin*. London: T. Nelson and Sons, 1894.

Hall, Charles F. *Arctic Researches and Life Among the Esquimaux, Being the Narrative of an Expedition in Search of Sir John Franklin, in the Years 1860, 1861 and 1862*. New York: Harper and Brothers, 1865.

Holland, Clive, ed. *Farthest North: A History of North Polar Exploration in Eye-Witness Accounts*. London: Robinson Publishing, 1994.

Hope, Ascott. *Wonders of the Ice World*. London: Gall and Inglis, (n.d.) c. 1891.

Hutton, S. K. *By Eskimo Dogsled and Kayak.* London: Seeley, Service and Co., 1919.

Kenyon, Walter A. *Tokens of Possession: The Northern Voyages of Martin Frobisher.* Toronto: Royal Ontario Museum, 1975.

Kingston, W.H.G. *Arctic Adventures.* London: George Routledge, (n.d.) c. 1890.

Lopez, Barry. *Arctic Dreams: Imagination and Desire in a Northern Landscape.* New York: Charles Scribner, 1986

Loomis, Chauncey. "The Arctic Sublime," in W. C. Knoepflmachel and J. B. Tennyson, ed. *Nature and the Victorian Imagination.* Berkley: University of California Press, 1977.

Lyon, Captain G. F. *The Private Journal of G. F. Lyon of H.M.S. Hecla.* London: John Murray, 1824.

Maclaren, I. S. "The Aesthetic Map of the North, 1845–1859." *Arctic* 38:2 (June 1985), 89–103.

Marsh, Donald B. *Echoes from a Frozen Land.* Edmonton: Hurtig, 1987.

McClintock, F. Leopold. *The Voyage of the Fox in the Arctic Seas in Search of Franklin and his Companions.* 5th ed. London: John Murray, 1881.

Moss, John. "The Cartography of Dreams." *Journal of Canadian Studies,* 28:3 (Fall 1993), 140–158.

———. "Imagining the Arctic: From Frankenstein to Farley Mowat," *Arctic Circle,* March/April 1991.

———. *Enduring Dreams: An Exploration of Arctic Landscape.* Concord, Ontario: Anansi, 1994.

Mowat, Farley. *The Desperate People.* Toronto: McClelland and Stewart, 1959.

———. *The People of the Deer.* Toronto: McClelland and Stewart, 1952.

Munn, Captain Henry Toke. *Tales of the Eskimo: Being Impressions of a Strenuous, Indomitable, and Cheerful Little People.* London: W. and R. Chambers, (n.d.) c. 1925.

Parry, William Edward. *Journal of a Second Voyage for the Discovery of a Northwest Passage from the Atlantic to the Pacific: Performed in the years 1821–22–23, in His Majesty's Ships Fury and Hecla.* London: John Murray, 1824.

Rasing, W. C. E. *'Too Many People,' Order and Nonconformity in Iglulingmiut Social Process.* Imigen, Norway: Recht and Samenleving, 1994.

Rasmussen, Knud. *Across Arctic America: Narrative of the Fifth Thule Expedition.* New York: G.P/ Putnam's Sons, 1927.

———. *Report of the Fifth Thule Expedition, 1921–1924.* Vol. VII, VIII. Copenhagen: Nordisk Forlag, 1929–1942.

Riffenburgh, Beau. *The Myth of the Explorer: The Press, Sensationalism and Geographical Discovery.* London: Belhaven Press, 1993.

Rink, Dr. Henry. *Tales and Traditions of the Eskimo.* 2nd ed. London: William Blackwood and Sons, 1875.

Ross, John. *A Voyage of Discovery. . . .* London: John Murray, 1819.

Scoresby, Capt. Wm. *The Arctic Regions.* New York: American Sunday School Union, c. 1860.

Soper, J. Dewey. *Canadian Arctic Recollections: Baffin Island, 1923–1931.* Saskatoon: University of Saskatchewan, 1981.

Stefansson, Vilhjalmur. *The Friendly Arctic.* New York: Macmillan, 1939

Tippett, Maria. *Between Two Cultures: A Photographer Among the Inuit.* Toronto: Viking, 1994.

Wharton, Captain Wm. B. *Tales of the Frozen North.* Philadelphia: John Potter and Company, 1895.

Woodman, David C. *Unravelling the Franklin Mystery: Inuit Testimony.* Kingston: McGill-Queen's University Press, 1991.

Selected Inuit Legends, Stories, and Novels

Cowan, Susan, ed. *We Don't Live In Snow Houses Now.* Ottawa: Canadian Arctic Producers, 1976.

Gedalof, Robin, ed. *Paper Stays Put: A Collection of Inuit Writing.* Edmonton: Hurtig, 1988.

Ipellie, Alootook. *Arctic Dreams and Nightmares.* Ottawa: 1994.

———. "Nunatsiaqmuit: People of the Good Land." *Inuit Art Quarterly,* (Spring 1992) 14.

Markoosie. *Harpoon of the Hunter.* Kingston: McGill-Queen's University Press, 1970.

Nuligak. *I, Nuligak.* Toronto: Peter Martin, 1966.

Nungak, Zebedee, and Eugene Arima. *Inuit Stories: Povungnituk.* Ottawa: Canadian Museum of Civilization, 1988.

Petrone, Penny, ed. *Northern Voices: Inuit Writing in English.* Toronto: University of Toronto Press, 1988.

Pitseolak, Peter, and Dorothy Harley Eber. *People from Our Side.* Kingston: McGill-Queen's University Press, 1993.

Toonga, Armand. *Shadows.* Ottawa: Oberon Press, 1975.

Tulurialik, Ruth Annaqtuusi, and David F. Pelly. *Qikaaluktut: Images of Inuit Life.* Toronto: Oxford University Press, 1986.

Selected European, American, and Canadian Fiction

Anonymous. *Northern Regions—Uncle Richard's Voyages for the Discovery of a Northwest Passage.* London: J. Harris, 1826.

Ballantyne, R. M. *Fast in the Ice or Adventures in the Polar Regions.* New York: D. Appleton, 1871.

———. *Ungava, A Tale of the Esquimaux.* London: G. Nelson and Son, (1879).

———. *World of Ice.* London: T. Nelson and Sons, n.d.

Ede, Charles, R. N. *The Home Amid the Snow (or) Warm Hearts in Cold Regions.* London: T. Nelson and Sons, 1878.

Peter Høeg, *Smila's Sense of Snow.* Toronto: Doubleday, 1993.

Horwood, Harold. *White Eskimo.* Toronto: Doubleday, 1972.

Houston, James. *White Dawn.* New York: Harcourt Brace Jovanovich, 1971.

Munroe, Kirk. *Under the Great Bear.* New York: Doubleday, 1900.

Ralphson. G. Harvey. *Boy Scouts Beyond the Arctic Circle or The Lost Expedition.* Chicago: M. A. Donahue and Company, 1913.

Oxley, J. MacDonald. *North Overland with Franklin.* Toronto: Musson, n.d.

Richards, Milton. *Dick Kent with the Eskimos.* New York: Salfield Publishing, 1927.

St. John, Percy B. *The Arctic Crusoe: A Tale of the Polar Sea.* Boston: Lee and Shepard, 1875.

Sullivan, Alan. *Brother Eskimo.* London: Sir Isaac Pitman and Sons, 1918.

van Herk, Aritha. *Places Far from Ellesmere,* Red Deer, Alta: Red Deer College Press, 1990.

Verne, Jules. *The Desert of Ice or the Further Adventures of Captain Hatteras.* Philadelphia: Porter and Coates, 1874.

———. *The English at the North Pole.* London: Ward, Lock and Co., c. 1873.

Wade, Mary Hazelton. *Etu, Our Little Eskimo Cousin.* Boston: Page, 1902.

Wiebe, Rudy. *A Discovery of Strangers.* Toronto: Knopf, 1994.

The Sea Goddess Sedna:
An Enduring Pan-Arctic Legend
from Traditional Orature
to the New Narratives of the
Late Twentieth Century

MICHAEL P. J. KENNEDY

Within the rich Inuit tradition, there is a legend of a female spirit who dwells at the bottom of the sea. For generations, Inuit orature has related how this woman came to be mistress of the sea creatures. The explanations of who she was vary, as do the interpretations of how she came to have dominion over the denizens of the ocean and provide seafood sustenance for the Inuit. Despite variations in its content, the Sea Goddess myth is pan-Arctic in scope, extending in one form or another from East Greenland[1] along the coast of West Greenland[2] into the North Greenland polar regions,[3] west into Labrador,[4] the Canadian North,[5] and farther west into Alaska[6] and Siberia .[7]

With the coming of Europeans and others from the south, this narrative from Inuit oral tradition was translated and transcribed. Central to the Sea Goddess legend is a being at the bottom of the ocean who decides whether to release the sea creatures for the Inuit to hunt for food. This woman has had many names ascribed to her including The Ghastly Woman or Infernal Goddess,[8] Aywilliayoo or Protectress of the Sea Animals,[9] Arnarkuagsak or Old Woman,[10] Sid-ne or Spirit Below,[11] Sidney,[12] Nerrivik or The Food Dish,[13] Nuliajuk or Kavna (She Down There),[14] Takanaluk Arnaluk or Mother of the Sea Beasts,[15] and Sedna.[16] The Sea Goddess legend is a creation story which reveals the origin of the creatures of the ocean. The core tale of a woman having the digits of her hand being cut off as she clings to a boat in an attempt to save her own life is pan-Arctic in scope. According to Greenlandic legend,[17] Smith Sound Inuit tradition,[18] Central Inuit orature,[19] the Iglulik of Melville Peninsula,[20] and the Chukchee people of Siberia,[21] it is the father who cuts off the fingers of his daughter. Some traditions,[22] including that of the Cumberland Sound Inuit, tell of how the father also punctures his daughter's eye.[23]

For the Polar Inuit of Greenland observed by Rasmussen in 1903–1904, it was the girl's grandfather who cut off her entire hand.[24] Peter Freuchen and Knud Rasmussen describe how for other Inuit the legend is that of an orphan girl who is abandoned by her community.[25] When the girl swims to the community's boat and grabs it in an attempt to go with them, her fingers are cut off by those in the boat.[26]

The basic plot of a woman clinging to the side of a boat and having the fingers of one hand cut off to become the creatures of the sea is central to most versions of the Sea Goddess legend. The durability of this segment of the legend is indeed significant in light of the variety of tales which lead up to it. In some versions, the woman clinging to the boat is a woman who has been married to a bird,[27] usually a fulmar[28] or a petrel.[29] In other renderings, she is the woman who has wed a dog [30] and is the mother of some non-Inuit races.[31] Despite the variance in narrative content among the tales, the Sea Goddess has endured time, distance, and the intrusion of new religion and culture and ways of life. The Woman at the Bottom of the Sea story continued to be a tradition among Inuit people during post-contact years. Indeed, it remains today a touchstone with an Inuit past where the very survival of the people was dependent upon the sea and, in turn, this Mistress of the Sea Creatures.

Traditional Inuit orature was transcribed by anthropologists and other non-Inuit recorders of the spoken word into literary narratives which met the needs of eighteenth-, nineteenth-, and early twentieth-century Europeans and North Americans. However as the twentieth century progresses and the borders of traditional narrative expand, so too has the expression of the Sedna myth expanded to encompass new narratives which provide people from the latter half of this century with new approaches to the legend.

The new narratives of the last decades of the Twentieth Century include several re-tellings of the Sedna legend in traditional prose and songs transcribed into English. A. Grove Day's 1951 volume *The Sky Clears: Poetry of the American Indians* refers to Sedna, the powerful old woman who lives in the sea.[32] Erik Holtved's 1951 "The Polar Eskimos" contains direct reference to Nerrivik with the story being retold in both phonetic and English forms.[33] "The Girl and the Dog" story also appears in the Holtved piece.[34] Edmund Carpenter's *Anerica*, published in 1959, contains reference to "the huge, hairless, dog-husband of Sedna, goddess of the fruitful sea."[35] The 1961 *Peter Freuchen's Book of the Eskimos* includes the story of Neqivik, the orphan girl, as related in traditional prose.[36] Richard Lewis's 1971 *I Breathe a New Song: Poems of the Eskimo* discusses poetic myths, including that of Sedna and the cruel bird as told to Knud Rasmussen.[37]

Nuliajuk, "the Mother of the Sea and Ruler of all beasts on sea and land" is depicted in Edward Field's 1973 *Eskimo Songs and Stories*.[38] Edith Fowke's *Folklore of Canada*, published in 1976, contains the Boas version of

Sedna and the Fulmar.[39] *Paper Stays Put: A Collection of Inuit Writing* refers to Sedna as "the most powerful and dangerous of ancient Inuit spirits" and also features an ink sketch of her by Alootook Ipellie.[40] The reference and drawing accompany "The Half-Fish," a story told by northern Quebec Inuk Taivitialuk Alaasuaq. The Sedna legend and the girl and the dog story are part of the extensive historical notes in *Eskimo Stories: Unikkaatuat* in which the Alaasuaq tale is also published.[41] In 1986, W. H. New edited *Canadian Short Fiction: From Myth to Modern* comprising over fifty stories including a version of the Sedna story. The rendition used was collected by Edward M. Weyer: it describes the young woman and the dog and the woman and the petrel story as documented by Rasmussen on Melville Peninsula in his *Intellectual Culture of the Iglulik Eskimo.*[42] In California, Lawrence Millman published *A Kayak Full of Dreams* in 1987. It contains a version of the fulmar narrative.[43] The same account appears in *Northern Voices,* a 1988 anthology of Inuit literature edited by Penny Petrone that was republished in 1992.[44]

The continued popularity of the Sedna legend is shown by the many publications that collect Inuit songs and orature yet present them in fairly traditional narrative form. In his Introduction to *Arctic Dreams and Nightmares,* Alootook Ipellie discusses how contemporary Inuit writer-artists have "adapt[ed] their imagination and their story-telling tradition to suit today's artistic demands."[45] Indeed, traditional narratives used to relate traditional tales have been expanded to include a wider range of communication.

In the past, legends such as that of Sedna were presented as sagas "larger than life."[46] Yet as early as the initial decade of this century, Arthur Ransome, in his book on the evolution of storytelling, observes: "storytelling has grown into a means of expression with a gamut as wide as that of poetry, which is as wide as that of humanity."[47] Contemporary literary guides such as Chris Baldick's *Concise Oxford Dictionary of Literary Terms* and Holman and Harmon's *A Handbook to Literature* illustrate further how even at a basic level the concept of narrative has expanded beyond that of decades past. Baldick refers to narrative as the "telling of some true or fictitious event."[48] Holman and Harmon explain how narrative is "anything that is narrated;" that is, "to recount events."[49] These two broad definitions include the traditional orature and transcribed accounts of the Sedna legend, but they include, as well, expanded means of expression of the Sea Goddess legend.

Gerard Genette's *Narrative Discourse: An Essay in Method* discusses narrative statement as being: "the oral or written discourse that undertakes to tell of an event or series of events." He proceeds to discuss how "analysis of narrative" involves "a totality of actions and situations taken in themselves, without regard to the medium, linguistic or other, through which knowledge of the totality comes to us. . . ."[50] Didier Coste in *Narrative as Communication* states that "a message is narrative not because of the way in which it is conveyed (its 'mode,' in Genette's terminology) but because it has narrative meaning." "Narrative communication, however, does not necessarily take a verbal form—not until it becomes an object of knowledge."[51]

One of the most creative modern adaptations of the Sedna myth is Alootook Ipellie's "Summit with Sedna, the Mother of Sea Beasts." This was published in *An Anthology of Canadian Native Literature in English* edited by Daniel David Moses and Terry Goldie in 1992. It was later included in Ipellie's collection of stories entitled *Arctic Dreams and Nightmares,* published in 1993. Ipellie imaginatively presents a contemporary Sedna who has been the victim of childhood sexual abuse. As an adult, she is sexually frustrated, alone at the bottom of the sea. With feelings of futility, she withholds the sea creatures from the Inuit. In response, the shaman goes below and braids her hair, placing Sedna in a trance wherein she "met her male equivalent, Andes, a God of the Sea, who presided over all the sea beasts on the other side of the universe. In her dream of dreams, Sedna finally had a sexual encounter measurable in ecstatic terms."[52] She then releases the sea beasts, thereby providing food for the people above. This version is not concerned with how Sedna got to bottom of the sea nor with the creation story of the Woman and the Dog or the mutilation of Sedna's fingers to create the sea creatures. Instead, Ipellie concentrates his magic-realistic narrative on her status today as keeper of the sea creatures. His story explores psychological and sociological implications of sexual frustration using the traditional narrative of the Sedna legend as context.

Although traditional prose accounts such as those edited by Carpenter, Gedalof, and Millman use drawings to supplement their text, two volumes directed specifically at a children's audience make a more complete commitment to the integration of visual with the written word which, in the critical language of Gerard Genette, "create an event."[53] In both *Sedna: An Eskimo Myth* by Beverly Brodsky McDermott, published in 1975, and in *Song of Sedna* by Robert San Souci which first appeared in 1981 and was republished in 1994, the Sedna legend has been somewhat sanitized to meet the perceived needs of a children's audience. Full narrative meaning is the product of integrated verbal text and visual presentation.

McDermott's account begins with the revelation that "The Inuit were hungry and sick" as the hunters waited for Sedna the "powerful sea spirit."[54] Unlike previous accounts of the Sea Goddess, this children's story has Sedna herself as storyteller. Narrating her own story, the Woman Below the Ocean relates how she was deceived by the one she thought was her perfect lover: "Much later I discovered that he was a cunning spirit, a sea bird who had transformed himself into a man. To take on human shape, he had shed his feathers and removed his beak."[55] In this children's story, Sedna is rescued from the sea bird by her father, but they are chased across the water by the bird:

My father shivered when he looked up and saw the sky grow black. Helpless against the fierce bird spirit, he threw me into the icy waters. I struggled to breathe and clung to the boat. To save himself my father struck at my hands. My fingers broke into little pieces and fell into the sea. As I watched, I saw my fingers become shiny seals, fat walruses, and great whales. And so I became mother of all sea beasts.[56]

The cutting off of the finger digits and the sexual relationship with the bird are depicted in euphemistic narrative aimed at young readers. Yet it is the presentation of events from Sedna's point of view which marks this narrative as different from those previously discussed. Narrative technique has been adapted to make Sedna a more personable being; to transport the reader closer to the events which take place. Although not as psychologically forthright as Ipellie's Sea Goddess, this version elicits reader sympathy or empathy through effective use of first person narration.

Another adaptation of the Sedna story is Robert San Souci's illustrated book for children entitled *Song of Sedna*. Throughout the volume, colour illustrations supplement the prose, thereby creating new meaning beyond the verbal. Like several previous versions of the legend, the young woman is described as being very selective in her choice of a mate. Finally, a "handsome young hunter," Mattak, arrives and wins her heart. Mattak takes her away to his homeland where she discovers that he is actually a "bird-spirit."[57] In addition to the woman and the bird story, echoes of the girl and the dog legend appear. Sedna has a faithful husky dog "Setka, who had the blood of the wolf in him."[58] Unlike the stories of Boas ("Eskimo of Baffin Land") or Rasmussen (*Intellectual Culture of the Iglulik*), which combine the woman and dog and woman and bird legends, this children's story does not touch upon any sexual liaison between the dog and Sedna. However, the dog disappears on the day Mattak arrives, implying that Sedna is moving on to a new relationship which excludes her beloved husky. The subsequent unhappiness of Sedna with the bird-spirit and the attempted rescue of her by her father in a boat are in keeping with the traditional woman and bird legend.

In deference to the new narrative aimed at a children's audience, Mattak follows Sedna and her father Noato in a boat which magically turns into a fire-breathing dragon. Vivid illustrations of the dragon and the bird-spirit enhance the narrative. Indeed, they alter the effect of the story considerably through visual impact. Mattak stirs up the sea, threatening the lives of the escaping pair. In fear, Noato hurls his daughter into the sea. Again, because the book is aimed at children, the Sedna legend is somewhat sanitized: there is no mention of the father cutting off Sedna's fingers: "Three times Sedna attempted to climb back into the boat, and each time her fainthearted father pushed her away...." "Exhausted, finally, Sedna gave up the struggle and sank down to the bottom of the sea."[59] Sedna ends up at the bottom of the ocean where she is proclaimed "goddess of the sea." Joining her, through her manipulation of the waves, are her father and her dog, Setka.

In both the children's stories above, narrative has been expanded to create new meaning to meet the needs of contemporary children. This is accomplished through the use of dramatic illustrations as well as the omission of the less attractive elements of the sexual liaison between Sedna and the dog and any graphic description of the chopping off of Sedna's fingers by her father.

A recent adaptation of the Sedna legend is Australian David Holman's play *Whale*. In this children's drama, which was produced in spring 1993 and again in the program of plays for 1995 at Toronto's Young People's Theatre, Holman combines the tradition of Sedna with the "real events of October 1988 when three California grey whales were trapped under the Arctic ice-cap at Point Barrow, Alaska."[60] Here narrative meaning is expanded through the use of theatrical conventions to create a new experience. In addition, a contemporary environmental/social issue is grafted onto the Sedna legend. The Sedna myth serves as the backdrop for the primary narrative dealing with the stranded whales.

The playwright presents a vengeful Sea Goddess who is angry at all humans for the fate she suffered at the hands of those who cut off her fingers: "To have revenge on the Inuit who caused her such suffering she entangles her creatures in her beautiful hair and does not allow them to surface when they are food for the Inuit." "The struggle with icebreakers and helicopters to rescue the whales is set against a mythological background of attempts to appease Sedna and make her happy, so [she] finally releas[es] the whales from her kingdom."[61]

Didier Coste has stated that "narrative communication does not necessarily take a verbal form ... until it becomes an object of knowledge."[62] Knowledge of the Sea Goddess has a long history of being revealed through visual creations. Early sculptures of the half woman/half sea creature were observed by Edward Nelson and photographed for his *The Eskimo About Bering Strait* (1896–1897). The photographs show "a mythic creature, half seal and half human" from the western Arctic along the Bering Strait.[63] Other sculptures in soapstone and whalebone depicting the Sea Goddess have been documented throughout the Twentieth Century. Major exhibitions such as the "Sculpture of the Inuit: Masterworks of the Canadian Arctic," which was at the National Gallery in Ottawa (1969–1970), "The Art of Manasie Akpaliapik" at the Winnipeg Art Gallery (1994), the permanent collection at the Toronto Dominion Gallery of Inuit Art in Toronto, and individual Inuit carvings for sale at galleries across North America, attest to the continued depiction of the Woman Beneath the Sea in Inuit art. Further expansion beyond the purely visual to include verbal communication of the Sedna myth is documented in gallery programs and in a variety of books with photographs published to celebrate Inuit visual representations of the Sea Goddess.

Pudlo's 1963 stonecut entitled "Taleelayo" is reproduced and explained in James Houston's *Eskimo Prints*.[64] George Swinton's *Sculpture of the Inuit* first appeared in 1972, was reprinted in 1982 and 1987, and revised and expanded in 1992. In the latest edition, Swinton has a photograph of Manasie Akpaliapik's 1989 whalebone and narwhal-ivory work entitled: "Shaman Summoning Taleelayuk Animals." Included, too, is a synopsis by Darlene Wight of why the shaman goes to the Sea Goddess Taleelayuk.[65] Bodil Kaalund's *The Art of Greenland: Sculpture, Crafts, Painting* appeared originally in 1979. This volume includes photographs of "The Sea's Mother" sculpture by a West Greenlandic artist, as well as an overview of the legend.[66] In addition, there is a listing of the Sea Goddess's numerous designations: Sedna ("She Down in the Sea") for the Baffin Inuit, Nerrivik ("The Food Place") for the Polar Inuit, Arnaqquagssaaq ("The Old Woman") for the West Greenlanders, and Immap Ukuua ("The Sea's Mother") for the East Greenlanders.[67]

Carson Ritchie's *The Eskimo and His Art* refers to Sedna as Arnarkuagssak, "the old woman" who was the "patroness of hunters" for marine animals.[68] *Things Made by Inuit* is a 1980 catalogue with photographs of Inuit creations from Arctic Quebec. It includes photographs of sculptures of·Sedna by Aipili Qumaluk of Wakeham Bay and Timothy Arksapak of Povungnituk, and an ink sketch of Sedna by Eelayziapik of Povungnituk. These are enriched by a narrative explaining the "many variations of this myth" of Sedna.[69]

Lords of the Stone: An Anthology of Eskimo Sculpture by Alistair Macduff was published in 1982. The volume is divided according to geographical districts within the Arctic and has colour photographs of sculpted Sea Goddesses. Included are "Keeviak's Sea Journey," a black soapstone piece by Pukingnark of Baker Lake, "Whalebone Sculpture[s]" by Davidee Achealuk from Pangnirtung, "Talelayo" a whalebone work by Solomon Karpik also of Pangnirtung, and "Talelayo" by Seepee Ipellie of Frobisher Bay.[70] Narrative text accompanies the photographs to expand meaning.

Part of the durability of the Goddess of the Sea legend lies in the fact that it has met the needs of the people within whose culture it has been kept alive. The media used to depict the Sea Goddess has varied from light and dark soapstone and whalebone to ink sketches. Indeed, in a 1989 catalogue from the Inuit Gallery of Vancouver, George Kamookak's "Sea Goddess" is described as having been made with whalebone and hair. The ill-fated woman grasps an ulu in her one hand.[71] A more whimsical Woman of the Sea is Natar Ungalaq's "Sedna With a Hairbrush" owned by the National Gallery of Canada and featured in an issue of *Inuit Art Quarterly*.[72] Other contemporary art in soapstone such as Clyde River "Sednas" by Qalluk Palituq,[73] Paul Toolooktook of Baker Lake's "Sedna," David Ruben Piqtoukun"s "Dog Children,"[74] and the more exotic "Shaman Braiding Sedna's Hair" bronze of Abraham Ruben[75] have been created by artists from across the Arctic to give artistic physical presence to the Sedna legend.

These have been featured works at galleries across the country. They and other Sedna pieces have been described frequently in publications such as *Inuit Art Quarterly*. Volume nine, number four (winter 1994), for example, features no fewer than three different Sedna works, including a cover piece by Ovilu Tunnillie. The largest and most expensive sculpture celebrating the Sea Goddess is the magnificent Royal Trust Project "Sedna" made from indigenous marble found near Cape Dorset and created by four artists.[76] The narrative here has been expanded beyond the five separate pieces within the sculpture to include an information brochure with photographs and a written summary of the legend. As well, a film, *Sedna: The Making of a Myth* directed and produced by John Paskievich, relates the story of the creation and completion of the work. The Sea Goddess legend continues to capture the creative imagination of artists in the last decade of the twentieth century who deploy new narratives combining the verbal with the visual.

The Inuit Imagination: Arctic Myth and Sculpture by Harold Seidelman and James Turner is an excellent collection of photographs of sculptures and it includes an entire chapter dealing with "Sedna and the Shaman's Journey."[77] Narrative revelation of the pan-Arctic diversity of Sea Goddess traditions is expanded outward through the use of twenty-four colour photographs of sculptures of different depictions of the Sedna myth. The most extensive documentation of the Sea Goddess legend in all its forms as presented in visual arts is to be found in Nelda Swinton's *The Inuit Sea Goddess,* which was published in 1980. Swinton documents variations in the legend and illustrates well how numerous individual artists have embodied Sedna in their work. In this book photographs and descriptions of over fifty carvings, stonecuts, and engravings are invaluably combined with well-researched and documented historical narrative. Tables provide an historical and geographical perspective for the evolution of the legend, adding to the expanded narrative.

The Sea Goddess legend has been captured, too, by Inuit craftspeople through the creation of cloth dolls. Traditional packing dolls were developed initially at Spence Bay and later produced both at Spence Bay and Holman Island. The Sedna legend continues to be perpetuated in visual art supplemented by narrative as the crafted dolls are accompanied by a written description of the Sea Goddess legend.

Despite variations in content, the Sea Goddess myth is pan-Arctic in scope, extending from Greenland across the Canadian North to Siberia. It has endured time, distance, and the intrusion of alien religion and culture. The legend of the Woman Beneath the Sea has evolved from a basic spiritual belief of the Inuit linked to the provision of food through hunting, to a story which has been transcribed from the oral and adapted in presentation to remain relevant for a variety of Inuit and non-Inuit contemporary audiences. Today, the Sedna legend continues through the imaginative and expanding nature of narrative which includes traditional prose, psycho-socio-magic realism, children's illustrated stories, theatrical production, and texts that combine with visual arts to create new meaning. The narrative of the Mistress of the Sea Creatures has been expanded to encompass contemporary themes told in imaginative ways. The legend of Sedna endures.

NOTES

(Because there are so many concentrated patterns of citations in this paper, all page references have been placed in these notes, rather than in parentheses within the text. jm)

1. Thalbitzer, 1923, 83, 314; Osterman 73, 81–82.
2. Egede 201–205; Crantz 186–190; Rink, 1875, 39–41, 466; Rink, 1877, 199–201.
3. Rasmussen, 1908, 151–152; Rasmussen, Greenland 1921, 158–159; Holtved 60–70.
4. Hawkes 126–127, 152.
5. Kroeber, Smith Sound 1899, 179; Lyon 361–363; Hall, 1864, 524, 529; Hall, 1879, 101, 103, 188; Boas, 1888, 583–599; Boas & Rink,123–128; Boas, 1901, 163–167, 327–328; Rasmussen, 1927, 31–34; Jenness, 1924, 71A; Jenness, 1925, 490–491; Jenness, 1928, 123; Rasmussen, 1929, 63–71, 123–127; Rasmussen, 1930, 48, 101; Rasmussen, 1932, 24–27, 36–37, 172–173.
6. Boas, 1894, 205–207.
7. Bogoras 315–318.
8. Egede 201, 204.
9. Lyon 361–364.
10. Rink, 1875, 40.
11. Hall, 1864, 524.
12. Hall, 1879, 188.
13. Rasmussen, 1908, 151–152.
14. Rasmussen, 1930, 48.
15. Rasmussen, 1929, 63–68.
16. Boas, 1888, 583–591; Smith 209–210; Wardle 568–580; Fisher 27–42; Carpenter, 1955, 69–73; Sonne 3–34.
17. Holtved 62.
18. Kroeber 179.
19. Boas, 1888, 584; Boas & Rink 125; Boas, 1901, 163–165.
20. Rasmussen, 1929, 66.
21. Bogoras 316.
22. Carpenter, 1955, 70.
23. Boas, 1901, 163–165.
24. Rasmussen, 1908, 152.
25. Freuchen 234; Field 47.
26. Field 47.

27. Rasmussen, 1921, 113; Rasmussen, Greenland 1921, 158.
28. Boas, 1888, 583–584; Holtved 60–61.
29. Rasmussen, 1927, 27–28; Rasmussen, 1908, 151.
30. Boas & Rink 125; Boas, 1901, 207; Jenness, 1924, 80A-81A; Rasmussen, 1930, 101; Kroeber, Smith Sound 1899, 168; Hawkes 152; Thalbitzer, 1914, 270–271.
31. Rasmussen, 1930, 118; Thalbitzer, 1923, 397.
32. Day 39.
33. Holtved 60–63.
34. Holtved 64–70.
35. Carpenter, 1959, n.p.
36. Freuchen 234–325.
37. Lewis 18–19.
38. Field 47.
39. Fowke 40–42.
40. Gedalof 94–95.
41. Nungak & Arima, 1969, 113–117.
42. Rasmussen, 1929, 63–66; New 24–25.
43. Millman 19–20.
44. Petrone 42–44.
45. Ipellie xv.
46. Ransome 9.
47. Ransome 311.
48. Baldick 145.
49. Holman & Harmon 308.
50. Genette 25.
51. Coste 5.
52. Ipellie 41.
53. Genette 25.
54. McDermott n.p.
55. McDermott n.p.
56. McDermott n.p.
57. San Souci n.p.
58. San Souci n.p.
59. San Souci n.p.
60. Holman, Preface 1992, n.p.
61. Holman, 1992, viii.
62. Coste 5.
63. Nelson 447–448.
64 Houston 68–69.
65. Swinton 262.
66. Kaalund 72.
67. Kaalund 35.
68. Ritchie 34.
69. Myers 32–33.
70. Macduff 83, 100–101, 103, 110.
71. *Kitikmeot,* photograph 25, n.p.
72. *Inuit Art Quarterly* 8 No. 3 (fall 1993).
73. *Inuit Art Quarterly* 9 No. 1: 2.
74. *Inuit Art Quarterly* 9 No. 2: 32, 63.
75. *Inuit Art Quarterly* 8 No. 3: 34.
76. Weihs 7.
77. Seidelman & Turner 71–87.

WORKS CITED AND CONSULTED

Baldick, Chris. *The Concise Oxford Dictionary of Literary Terms.* Oxford: Oxford University Press, 1990.

Boas, Franz. *The Central Eskimo.* Washington, D.C.: Bureau of Ethnology, 1888. Toronto: Coles Canadiana Collection, 1974.

———. "Eskimo of Baffin Land and Hudson Bay (Tales from Cumberland Sound and Tales from the West Coast of Hudson Bay)." *Bulletin of the American Museum of Natural History.* 15 part I (1901): 163–332.

———. "Notes on the Eskimo of Port Clarence, Alaska." *Journal of American Folk–Lore* 7, 26 (July-September 1894): 205–208.

——— and Henry Rink. "Eskimo Tales and Songs." *Journal of American Folk–Lore* 2, 5 (April-June 1889): 123–131.

Bogoras, Waldemer. "The Chukchee." *Memoirs of the American Museum of Natural History: 1904–1909.* Vol.11 Jesop North Pacific Expedition. New York: G. E. Stechert & Co., 1909.

Carpenter, Edmund, ed. *Anerca.* Toronto: J. M. Dent, 1959.

———. "Changes in the Sedna Myth Among the Aivilik." *Anthropological Papers of the University of Alaska.* 3 No. 2 (1955): 69–73.

Colombo, John Robert, ed. *Poems of the Inuit.* Ottawa: Oberon Press, 1981.

Coste, Didier. *Narrative as Communication.* Minneapolis: University of Minnesota Press, 1989.

Crantz, David. *The History of Greenland: Including an Account of the Mission Carried on by the United Brethren in that Country. From the German of David Crantz with a Continuation to the Present Time; illustrative Notes; and an Appendix, Containing a Sketch of the Mission of the Brethren in Labrador.* 2 vol. London: Longman, Hurst, Rees, Orme, and Brown, 1820.

Cranz [sic.], David. *Historie von Gronland Enthaltend Die Beschreibungdes Landes und der Einwohner & c. insbesondere die Geschichte der dortigen Mission der Evangelischen Bruder zu Neu–Herrnhut und Lichtenfels.* Mit acht Kupfertafeln und einem Register. Barby bey Heinrich Detlef Ebers, und in Leipzig in Commission bey Weidmanns Erben und Reich, 1765.

Crowe, Keith J. *A History of The Original Peoples of Northern Canada.* 1974. Kingston: McGill–Queen's University Press (Arctic Institute of North America), 1986.

Day, A. Grove. *The Sky Clears: Poetry of the American Indians.* New York: Macmillan Company, 1951.

Egede, Hans. *A Description of Greenland: A New Edition with an Historical Introduction and a Life of the Author.* London: T. and J. Allman, 1818.

Field, Edward, trans. *Eskimo Songs and Stories Collected by Knud Rasmussen on the Fifth Thule Expedition,* illust. Kiakshuk and Pudlo. New York: Delacorte Press, 1975.

Fisher, James. *The Fulmar.* London: Collins, 1952.

Fisher, John F. "An Analysis of the Central Eskimo Sedna Myth." *Temenos* 2 (1975): 27–42.

Fowke, Edith, ed. *Folklore in Canada.* Toronto: McClelland and Steward Limited, 1976.

Freuchen, Dagmar, ed. *Peter Freuchen's Book of the Eskimos.* Cleveland: The World Publishing Company, 1961.

Gedalof, Robin. *Annotated Bibliography of Canadian Inuit Literature.* 1978. Ottawa: Indian and Northern Affairs, 1979.

———. *Paper Stays Put: A Collection of Inuit Writing,* illust. Alootook Ipellie. Edmonton: Hurtig Publishing, 1980.

Genette, Gerard. *Narrative Discourse,* trans. Jane E. Lewin. Ithaca: Cornell University Press, 1980.

Hall, Charles Francis. *Life with the Esquimaux: a Narrative of Arctic Experience in Search of Survivors of Sir John Franklin's Expedition (1860–1862)*. 1864. Edmonton: Hurtig, 1970.

———. *Narrative of the Second Arctic Expedition made by Charles F. Hall: His Voyage to Repulse Bay, Sledge Journeys to the Straits of Fury and Hecla and to King William's Land, and Residence among the Eskimos during the Years 1864–1869*, ed. J. E. Nourse (United States Naval Observatory). Washington: Government Printing Office, 1879. London: Trubner and Company, 1879.

Hawkes, E.W. *The Labrador Eskimo*. No.14, Anthropological Series, Memoir 91. Ottawa: Department of Mines, Geological Survey, 1916.

Holm, G. "The Ammassalik Eskimo: Contributions to the Ethnology of the East Greenland Natives (Exploration of 1883–85)." See Thalbitzer. *Meddelelser Om Gronland*. Bind 39 (1914).

Holman, C. Hugh and William Harman, eds. *A Handbook to Literature*. 6th ed. New York: Macmillan Publishing Company, 1992.

Holman, David. *Whale*. London: Methuen Drama, 1989. Oxford: Heinemann Plays, 1992.

Holtved, Erik, ed. "The Polar Eskimos: Language and Folklore." *Meddelelser om Gronland*. Bind 152 Nr. 1. (1951).

Houston, James A. *Eskimo Prints*. Barrie, Mass., 1967.

———. *Songs of the Dream People; Chants and Images from the Indians and Eskimos of North America*. New York: Atheneum, 1972.

Inuit Art Quarterly 8, 3 (Fall 1993).

Inuit Art Quarterly 9, 1 (Spring 1994).

Inuit Art Quarterly 9, 2 (Summer 1994).

Inuit Art Quarterly 9, 4 (Winter 1994).

Ipellie, Alootook. *Arctic Dreams and Nightmares*. Penticton: Theytus Books, 1993.

Jenness, Diamond. *The Copper Eskimos*. Vol. 12 of *Report of the Canadian Arctic Expedition 1913–1918 (Southern Party, 1913–1916)*. Ottawa: The King's Printer (F. A. Acland), 1923.

———. *Eskimo Folklore*. Vol. 13 of *Report of the Canadian Arctic Expedition 1913–1918 (Southern Party, 1913–16)*. Ottawa: The King's Printer (F. A. Acland), 1924.

———. *Eskimo Songs*. Vol. 14 of *Report of the Canadian Arctic Expedition 1913–1918 (Southern Party, 1913–16)*. Ottawa: The King's Printer (F. A. Acland), 1925.

———. *The People of the Twilight*. New York: The Macmillan Company, 1928.

Kaalund, Bodil. *The Art of Greenland: Sculpture, Crafts, Painting*, trans. Kenneth Tindall. Berkeley: University of California Press, 1979.

Kalluak, Mark. *How Kabloonat Became, and Other Inuit Legends*, illust. Mark Kalluak. Yellowknife: Programme Development Division, Department of Education, Government of the Northwest Territories, 1974.

Kannuk, Simeonie, interviewer. "Natar Ungalaq Talks about his Art and his Goals." *Inuit Art Quarterly* 8, 3 (Fall 1993): 16–23.

Kennedy, Michael P. J. "Inuit Literature in English: A Chronological Survey." *Canadian Journal of Native Studies*. 13, 1 (1993): 31–41.

Kernohan, Kathryn, A.G. *Eskimo Poetry*. Dissertation. Ottawa: Carleton University, 1972.

Kitikmeot. Vancouver: Inuit Gallery of Vancouver, 1989.

Kroeber, A. L. "Animal Tales of the Eskimo." *Journal of American Folk-Lore* 12, 44 (January–March 1899): 17–23.

———. "Tales of the Smith Sound Eskimo." *Journal of American Folk-Lore* 12, 46 (July–September 1899): 166–182.

"Legend of Nuleeaut." *The Packing Animals of Spence Bay*. Single sheet—n.p, n.d. Acquired Inuvik, 1994.

Legends and Life of the Inuit. Director: Richard Robesco. National Film Board of Canada, 1993.

Lewis, Richard, ed. *I Breathe a New Song; Poems of the Eskimo,* Intro. Edmund Carpenter and illustrated by Oonark. New York: Simon and Schuster, 1971.

Lowenstein, Tom, trans. *Eskimo Poems from Canada and Greenland from Material Originally Collected by Knud Rasmussen.* London: Anchor Press, 1973.

Lyon, Captain G.F. *The Private Journal of Captain G. F. Lyon of H.M.S. Hecla, During the Recent Voyage of Discovery under Captain Parry.* London: John Murray, 1824.

Macduff, Alistair. *Lords of the Stone: An Anthology of Eskimo Sculpture,* illust. George M. Galpin. North Vancouver: Whitecap Books, 1982.

McDermott, Beverly Brodsky. Adapter and illustrator. *Sedna: An Eskimo Myth.* New York: The Viking Press, 1975.

McGrath, Robin. *Canadian Inuit Literature: Development of a Tradition.* Ottawa: National Museums of Canada, 1984.

Millard, Peter. "On Quality in Art: Who Decides?" *Inuit Art Quarterly* 7, 3 (Summer/Fall 1992): 4–14.

Millman, Lawrence, compiler. *A Kayak Full of Ghosts: Eskimo Tales.* Santa Barbara: Capra Press, 1987.

Moses, Daniel David and Terry Goldie, eds. *An Anthology of Canadian Native Literature in English.* Toronto: Oxford University Press, 1992.

Myers, Marybelle, ed. *Things Made by Inuit.* Quebec: La Federation des Cooperatives du Nouveau–Québec, 1980.

Nelson, Edward William. "The Eskimo About Bering Strait." *Eighteenth Annual Report of the Bureau of American Ethnology* (1896–97). Part 1 of 2. Washington: Government Printing Office, 1899.

New, W. H. *Canadian Short Fiction: From Myth to Modern.* Scarborough: Prentice–Hall Canada, 1986.

Nungak, Zebedee and Eugene Arima. *Eskimo Stories from Povungnituk, Quebec: Unikkaatuat.* Bulletin 235, Anthropological Series 90. Ottawa: National Museums of Canada, 1969.

———. *Inuit Stories/Legendes Inuit Povungnituk.* 1988. Hull: Canadian Museum of Civilization, 1992.

Ostermann, H. "Knud Rasmussen's Posthumous Notes on the Life and Doings of the East Greenlanders in Olden Times." *Meddelelser om Gronland.* Bind 109, .1 (1938).

Paniaq, Igloolik. "The Woman who Married a Dog." *Inuktitut* (Spring 1987): 41–43.

Petrone, Penny, ed. *Northern Voices: Inuit Writing in English.* 1988. Toronto: University of Toronto Press, 1992.

Ransome, Arthur. *A History of Story–Telling: Studies in the Development of Narrative.* London: T.C. and E. C. Jack, 1909.

Rasmussen, Knud. *Across Arctic America: Narrative of the Fifth Thule Expedition.* London: G. P. Putnam's, 1927.

———. *Eskimo Folk Tales,* ed. W. Worster. London and Copenhagen: Gyldendal, 1921.

———. *Greenland by the Polar Sea: The Story of the Thule Expedition from Melville Bay to Cape Morris Jesup* [Fourth Thule Expedition], trans. Asta and Rowland Kenney. London: William Heinemann, 1921.

———. *Iglulik and Caribou Eskimo Texts.* Vol. 7, 3 of *Report of the Fifth Thule Expedition 1921–24.* Copenhagen: Glydendalske Boghandel, Nordisk Forlag, 1930.

———. *Intellectual Culture of the Copper Eskimos.* Vol. 9 of *Report of the Fifth Thule Expedition 1921–24.* Copenhagen: Gyldendalske Boghandel, Nordisk Forlag, 1932.

———. *Intellectual Culture of the Iglulik Eskimos.* Vol. 7, 1 of *Report of the Fifth Thule Expedition 1921–24.* Copenhagen: Gyldendalske Boghandel, Nordisk Forlag, 1929.

————. *Observations on the Intellectual Culture of the Caribou Eskimo.* Vol. 7, 2 of *Report of the Fifth Thule Expedition 1921–24.* Copenhagen: Gyldendalske Boghandel, Nordisk Forlag, 1930.

————. *The People of the Polar North: A Record,* ed. G. Herring. London: Kegan Paul, Trench, Trubner and Company Limited, 1908. Philadelphia: J.B. Lippincott Company, 1908. New York: A.M.S. Press, 1976.

Rink, Dr. Henry. *Danish Greenland: Its People and Products.* Edited by Robert Brown. London: Henry S. King and Company, 1877. Introduction by Helge Larsen. Montreal: McGill–Queen's University Press, 1974.

————, ed. *Tales and Traditions of The Eskimo (with a Sketch of their Habits, Religion, Language, and other Peculiarities).* Edinburgh: Blackwood and Sons, 1875. New York: A. M. S Press, 1975.

Ritchie, Carson I.A. *The Eskimo and His Art.* Toronto: McClelland and Stewart Limited, 1974.

Roberts, Helen Heffron and Diamond Jenness. *Eskimo Songs: Songs of the Copper Eskimos.* Vol. 14 of *Report of the Canadian Arctic Expedition 1913–18: (Southern Party 1913–16),* Ottawa: The King's Printer (F. A. Acland), 1925.

Royal Trust Sedna [brochure]. Toronto: Royal Trust, n.d.

Sabo III, George and Deborah Rowland Sabo. "Belief Systems and the Ecology of Sea Mammal Hunting Among Baffinland Eskimo. "*Arctic Anthropology* 22, 2 (1985): 77–86.

San Souci, Robert D., Adaptor. *Song of Sedna.* 1981, illust. Daniel San Souci. New York: Bantam Doubleday Dell Books (Picture Yearling Books), 1994.

Sculpture of the Inuit. November 1969–January 1970. Art Exhibition Catalogue. Ottawa: Canadian Eskimo Arts Council, c. 1969.

Seidelman, Harold and James Turner. *The Inuit Imagination: Arctic Myth and Sculpture.* Vancouver: Douglas and McIntyre, 1993.

Smith, Harlan A. "Notes on Eskimo Traditions." *Journal of American Folk–Lore.* 7, 26 (July–September 1894): 209–216.

Sonne, Birgitte. "The Acculturative Role of Sea Woman: Early Contact Relations Between Inuit and Whites as Revealed in the Origin Myth of Sea Woman." *Meddeleser om Gronland: Man and Society* 13 (1990): 3–34.

Swinton, George. *Sculpture of the Inuit.* 1972. Revised and Updated Edition. Toronto: McClelland and Stewart, 1992.

Swinton, Nelda. *The Inuit Sea Goddess.* Montreal: Montreal Museum of Fine Arts, 1980.

Thalbitzer, William, ed. "The Ammassalik Eskimo: Contributions to the Ethnology of the East Greenland Natives [First Part]." *Meddelelser om Gronland.* Bind 39 (1914). New York: A. M. S. Press, 1979.

————, ed. "The Ammassalik Eskimo: Contributions to the Ethnology of the East Greenland Natives [Second Part]." *Meddelelser om Gronland.* Bind 40 (1923). New York: A. M. S. Press, 1979.

Wardle, H. Newell. "The Sedna Cycle: A Study in Myth Evolution." *American Anthropologist* 2 (1900): 568–580.

Weihs, Ronald. "Comfortable in Two Worlds: An Interview with Simata Pitsiulak." *Inuit Art Quarterly* 8, 1 (Spring 1993): 6–13.

Weyer, Edward M. Compiler. "The Sedna Myth." *Canadian Short Fiction: From Myth to Modern.* Scarborough, Ontario: Prentice Hall Canada Limited, 1986.

Wright, Darlene. *Manasie: The Art of Manasie Akpaliapik.* Winnipeg: Winnipeg Art Gallery, 1990.

Stories: "Skeleton Woman," "Woman of the Sea"

MARY CARPENTER

We have lost, in particular, the family stories. We have forgotten our ancient gods. And that is the wonderful thing about conferences: we watch, listen, and meet the ones who have not forgotten. Women have always carried the bundles for healing. We have always carried the medicine for all things. We carry the stories: dreams, words, songs, signs, symbols. We women are both vehicle and destination. I once lived in the Badlands of Vanier, Ontario, and met Inuit women who had a tremendous drive to compensate for long famines and exile. They were endangered by excessive and mindless striving toward people and goals that were not nurturant, substantive, or enduring. There is something about famine that causes judgement to be blighted. But my way to cope with this spiritual famine was to read more and judge less. I also didn't resign myself to this marginal place in life. If this has ever happened to you, unresign yourself and come out kicking ass.

To truly heal, however, we must say our truth; not only our regret and our pain, but also what harm was done, what anger, what disgust, and also what desire for self-punishment or vengeance was evoked in us. Take up that writing, go to that ocean. Do some learning and loving that strengthens you. This is right, good, and healing. I know that I have been privileged to have been the daughter of an accomplished and proven hunter, Ayoogaliuk, and to have grown up in wilderness areas and observed what animals do when they are badgered. They bound, they pounce, they run, they dive, they scramble, they play dead, and they go for the throat—whatever needs to be done to survive and thrive.

I refuse to normalize the abnormal that's happening in Inuit country, even when there is clear evidence that it is to my own detriment to do so; this applies to all battering of physical, emotional, creative, spiritual, and instinctive natures. When the instincts are injured, humans will normalize assault after assault, acts of injustice and destruction toward themselves, their offspring, their loved ones, their land, and even their gods. Walk away. Heal. Anyone who does not support your art, your life, is not worth your time. We want to put ourselves in situations where, like the plants and trees, we can turn toward the sun. But there has to be a sun. Friends who love you and have warmth for your creative life, are the very best suns in the world.

The poorest bargain of our lives is the one we make when we forfeit our deep knowing life for one that is far more frail. Learn from the wild animals who never give up: their teeth, their claws, their sense, their scents. When we surrender our wilder natures for a promise of something that seems to be richer, but that turns out to be hollow, we have given up on ourselves, and die fast. We make this bargain without realizing the sorrow, the pain, and the dislocation it will cause us. If we listen to our dream voices, to images, to stories, to our art, to those who have gone before, and to each other, something will be handed to us.

The first story I'm going to tell you is from the Alaskan Inuit. I am Inuvaliut from the Western Arctic—Tuktoyaktuk, Sachs Harbour—and I learned this story in the whaling camps at Kittigazuit. When you hear the story, I know your Western ears might conjure up Halloween imagery. Put that aside. The symbols in here are powerful and I'd like to guide you. Tears are part of the mending of rips in the psyche where energy has leaked and leaked away. And crying is good; it enables the process to continue instead of collapsing. The purity of true tears is that it causes the predator's power to be broken. The listener is a person who can listen with a full heart and can wince, shiver, and feel a ray of pain cross the heart and not collapse. The heart symbolizes essence. The songs heal wounds; through songs the dead are called or resurrected. Love is each partner transforming the other. To support only one kind of beauty is to be somehow unobservant of nature. Drums conjure up the spirit world where men are fulmars and women are sea goddesses. And the elders dance like shadows in front of you. They are old and substantial.

Skeleton Woman

The young woman had done something her father did not approve of, although no one in the village could remember what it was, but her father had dragged her to the cliffs and thrown her over and into the sea. There the fish ate her flesh away and plucked out her eyes. As she lay under the sea, her skeleton turned over and over in the currents.

One day, a young and handsome hunter-fisherman, who had drifted far, far from home, came fishing. He was not aware that the local fishermen stayed away from this inlet, as they believed that it was haunted. As the man's hook drifted down, down, down through the water, it caught—of all places—in the bones of skeleton woman's ribcage. The hunter-fisherman thought, "Oh, finally, I've finally caught the big one!" In his mind he was thinking of all the people this great fish would feed, how long it would last, how long it might free him from the chore of fishing.

As he struggled with this great weight at the end of the hook, the sea stirred to a thrashing broth and his kayak bucked and shook, for she who was beneath struggled to disentangle herself. But the more she struggled, the more she tangled in the line. No matter what she did, she was dragged upward, tugged up by the bones of her own ribs. The hunter-fisherman had turned to scoop up his net so he did not see her bald head rising above the waves. He did not see the little coral creatures glinting in the orbs of her skull. He did not see the crustaceans on her old ivory teeth. When he turned back with his net, her entire body, such as it was, had come to the surface and was hanging from the tip of his kayak by her long, front teeth.

"Ah!" cried the man. His heart fell into his knees. His eyes hid in terror on the back of his head. His ears blazed bright red. "Ah!" he screamed as he knocked her off the prow with his oar, and began paddling like a demon toward the shoreline, not realising that she was tangled in the fishing line. He was frightened all the more, for she appeared to stand upon her feet while chasing him all the way to shore. No matter which way he turned his kayak, she stayed right behind. Her breath rolled over the water in clouds of steam and her arms flailed out as if to snatch him down, down, down into the depths.

"Ah!" he wailed as he ran aground. In one leap he was out of his kayak, clutching his fishing stick and running. And the coral white corpse of skeleton woman, still snagged in the fishing line, bumpity-bumped behind right after him. Over the rocks he ran and she followed. Over the frozen tundra he ran and she kept right up. Over the frozen meat laid out to dry he ran, cracking them to pieces as his mukluks bore down. Throughout it all, she kept right up. In fact, she grabbed some of the frozen fish as she was dragged behind. This she began to eat for she had not gorged in a long, long time. Finally, the man reached his snow house and in one leap dove into the tunnel and, on his hands and knees, scrambled his way into the interior. Panting and sobbing he lay in the dark. His heart a drum, a mighty drum. Safe at last. Thank the spirits. Raven, yes, thank raven. Sedna, yes thank all bountiful Sedna. Safe. Safe. Safe at last.

Safe? Ha. Imagine. Imagine when he lit his whale oil lamp and there she—it—lay in a tumble on his snow floor, one foot over her shoulder, one knee inside her ribcage, one ankle over her elbow! He could not say later what it was—perhaps the firelight had softened her features, or the fact that he was a very lonely man—but a feeling of some kindness came into his breathing. Slowly, slowly, slowly, he reached out his grimy hands and, using words softly like mother to child, began to untangle her from the fishing line.

Singing "Oh na na, na goo younga." First he untangled the toes and then the ankles. "Oh na na, na goo younga." On and on he worked into the night, finally dressing her in furs to keep her warm. Skeleton Woman's bones were now in the order a human should be. The man reached into his leather cuffs for his flint and used some of his hair to make a little more fire. From time to time he would gaze at her as he oiled the precious wood of his fishing stick and rewound the gut line. But she in the furs uttered not a word. Not a single word. She did not dare, lest this hunter pick her up and throw her down into the rocks and break her bones to pieces utterly.

At last the man became drowsy, and slid under his sleeping skins. Sometimes, as humans sleep, a tear escapes the dreamer's eye. We never know what sort of dream causes this to happen, but we know that it is either a dream of great sadness, or a dream of great longing. This is what happened to the man. Skeleton Woman saw the tear glisten in the fire-light. Suddenly she became so thirsty, she tinkled and clanged and crawled over to the sleeping man and put her mouth to his tear. The single tear became like a river and she drank and she drank and she drank and she drank until her many, many years-long thirst was slaked.

While lying beside the sleeping man, Skeleton Woman reached over and took out his heart, the mighty drum. She sat up and began to bang on both sides of it: bong bong, bong bong, bong bong. And as she drummed, she began to sing: "Flesh flesh, flesh flesh, flesh flesh." And the more she sang, the more her body filled out with flesh. She sang for hair and good eyes and nice fat hands. She sang the divide between her legs and breasts long enough to wrap for warmth, and all the things that a woman needs. And when she was all done, she also sang the sleeping man's clothes off and crept into his bed beside him, skin against skin. She returned the mighty drum, his heart, to his body. And that is how they awakened, wrapped one around the other, tangled from their night in another way now. A good and lasting way.

The people who do not remember how Skeleton Woman came to her first misfortune say that she and this young, handsome, hunter-fisher-man went away and were always well fed by the creatures she had known in her life underwater. The people say that this is true, and that is all they know.

Nuriviq: A Woman of the Sea

In the time of the earliest forefathers, there lived a handsome young woman known far and wide for her long thick hair. When she bunched this hair in a top-knot, it was almost the size of the rest of her body. Entire weeks she would spend combing it. Also, she had nice, fat hands which many, many men admired.

One day the woman was picking berries when a fulmar flying overhead happened to see her. Immediately he swooped down and said, "Marry me, my dear." "Ha!" she laughed, and said that seabirds weren't much to her taste. The fulmar went away and changed himself into a man. He put on a garment of the richest sealskin, a colourful tunic, and sunspectacles made from walrus tusks. Now he came back and appeared at the woman's door. Once again he put the question to her. "Ah, you're some fine piece of a man!" she said, and she left with him, despite her parents' objections.

Now the woman lived with the fulmar in a little rock hut at the end of the sea. As she was very fond of blubber, each day the fulmar would bring her a fresh seal. As she was very fond of singing, he would sing to her while they made love. And so they had a happy marriage. But one day the fulmar's spectacles fell off and the woman saw his eyes. She said, "You're just an ugly fellow, like all the others."

At this time, her parents were paddling around in search of her. At every cove and headland they called out: "Daughter, daughter, where have you gone?" They searched the shore all the way to the inland ice. At last they arrived at the little rock hut at the end of the sea and beseeched her to return with them. She agreed to go because, she said, "I can't stand my husband's hideous eyes."

Now the fulmar was looking for the woman himself. First he couldn't find her. But then he put on the walrus tusk spectacles and saw the little boat in the sea below, whereupon he flapped his wings wildly more and more and a terrible storm rushed over the waters. Wind swept down the mountains. The boat looked as if it might capsize. The woman's parents said, "You brought on this storm. If you don't get out, we'll all drown." "Out, out with you," they said.

She protested that the storm was her husband's fault. It did no good. Her parents tossed her overboard, but she caught hold of the gunwale and clung to it. Now her father took out his knife and chopped off a few of her fingers. Still, she clung there. He chopped off a few more. Still she clung. Now her father chopped off both her hands. She tried to hold on with her stumps, but she had no grip, and as a result, she slipped away. Immediately, the water subsided and her parents were able to paddle home safely, happy that they'd survived, despite the fact that they had sacrificed their daughter.

The woman sank to the bottom of the sea. There she acquired the name Nuriviq: food dish. Her chopped off fingers came back to her as fish, seals, walruses, and whales, all making their homes in her hair. But she couldn't comb this hair as she'd been able to before. She didn't have any hands. All she could do was sit there at sea bottom, legs drawn up to her chest, and watch her hair grow more and more filthy with each passing day. Thus it is that shamans must swim down to the depths of the sea and comb Nuriviq's hair for her. And in her gratitude, she offers humankind all the creatures of the sea. The bounty in her long, spreading hair is endless.

CONTRIBUTORS

MARY CARPENTER	Storyteller Ottawa
NELLIE COURNOYEA	Former Premier of the Northwest Territories Yellowknife
MARLENE GOLDMAN	University of Toronto
SHERRILL E. GRACE	University of British Columbia
WAYNE GRADY	Editor, writer, translator Kingston
LORRIE GRAHAM	University of Ottawa
SHELAGH D. GRANT	Trent University
KENNETH HOEPPNER	Mount Royal College
HAROLD HORWOOD	Writer, former Newfoundland legislator Annapolis Royal
RENÉE HULAN	McGill University of British Columbia
ALOOTOOK IPELLIE	Writer, artist Ottawa
H. G. JONES	University of North Carolina at Chapel Hill
MICHAEL P. J. KENNEDY	Kelsey College University of Saskatchewan
CONSTANCE MARTIN	Arctic Institute of North America University of Calgary
JOHN MOSS	University of Ottawa
FARLEY MOWAT	Writer Port Hope

EDWARD PARKINSON	McMaster University
ANGELA ROBBESON	University of Ottawa
GRAHAM ROWLEY	Exploration leader, DIAND advisor, writer Ottawa
ARON SENKPIEL	Yukon College
JOAN STRONG	Carleton University
ARITHA VAN HERK	University of Calgary
RUDY WIEBE	University of Alberta
TIM WILSON	University of Ottawa
DAVID C. WOODMAN	Queen's Harbour Master Expedition leader, Royal Canadian Geographical Society, writer